D1083783

New Ways and Means

New Ways and Means

Reform and Change in a Congressional Committee

Randall Strahan

The University of North Carolina Press
Chapel Hill and London

The paper in this book meets the guidelines for
permanence and durability of the Committee on
Production Guidelines for Book Longevity
of the Council on Library Resources.

94 93 92 91 90   5 4 3 2 1

Library of Congress Cataloging-in-Publication Data

Strahan, Randall.
    New ways and means : reform and change in a congressional
committee / by Randall Strahan.
        p.   cm.
    Includes bibliographical references.
    ISBN 0-8078-1890-9 (alk. paper)
    1. United States. Congress. House. Committee on Ways
and Means.   2. United States—Politics and government—
1974–1977.   3. United States—Politics and government—
1977–   . I. Title.
JK1430.W32S76   1990
328.73'07658—dc20   89-22660
                                                 CIP

Chapter 6 of this work appeared earlier in somewhat different
form as "Agenda Change and Committee Politics in the Postreform House," *Legislative Studies Quarterly* 13 (May 1988),
and is reproduced here by permission of the Comparative Legislative Research Center. Part of Chapter 7 appeared earlier in
somewhat different form as "Members' Goals and Coalition-
Building Strategies in the U.S. House: The Case of Tax Reform," *Journal of Politics* 51, no. 2 (May 1989), and is reproduced here by permission of the University of Texas Press.

For Annie

Contents

Tables

Figures

Preface

The decade of the 1970s was one in which institutional change in Congress occurred on an impressive scale. In one of the most comprehensive accounts of this era in congressional politics, James L. Sundquist has written: "The 1970s were a period of upheaval, of change so rapid and so radical as to transform the pattern of relationships that had evolved and settled into place over the span of half a century or more."[1] Roger H. Davidson and Walter J. Oleszek likewise concluded in their study of reform politics in the House of Representatives: "The 1970–1975 period was clearly an era of congressional change, perhaps not equalled at any time since the [1910] downfall of Speaker Cannon."[2]

With over a decade having passed since the high-water mark of congressional reform activity was reached during the mid-1970s, there is now a considerable body of literature devoted to this period and its effects on congressional politics.[3] If most observers can agree that the 1970s were a period of unusual turbulence and extensive structural reorganization, there is much less agreement on the significance of the changes that occurred during this time. Some, including Samuel C. Patterson, caution that changes during the 1970s should be viewed within the long-term pattern of institutional stability and adaptive change that has long been a distinctive characteristic of congressional politics.[4] Others, such as Lawrence C. Dodd, have concluded that the 1970s reforms "were not just mild alterations of existing arrangements; they constituted a fundamental transformation of congressional structure."[5] Concerning the consequences for national policymaking, one interpretation holds that the most important legacy of the reform era has been a degree of institutional fragmentation in Congress that enhances the influence of particularistic interests at the expense of broader, long-term interests and threatens to immobilize the national legislative process.[6] Others see in the aftermath of the reforms a strengthened policymaking capability in Congress. To quote Patterson: "Congress has acquired impressive staffs and information processing facilities; improvements have been made in its system of committees; . . . mainly on account of its extensive and expert staffs, it is substantially more impervious to special-interest pressure." Congress, in this view, "is far more formidable as a political body than it was in the quiescent days of the 1950s and 1960s."[7]

This study seeks to contribute to the assessment of effects of this important reform era through a case study of change in a major House committee, the Committee on Ways and Means. Historically the Ways and Means Committee has been one of the most important standing committees in Congress. One historian described the pre–Civil War committee as "an Atlas bearing upon its shoulders all the business of the House."[8] First established as a permanent standing committee in 1795, Ways and Means has controlled jurisdiction over revenue legislation since its inception, and up until 1865 it reviewed spending bills as well.[9] Due to the importance of revenue issues (primarily tariffs) in the congressional agenda of the nineteenth century, the committee became increasingly intertwined with the developing party organization in the House. After the mid-nineteenth century, the chairman of Ways and Means was frequently named majority floor leader under speakers of both parties.[10]

In the aftermath of the 1910–11 reforms in the House that reduced the power of the speakership, the Ways and Means Committee became even more closely linked to majority party organization in the chamber. Democrats who organized the House in 1911 removed remaining committee assignment powers from the Speaker (power to name Rules Committee members had been revoked in 1910) by providing for election of all committees and their chairmen by the House. In practice the power to make committee assignments for the Democrats shifted to the Democratic members of Ways and Means, who exercised that function until it was removed during a new wave of reforms in 1974.[11] After the reduction in power of the speakership in 1910–11, the most important figure became Oscar Underwood (D-Ala.), who served as both majority floor leader and chairman of Ways and Means.

During Underwood's tenure as floor leader (1911–15) the Democratic caucus, the Rules Committee, and the Ways and Means Committee all became important instruments of a remarkable period of party government in the House.[12] Working to develop legislation for submission to the caucus, Democratic members of Ways and Means "became, in effect, the policy committee of the party."[13] The practice of naming the floor leader chairman of Ways and Means continued until Republicans regained control of the House in 1919, from which time the two positions have remained separate. But continuing to exercise the important organizational function of making committee assignments for House Democrats and presiding over a jurisdiction that included, after the 1930s, Social Security and related social welfare programs, as well as tax and trade policy, Ways and Means had by the 1970s long been viewed as one of the most important committees—if not the most important—in the House.[14]

In part because of this central role in House politics, during the 1970s reform era the Ways and Means Committee became a focal point for criticism of institutional arrangements in Congress, and became one of the primary targets of reformers. Because the committee was such a central object of reform efforts and because of the continuing importance of the economic and social welfare issues over which it exercises jurisdiction, the postreform Ways and Means Committee provides an important case for considering the consequences of the 1970s reforms.

Even in the case of a single congressional committee, identifying and evaluating the effects of institutional changes are extraordinarily difficult tasks.[15] Important factors other than institutional arrangements rarely remain constant in the real world of congressional politics, making pre- and postreform comparisons problematic. Leaders change, new issues arise, and other changes affecting committee politics occur.[16] Still, both for the light that may be shed on our theories about how institutions work, and for whatever small contribution may be made to the inevitable debates on reform that will occur in the future, attempts to sort out the effects of reforms on the functioning of political institutions merit the attention of political scientists.

In the case of the Ways and Means Committee, the task of evaluating change in committee politics is aided greatly by the excellent studies of the prereform committee written by John F. Manley and Richard F. Fenno, Jr., and by a series of essays by Catherine E. Rudder and the comparative committee study by Steven S. Smith and Christopher J. Deering that have begun the task of reexamining the politics of the committee in the postreform years.[17] The Manley and Fenno studies offer a good historical baseline against which to compare patterns in committee politics over the 1975–86 period that serves as the time frame for this study, and the more recent works provide some clear points of departure for the more intensive analysis this study seeks to provide. Although the book draws heavily from both Manley and Fenno in making comparisons over time, and from Fenno's theoretical framework for analyzing the effects of institutional change on committee politics, it does not attempt to match the scope of either study or to serve simply as an "update" of either author's analysis.

Instead, the basic objectives of the analysis of change in the House Ways and Means Committee are threefold. First, the book will examine why the Ways and Means Committee—though described by informed observers in the 1960s as both prestigious and closely attuned to the politics of the parent chamber—became one epicenter of the institutional upheavals that rocked the House during the 1970s. Second, the analysis will consider the effects of reform-era institutional changes on committee politics by looking at House-committee relations over the postreform period, at committee leadership, and at committee decisionmaking in the area of federal tax legislation over the 1975–86 period. Finally, the study seeks to evaluate how reform-era changes in the Ways and Means Committee and the House have affected capabilities of the parent legislature for deliberation.

Though much attention and scholarly work has been focused in recent years on group and policy-driven explanations of political behavior, there has developed more recently a new interest among political scientists in institutions and institutional analysis.[18] If by institutional analysis is meant the study of how formal structures or informal but well-established norms and incentives channel individual behavior, institutionalism has long been an important part of congressional scholarship.[19] As a study of the causes and effects of institutional change, this book falls squarely within that tradition. However, the argument of the book suggests that if institutional arrangements normally establish certain tendencies or outside constraints on behavior, policy-related factors, or changing issues on the governmental agenda, may offset or even reverse certain institutional tendencies in congressional politics. The Ways and Means case also indicates that, under certain conditions, leaders may be more important in shaping congressional politics than the view of leadership presented in many recent studies might suggest. In short, institutional changes matter, policy or agenda factors matter, and leaders matter in explaining why the politics of the Ways and Means Committee have changed in the aftermath of the reforms of the 1970s.

The analysis of the Ways and Means Committee reforms enacted during the 1970s and of committee politics over the 1975–86 period draws on secondary literature on the reform era, contemporary journalistic accounts, the public record (including recorded committee votes obtained from the committee's files), and on a series of personal interviews conducted by the author with current and former Ways and Means Committee members, staff, and lobbyists who were active in the House reform movement during the 1970s or who have dealt with the committee regularly on tax issues.[20] An attempt has been made whenever possible to confirm interview data with other types of evidence. But given the difficulty today of gaining access to members of Congress for interviews, and the importance of trying to understand the institution from the *members'* perspective, I have also attempted to incorporate as much of the interview material in the text as possible.

The organization of the book is as follows. Chapter 1 presents an overview of the basic questions addressed in the book—why the Ways and Means Committee became a target of House reformers, what effects the reforms have had on the operation of the committee, and how reform-era changes have affected the deliberative capabilities of the committee and the House. Chapter 2 profiles the prereform committee and examines the sources of the breakdown in the 1970s of the broader set of institutional relationships within which the committee had functioned. Chapter 3 provides an overview of the reforms that were targeted at Ways and Means or that had important implications for the committee's operation. Focusing primarily on factors suggested by the purposive theoretical frameworks developed by David R. Mayhew and Richard F. Fenno, Jr., Chapter 4 looks at House-committee relations and the institutional context within which the Ways and Means Committee has operated since 1974. Chapter 5 examines committee leadership in the wake of reform and the fall from grace of the committee's legendary chairman, Wilbur D. Mills. Chapters 6 and 7 are then devoted to an analysis of committee decisionmaking on major tax legislation over the 1975–86 period, including especially close attention to the role of the Ways and Means Committee in the enactment of comprehensive tax reform during 1985–86. Finally, the concluding chapter (Chapter 8) considers the implications of the Ways and Means case for viewing committee politics from the perspectives of Mayhew's electoral connection model and Fenno's more complex theoretical framework, and returns to the question of the effects of changes in this key committee for the effective performance of the deliberative function of the House of Representatives.

Acknowledgments

Of the many debts incurred in the course of writing this book, by far the two largest are to my wife, Annie Guthrie Strahan, who helped me keep this project in proper perspective over what must seem to her an even longer time than it does to me, and to Professor Charles O. Jones, who first steered me toward the idea of a dissertation on the Ways and Means Committee and has been an invaluable source of encouragement and advice as first the dissertation and then the book manuscript have taken form. James W. Ceaser and Martha Derthick provided extensive comments on the study at the dissertation stage and have also provided helpful suggestions on various parts of the manuscript. I have also been fortunate to have a group of colleagues at Emory University—Alan I. Abramowitz, Richard F. Doner, Micheal W. Giles, Karen O'Connor, Eleanor C. Main, and Robert A. Pastor—who have generously given of their time to read, comment on, and talk with me about parts of the study. Comments on papers I have written on Ways and Means Committee politics or on chapter drafts from M. Kenneth Bowler, William F. Connelly, Jr., Joseph Cooper, Richard L. Hall, Dan Palazzolo, Ronald M. Peters, Jr., Paul J. Quirk, Catherine E. Rudder, Steven S. Smith, and Joseph White have encouraged me to rethink the arguments and evidence presented in the study. John F. Witte, James M. Verdier, and Allen Schick read the final version of the manuscript and inspired a number of improvements. Paul Betz, social sciences editor at the University of North Carolina Press, has been extraordinarily helpful in seeing the project through from beginning to end.

I am also grateful to those who have provided support for the research on which the book is based. First and foremost, I wish to express my gratitude to my parents, Gladys F. and Richard D. Strahan, whose support encouraged me early on to indulge my curiosity about politics. The Brookings Institution made available office space during the spring of 1985 when the initial round of interviews was conducted. A series of Faculty Development Awards from Emory College has allowed each of the summers since I came to Emory in the fall of 1985 to be devoted to research and writing. A research grant from the Smith Richardson Foundation allowed a semester off to work on this project in the fall of 1987. Fellowships from the Lynde and Harry Bradley Foundation during academic years

1986–87 and 1987–88 helped fund travel back and forth to Washington. In Washington, Michael and Caron Jackson repeatedly opened their home to me, often on short notice. I also wish to thank Gregg Ivers, Tan Qing-shan, Andrea Robinson, and especially Kenneth Cribbs for their conscientious work as research assistants.

With the exception of Chairman Dan Rostenkowski, all of the current and former members and staff of the House Committee on Ways and Means who were interviewed for this study were promised anonymity. I wish to express my sincere thanks to Chairman Rostenkowski and the other members and staff of the committee who were willing to set aside time (which has become one of the scarcest commodities on Capitol Hill these days) to sit down and talk about committee politics.

Finally, I need to say that the errors, misinterpretations, and oversimplifications that remain are my responsibility alone.

R. W. S.
Decatur, Georgia
1989

New Ways and Means

Chapter 1

Change in Congress

When change in any political institution or process is examined, two basic questions arise: Why did change occur and what effects or consequences followed? Changes in the structure and operation of the House Committee on Ways and Means during and after the congressional reform era of the 1970s present some interesting questions of both types for students of congressional politics. Described by congressional scholars who studied the House of Representatives during the 1960s as a prestigious group that was skillfully led and closely attuned to the politics of the parent chamber, the panel in the early 1970s became a focal point for a major reform movement in the House. Thus the initial question that is of interest in this case of change in Congress is why this estrangement occurred between the committee and its parent body, and how discontent with the existing organization and role of the panel became translated into structural reform.

The politics of the Ways and Means Committee in the aftermath of its restructuring in the mid-1970s presents a second, in some ways more complicated puzzle. In the initial postreform years, a more conflictual committee politics and relatively frequent amendment or rejection of committee bills by the full House suggested that reform-era changes had severely eroded the capabilities of the Ways and Means Committee for framing responsible policy choices for the parent chamber on the economic and social welfare issues within its jurisdiction.[1] The participation of the committee in bidding up revenue losses when competing unsuccessfully with the Reagan administration for control of tax reduction legislation in 1981, together with the failure to exercise the constitutionally based initiating function for the House on revenue legislation needed in 1982 to control spiraling deficits, seemed to confirm the conclusion that within the postreform House the Ways and Means Committee could no longer manage effectively its traditional function of balancing particular interests of members and clientele groups with fiscal concerns or other broader policy goals. But the role of the committee in taking the lead on a major deficit reduction package in 1984 and a comprehensive tax reform bill in 1985–86 seemed directly to contradict such an interpretation of the effects of the 1970s reforms. By the mid-1980s, the committee appeared to have reestablished its traditional focus on fiscal responsibility and its prereform role as the principal forum for deliberation on tax issues in the House.[2] If structural/procedural reforms undermined the influence of the Ways and Means Committee in House decisionmaking during the late 1970s, why has the committee been more fiscally responsible and able to reassert its influence during the 1980s?

This chapter outlines a framework for exploring these and other issues related to change in the House Ways and Means Committee during the 1970s and 1980s. Two questions form the basis for the chapter, as well as the book: Why were extensive reforms targeted at this key House committee during the 1970s, and what effects did these reforms and other institutional changes that occurred in the House during the mid-1970s have on the behavior of the committee and its relationship to the parent house?

Why Did Change Occur? The Restructuring of the Ways and Means Committee

Throughout the post–World War II period the Ways and Means Committee was by all accounts one of the most powerful and respected standing committees in Congress. Yet one of the major conclusions of John F. Manley's exhaustive study of the committee's operation during the 1960s was that the committee, though allowed considerable procedural autonomy, was in fact highly responsive to majorities in the parent chamber. "What is most impressive about House-Committee relations," Manley wrote in 1970, "is not the autonomy of the Committee from the House, but the sensitivity of Ways and Means to widely-held sentiments in the House."[3] But within only a few years this observation no longer described House-committee relations. Instead, the panel had come to be seen by many in the House as unresponsive and obstructionist—in one former member's view, "a 'bastille' that symbolized the inequities of the old order."[4] The result was, as part of a broader assault on the autonomy of standing committees and their chairmen during the 1970s, a series of reforms directed specifically at Ways and Means—including expansion of the committee, removal of its long held committee assignment power for House Democrats, adoption by the House of a resolution that required creation of subcommittees, and enactment of a new caucus procedure to make it easier to propose amendments to Ways and Means bills on the House floor.

As will be shown in Chapter 3, the discontent in the House that became focused on the Ways and Means Committee in the 1970s was due in part to political misjudgments and erratic behavior on the part of then-chairman Wilbur D. Mills. But more important for understanding why the committee fell into such disfavor and hence became a target for structural reform was the transformation that was occurring in the political context within which the committee functioned. Explaining the reforms targeted at this previously well-regarded committee requires looking at some of the broader political forces at work in American politics and in the House during the period as well as the particular controversies that swirled around the committee and its chairman.

Although some contemporary documentary sources and new interview materials are used in the examination of the Ways and Means reforms in Chapters 2 and 3, the extensive literature now available on the 1970s reform era makes the task of explaining the origins of the structural changes affecting the committee primarily one of bringing together and developing connections in these earlier accounts of reform politics. Joseph Cooper's work on how the political environment of the House influences its structural and operational characteristics is especially helpful in weaving the existing studies of congressional reform into a more focused account of the transformation of relations between the House and the Ways and Means Committee during the 1970s and the structural reforms that followed.

Drawing on organization theory, Cooper has argued that the structural and operational characteristics of the House are "a product of the combined impact of certain *fixed parameters*, which are imposed by critical and enduring aspects of the House's environment, and the . . . states of certain *situational variables*, which are also components of that environment."[5] The "situational variables" Cooper identifies—the state of environmental demand, the state of electoral politics, the state of executive roles and resources, and the state of democratic decisionmaking values—offer a useful organizing framework for exploring the political forces that drove House reform during the 1970s. With minor modifications to make some of the categories less abstract, Cooper's model provides the theoretical framework for the explanation in Chapter 2 of how a prestigious and reputedly responsive committee could become in a relatively short period of time a principal target of congressional reformers.

The Consequences of Reform

After examining the principal reforms affecting the Ways and Means Committee and the political context from which they emerged, the book turns to the questions of the effects of reform on the behavior of the committee and on the contribution of the committee to the performance of the deliberative function of the House of Representatives. In addressing these different types of questions about change in Congress, this study takes an admittedly eclectic approach. The theory of congressional politics developed by Cooper and used in this case to explain the emergence of committee reforms is drawn from a school of legislative scholarship which views political behavior in relation to the needs of a collectivity (the legislature, its subunits or component groups) that responds to internal and external forces while performing certain functions for a larger political or social system.[6]

A more recent development in the study of legislative politics has been the introduction of rational choice or purposive theories similar in form to those developed by economists. In studies by the rational choice school and its offshoots, the emphasis has shifted from a focus on collective influences on legislative behavior (norms, roles, institutional needs and functions, etc.) to a conceptualization of legislative behavior as the rational pursuit of self-interested goals of individual legislators.[7] In contrast to the first section of this study, which draws on Cooper's theory of how the structure and operation of the House as an institution are shaped by the political environment, the framework for the second part considers change from the perspective of purposive theory, that is, how institutional changes may affect the ways individual members pursue their goals in a committee setting.

The two most influential theories of congressional politics of the purposive type have been developed by David R. Mayhew and Richard F. Fenno, Jr.[8] Mayhew proposes that the essentials of congressional politics may be understood by viewing members of the institution as if they were "single-minded reelection seekers"; Fenno, on the other hand, contends that understanding members' behavior requires taking into account goals other than reelection, as well as the institutional and policy environments within which members seek to achieve their goals. As a result, each suggests a somewhat different focus for analyzing the effects of the institutional change, and in this case each leads to different expectations about its effects.

Only a brief statement of the implications of these two theories for the politics of the postreform Ways and Means Committee is necessary at this point. Both theories, and their relevance for understanding change in the Ways and Means case, are examined in greater detail in Chapter 4. It is sufficient to note here that according to Mayhew's theory, which may be termed the electoral connection model, reforms during the 1970s that reduced the power and prestige associated with membership on the Ways and Means Committee should produce certain predictable effects on committee members' behavior. The electoral connection model suggests that the cautious policymaking style of the prereform committee (see Chapter 2) should change in the direction of decisionmaking that reflects greater attention to distributing benefits to local constituencies and increased responsiveness to interest groups active in electoral politics. Fenno's theory is more complex than the electoral connection model, and hence the potential sources of change in committee politics suggested by this approach are also more complex. When viewed from this second theoretical perspective, the institutional changes of the reform era would be expected to result in the emergence of a more partisan, more ideological committee decisionmaking process—one in which members' efforts to advance their competing views of good public policy rather than the intensified pursuit of constituency and clientele benefits would become the most important new influence in committee politics.

The effects of institutional changes on committee politics will be examined primarily through an analysis of Ways and Means policymaking in the area of taxation over the 1975–86 period. Taxation is viewed by most committee members as the primary responsibility of the committee, and the abundant opportunities for providing electorally targeted constituency and clientele group benefits through the tax code make this an especially interesting policy area in which to test the usefulness of the electoral connection model. Using interview and roll call data, some comparisons will be made with other issue areas within the committee's jurisdiction, but the primary focus in examining the politics of the reformed committee will be on policymaking for taxation.

The initial impression produced by a look at patterns in tax policymaking is that neither the electoral connection model nor Fenno's framework appears to capture fully the dynamics of postreform committee politics. More conflict over partisan and policy goals among committee members, with limited evidence of increased responsiveness to interest groups or local constituency interests, appears in the initial years after the reforms, yet strong evidence in support of the Mayhew model seems to be present in a runaway "bidding war" that incorporated a large number of "special interest" provisions in tax reduction legislation in 1981 and in the failure of the committee to initiate the large tax increase that was ultimately enacted to stem burgeoning deficits in 1982. Yet relative autonomy from clientele groups was demonstrated by the committee in developing deficit reduction legislation in 1984 and on tax reform in 1985–86, in sharp contrast to what had occurred in the early 1980s. Chapters 6 and 7 are devoted to unraveling these puzzling patterns in committee tax decisionmaking over the 1975–86 period, with special emphasis on the unexpected breakthrough on comprehensive tax reform in 1985–86.

The 1970s Reforms and the Problem of Deliberation

A final question that merits consideration in relation to the institutional changes that occurred in the House and in the Ways and Means Committee during the 1970s is how these changes affected the capabilities of the House for performing its basic deliberative function in the constitutional system. Organizational and purposive theories are useful for exploring the causes of institutional reforms and postreform changes in committee behavior, but it is important also to consider change in relation to the responsibilities of the legislative body of which this committee is only a part. Examining the changes in the Ways and Means Committee from this perspective involves viewing the House as a political institution that, along with other legislatures in liberal democracies, must address a basic problem of maintaining a capability for deliberation.

This problem of deliberation arises from the organizational character-istics of legislatures and the responsibilities they are assigned in liberal democracies. As Nelson W. Polsby has argued, a legislature is defined in part by certain organizational or structural features: "It has more than one member and they meet and deliberate and vote as equals as a way of doing their business." Legislatures are distinguished also by the facts that "their formal enactments [are] officially binding on some meaningful population and . . . their legitimacy arise[s] by virtue of their direct relationship to that population."[9] Or, as Gerhard Lowenberg states in another definitional exer-cise, "The authority of their members depends on their claim to represent-ing the rest of the community, in some sense of that protean concept repre-sentation."[10] These, then, are the essential features of a legislature: 1) its members are formally equal (in terms of the ultimate majority that must give consent to decisions); 2) it makes authoritative decisions for a political community; and 3) its authority derives from some claim of acting for, being like, or being responsible to that community. The idea of representa-tion legitimizes the power of the legislature as the practical embodiment of the democratic principle of government by popular consent.

Because of their organization and the basis of their authority, legisla-tures with real power to govern in liberal democracies face a central prob-lem. Political and economic liberty allow diverse opinions and interests to develop and be expressed. As James Madison noted in *The Federalist* No. 10, "A landed interest, a manufacturing interest, a mercantile interest, a moneyed interest, with many lesser interests, grow up of necessity in civil-ized nations, and divide them into different classes, actuated by different sentiments and views."[11] And as Joseph M. Bessette observes (in describing the American founders' view of legislators), "The representatives . . . must share the basic values and goals of their constituents; their own delibera-tions about public policy must be firmly rooted in popular interests and inclinations."[12] Hence a fundamental problem emerges: Given the respon-sibility to represent the diverse interests and opinions that inevitably arise in a modern liberal democracy, how does a body of equals arrive at choices for the community as a whole? The central political problem for the legislature is that its basic functions—which have been termed with rough equivalence by students of legislative politics as representation and lawmaking, consent and action, responsiveness and responsibility, and expression and integra-tion[13]—are often in tension in a liberal democratic regime. An institution whose legitimacy rests on the representation of often divergent opinions and interests must also fulfill the responsibility for making authoritative rules for the entire community.

In essence, the problem of deliberation for the United States Congress is what Charles O. Jones has described as the problem of "how to move from a collectivity of representatives to a community of legislators."[14] At a minimum the problem is one of maintaining the capability for reaching agreement among legislators through bargaining and compromise. "At best, though," as Michael J. Malbin has argued, "deliberation can rise above mechanical split-the-difference compromising to produce serious discussions among people with different interests, from different backgrounds, each genuinely trying to serve a national interest, rather than a series of parochial interests."[15] Thus the problem of deliberation is one of maintaining capabilities for managing a process of bargaining and compromise among competing interests and, where possible, engaging representatives with different views in a reasoned debate on the public interest.[16]

Three basic conditions are necessary for legislative deliberation—the activity of reaching agreement among representatives on rules for the political community—to be effective.[17] The first is *information*. Legislators must make the effort to inform themselves about the issues that reach the legislative agenda, and if some action is thought to be necessary, have access to information needed to consider alternative courses of action. Second, deliberation requires *time*. Time is needed for legislators to familiarize themselves with the issues on the legislative agenda and to discuss with their colleagues the interests and principles at stake in issues that arise. Finally, effective deliberation requires *an appropriate institutional setting*. Agreement among representatives of divergent interests or points of view is most likely to occur in a forum small enough for serious discussion of differing positions, yet large enough to reflect the variety of views and interests present in the legislative body which must formally approve agreements that are reached. Agreement is also more likely to be achieved where legislators have opportunities to discuss issues and possible bases for agreement without direct scrutiny or pressure from groups or constituents which might encourage intransigence.

The United States Congress faces some distinctive problems in maintaining a capability for effective deliberation. First, Congress is a true bicameral legislature. Agreement must therefore be built within and between two very different legislative bodies. Although this study focuses on the House of Representatives, bicameralism is an important aspect of deliberation in Congress. Second, American political parties have rarely shown the cohesion to provide a consistent basis for legislative action. The more disciplined parties in parliamentary systems—at least when comfortable majorities or stable coalitions are present—provide an institutionalized mechanism or setting for reconciling particularistic perspectives of legislators and groups in society with the need to develop majority agreement on choices for the polity.[18] But cohesive legislative parties capable of providing an institutionalized setting of this type have been the exception in American history. Thus, in considering institutional settings where deliberative functions have been performed in the U.S. House, one is led to look elsewhere than the party organization and leadership. In practice, three different institutional "solutions" to the problem of maintaining deliberative capabilities in the modern House of Representatives may be identified, a brief review of which will complete the discussion of a framework for examining the consequences of the 1970s reforms.

The first is a *party-centered* pattern. Here, activities related to reviewing alternatives, structuring choices, and securing support for legislation are conducted primarily through party leadership and organization. Historically this pattern has two basic variations, neither of which has been seen in anything close to a pure form since the early decades of the twentieth century. The first was manifested in the period around the turn of the century, the so-called era of the czars. Speakers of this era possessing extensive formal powers and support by party majorities dominated deliberation in the House and in turn made the institution a relatively autonomous force vis-à-vis the executive in national policymaking. As David Brady has observed, during this period "the House was the seat of both policy formulation and policy approval."[19]

After reforms reduced the power of the speakership and the Democrats took control of the House in 1911, a second variation on the party-centered pattern emerged: strong party leadership oriented toward passage of the program of a president of the majority party.[20] Through the efforts of floor leader Oscar Underwood (who also chaired the Ways and Means Committee) and the use of a binding caucus, "the Democrats controlled the House as tightly as the Republicans had under Cannon."[21] The result, at least for the early years of the Wilson administration, was a rare example of party government centered in the White House and deliberations in the Democratic caucus, rather than in the office of the speaker. In later decades the majority party organization has remained an important influence in deliberative activities in the House, but it has never regained such a central role.[22]

By the 1920s factionalism had undercut the ability of party mechanisms to serve as the primary setting for deliberation in the House. The result, Cooper and Brady point out, "was to heighten the power and independence of the individual members and of key organizational units in the House."[23] These changes allowed for the emergence of a second "solution" to the problem of deliberation—a *committee-centered* pattern. Some House committees were important in the party-centered pattern of deliberation in the early twentieth century—especially Rules and Ways and Means. But these committees had functioned more as instruments of party majorities than as independent units active in discussing and framing policy choices and assembling coalitions for the parent body.

The careful empirical studies of Congress that began to appear in the 1960s showed that committees varied a great deal in their modes of operation. Some House committees operated primarily as ideologically charged partisan arenas with uneven success in developing legislation acceptable to the chamber as a whole; others specialized in particularistic clientele politics based on mutual noninterference or logrolling; still others became oriented toward producing legislation that could win support of House majorities by balancing particularistic forces with broader policy objectives. The most important examples of this last type were the Appropriations and Ways and Means committees.

In the period before the recent reform era, these House committees performed important deliberative functions in structuring policy choices for the House. Though it has been frequently argued (and correctly so) that standing committees in Congress are often unrepresentative of the views and interests of the entire chamber, tend to take a narrow view of complex policy issues, and thus are basically flawed as deliberative bodies,[24] it remains true that some House committees made important contributions to the performance of deliberative functions. This point is developed further in the discussion of the postwar institutional order in Chapter 2.

A third pattern through which deliberative functions have been performed is one in which activities of structuring choices and building agreement are centered outside the legislative body itself, in the presidency. Although relatively infrequent in its purest form—party leadership scholar Randall B. Ripley notes only two periods, 1915–19 (Wilson) and 1933–37 (Roosevelt), "when House leaders did not make a consistently major . . . input in planning the course of legislation"[25]—most would agree that a pronounced tendency in this direction is one of the most important twentieth-century developments in the American political system. James L. Sundquist, for example, writes: "By mid-century what may be called the presidential leadership model was firmly in place. The president was accepted even as the legislature's own leader, expected to set the goals for its legislative sessions, to assemble the agenda, to plan the strategy for the passage of individual bills, to negotiate the necessary compromises, and then even to round up the votes for their enactment."[26] A *presidency-centered* pattern may involve discussion with party and committee leaders or direct appeals to members. The defining characteristic is simply that the activities of structuring policy choices and building coalitions are dominated by the presidency rather than being carried out within the legislative body itself.

These historical patterns suggest three "types" of institutional settings within which the deliberative function of the House may be centered. Each, of course, presents different strengths and flaws as an institutional setting for deliberation. Viewed from the perspective of the problem of deliberation in the House, the reforms during the 1970s, including those involving the Ways and Means Committee, were in part an attempt to move the

House away from reliance on the presidency and the standing committees for performing deliberative functions for the chamber in favor of more participation by rank-and-file legislators and greater opportunities for party-centered deliberations. The success of the reformers in achieving these goals and the effects of reforms on the quality of deliberation in the areas that fall within the jurisdiction of the Ways and Means Committee will be examined in the concluding chapter as a final way of assessing the consequences of reform and institutional change in Congress during the 1970s.

Conclusion

Three types of questions, then, form the focus for this case study of change in Congress. First, why did the Ways and Means Committee, though reputed to be skillfully led and sensitive to the politics of the parent chamber, become a focal point for reform efforts in the House during the 1970s? Second, what effects did the institutional changes of the 1970s have on the committee's behavior in the area of tax policymaking, and how well do the most influential purposive theories explain members' behavior on the postreform committee? And finally, how did the restructuring of the Ways and Means Committee together with the other major House reforms of the 1970s affect the capabilities of the parent legislature for effective deliberation?

Chapter 2

The Decline of the Postwar Order

Studies of the Ways and Means Committee published in the early 1970s by John F. Manley and Richard F. Fenno, Jr., offer an excellent baseline for assessing change in committee politics in the wake of the 1970s reforms.[1] This chapter begins with a brief overview of the patterns in Ways and Means Committee politics found by these authors, then places the pre-reform committee within the broader network of institutional relationships in the House that were documented by scholars of post–World War II congressional politics. Finally, the chapter shows how, by the early 1970s, important aspects of this larger pattern of institutional arrangements—collectively termed the "postwar order"—were being challenged by changes in the political environment of the House.

Ways and Means Committee Politics: The Mills Era

Both Manley's exhaustive case study of the Ways and Means Committee and Fenno's comparative analysis of House committees portray a distinctive pattern of politics on the Ways and Means Committee in the late 1950s and 1960s. A more recent student of Ways and Means Committee politics, Catherine E. Rudder, has termed this period the Mills era, after Wilbur D. Mills, who served as committee chairman from 1958–74. Charged with responsibility for reviewing legislation involving taxation, trade, federal borrowing, and social welfare programs including Social Security and later Medicare, the Mills-era committee displayed a responsible ethos and consensual deliberative style in deciding these sometimes heavily lobbied and frequently partisan issues. Though centralized in its internal organization and possessing an unusual degree of procedural autonomy in the House, the Mills-era committee was distinguished also by sensitivity to the politics of the parent chamber. The procedural advantages allowed for Ways and Means bills, together with sensitivity to House majorities, resulted in a consistent pattern of approval of committee bills by the full House.

Ways and Means members of this era, Fenno observed, "carefully circumscribe internal partisanship and try to behave in what House members will regard as a responsible, responsive manner."[2] One aspect of this responsible ethos noted by both Manley and Fenno was an orientation toward balancing particular or short-term clientele and constituency interests with broader goals, including the maintenance of an adequate revenue base for the federal government, an open international trading system, and the solvency of the Social Security program.[3] As Martha Derthick has written on the politics of Social Security during this period: "Perhaps the most important function of the legislative committees was to reconcile the legislature's conflicting impulses and strike a balance between benefits and revenues. For this purpose, the Ways and Means Committee enforced a norm of 'fiscal soundness' that was absolutely central to policymaking for social security."[4]

A second, related characteristic of committee decisionmaking during the 1950s and 1960s was what Manley termed "restrained partisanship." Although partisanship was "built into" the committee through recruitment practices (discussed below) and the politics of the economic and social welfare issues in its jurisdiction, partisanship was usually limited to the final stages of decisionmaking. Thus, despite the frequent appearance of partisan splits in the final stages of committee work and in votes on the House floor, members of both parties usually took part in the deliberations through which committee bills took form.[5] In terms of policy outcomes the result was that most committee bills bore "the mark of the minority"; because of Republican participation in deliberations, committee bills usually had a more conservative cast than would have been the case if the Democratic majority had drafted them alone.[6]

Fenno's *Congressmen in Committees* and Manley's *The Politics of Finance* offered similar explanations for the distinctive decisionmaking style of the prereform Ways and Means Committee. Both emphasized *institutional* factors associated with the committee's prestige and influence in the House. This prestige was due primarily to the importance of the committee's tax jurisdiction and its committee assignment power for House Democrats. Members sought to get on the Ways and Means Committee, Manley and Fenno found, primarily because of this unique power and prestige in the House. With both parties' committee selection processes tending to choose experienced legislators from safe districts for this important committee, once on Ways and Means, committee members acted to protect the prestige that had attracted them to the panel in the first place. This meant guarding the House's prerogatives in the area of taxation by making decisions carefully, and acting in a manner likely to maintain support for the committee's autonomy and power in the House.

Viewed from the perspective of Fenno's theory of committee behavior (which is outlined in greater detail in Chapter 4), Ways and Means members sought to satisfy their individual goals as legislators within the constraints that existed in the committee's political environment. Members of Ways and Means were drawn primarily from House members with goals of internal influence or prestige, although most were also party regulars.[7] According to Fenno, the most important environmental constraints for Ways and Means members during the late 1950s and 1960s arose from the institutional context in the House. These constraints involved support among House members for a powerful committee to exercise institutional prerogatives in the tax area along with expectations of responsiveness to the parent chamber and legislative craftsmanship in Ways and Means bills.[8] The desire of House members for maintaining a responsive committee resulted in special attention to selection of Ways and Means members, while the desire for maintaining a powerful tax committee resulted in the acceptance of "a special degree of procedural autonomy" for the panel.[9] Thus formal procedures and organizational arrangements in the House that enhanced the ability of the prereform Ways and Means Committee to dominate deliberation on the issues in its jurisdiction (closed markups, closed rules prohibiting floor amendments, exclusive access to expert staff of the Joint Committee on Taxation) went hand in hand with institutional constraints defined by expectations of responsiveness to the parent chamber. The importance and visibility of the issues in the committee's jurisdiction also led to an unusual degree of involvement by party leaders in committee recruitment. Recruitment practices and the prominent place of party leaders in policy coalitions on issues handled by the committee led to expectations that committee members be responsive to partisan objectives as well as institutional prerogatives of the House.

When consensus on goals exists among committee members, according to Fenno's theory, a set of strategic premises or decision rules are developed on a committee to achieve its members' goals. With a consensus on the goal of achieving influence in the House and environmental constraints defined primarily by expectations that the committee remain responsive to the parent chamber in making policy choices, Ways and Means members developed the central strategic premise of writing bills that could pass the House. This led, in the House of the late 1950s and 1960s, to committee norms supportive of restrained partisanship and a deliberative style of decisionmaking. Although Fenno described the advancement of partisan policy goals as a secondary strategic premise of committee members due to the involvement of party leaders in recruitment and in coalition leadership on tax, trade, and social welfare issues, he stressed that the overriding concern with writing bills that could pass the House meant that Ways and Means tended to aim at consensus rather than partisan approaches to major policy issues.

The leadership of Chairman Wilbur D. Mills was an important factor in maintaining this distinctive decisionmaking style. As leader, Mills worked actively to achieve the basic objective shared by most Ways and Means members—protecting the prestige of the committee. For Mills, effective leadership meant ensuring that committee bills were substantively sound and capable of winning majority support on the House floor. As Manley described this approach, "Given the complexity of tax law and fiscal policy . . . he makes sure that the Committee is painstakingly thorough in the mark-up stage of the legislative process, that it studies the alternatives before reaching conclusions, and that it proceeds cautiously to lessen the chances of adversely affecting the economic status of the country, corporations, or individuals."[10]

Because subcommittees were abolished shortly after Mills became chairman, all of the committee's legislative activity was closely directed by the chairman. But by most accounts, Mills's influence was based more on mastery of substantive detail and skill at discovering grounds for agreement between committee and House members than use of formal powers or the threat of sanctions. Employing a relatively informal style in closed committee sessions, Mills sought the broadest possible consensus on bills the committee would report out, often avoiding personal endorsement of key provisions or formal votes until agreement began to emerge. One veteran member interviewed for this study described the Mills approach as "a system of consensus-building by infinite discussion." As a moderate, Mills "straddled" the major blocs in the committee and the House, and was therefore well positioned to play the role of compromiser.[11] Mills's relationship with his Republican counterpart on the committee during the 1960s, ranking minority member John W. Byrnes of Wisconsin, was marked by mutual esteem and set the tone for the moderate partisanship characteristic of the committee as a whole.[12] "Far from being cut off from influence on the Committee," Manley commented, "the Republicans feel that because of [the cooperation between] Mills and Byrnes they have as much say if not more than the Democrats."[13]

In Fenno's view, Mills made an especially important contribution to the operation of the prereform committee because of the particular balance he struck between the goals of maintaining committee prestige and pursuing partisan policy objectives. "As to winning on the floor," Fenno observed of Mills's cautious, consensus-building leadership style, "he performs optimally; as to policy partisanship, he performs less than optimally."[14] Anticipating what in fact occurred after Mills's departure from the chair, Fenno speculated: "A more liberal, less cautious chairman might increase policy partisanship and rely on smaller, partisan majorities—even at the risk of occasional floor defeat."[15] In addition, the committee sensitivity to House majorities emphasized by both Manley and Fenno depended to a considerable extent on the political judgment of the chairman. "Mills," Manley concluded, "has the primary responsibility for passing the bills reported by the Committee and he meets this responsibility by: sensing what kind of bill can pass the House; determining what kinds of changes should be made in the bill to ease its passage; and actively building a majority for the bill after it is reported by the Committee."[16]

The prestige of the Ways and Means Committee, along with other important factors affecting committee behavior such as recruitment patterns and committee procedures, were part and parcel of a set of institutional relationships and practices that were well established by the 1960s when Manley and Fenno did most of their research. A brief overview of this postwar order in the House and the political conditions under which it became institutionalized is necessary to show why the Ways and Means Committee became a focal point of criticism when these conditions began to change.

The Political Environment of the Postwar House

A useful framework for discussing how the political environment of the House influences structural and operational features of the institution has been developed by Joseph Cooper. Because Cooper's model provides the basic structure for the discussion of institutional change that follows, a summary of this theoretical framework serves as an introduction to the discussion of the political environment of the postwar House.

Drawing on the theoretical perspective of the sociology of organizations, Cooper's model starts from the premise that expectations in society about what tasks an organization should do and how it should do them place limits on how the organization can organize and operate.[17] These expectations create constraints of two types: *fixed parameters* and *situational variables*. The fixed parameters are defined by societal values related to the organization, structural linkages to the organization's environment, and the work that the organization is expected to perform. In the case of the United States Congress, Cooper argues, these parameters are defined by broadly shared liberal democratic values, constitutional arrangements that link Congress to the electorate and to the executive, and the basic lawmaking and oversight functions of Congress. These parameters create "highly stable and circumscribed ranges of variation" for institutional arrangements in the House, the most notable being limited possibilities for hierarchical organization due to accepted notions of democratic procedure and electoral arrangements that place selection (and removal) of members under the control of local constituencies.[18]

But within these parameters, institutional arrangements in the House at any given time are shaped by the interaction of four *situational variables*. These four variables are also related to values, structural links to the environment, and work, but involve aspects that are more subject to change and therefore have a more immediate impact on what the House is expected to do and how it is expected to do it. The four situational variables Cooper identifies are: 1) the state of environmental demand; 2) the state of electoral politics; 3) the state of executive roles and resources; and 4) the state of democratic decisionmaking values.

Within the bounds set by constitutional forms and basic values embedded in American political culture, the basic institutional configuration of the House at any given time, then, is shaped (though not strictly determined) by the interplay of four sets of environmental factors. Incorporating some minor changes in Cooper's language, these factors may be termed: electoral politics, the governmental agenda, executive-legislative relations, and public opinion on questions of institutional legitimacy. For the purpose of placing the behavior of the Mills-era Ways and Means Committee within a broader political and institutional context, a rough sketch of the connections between these environmental factors and the postwar institutional order in the House follows.

Electoral Politics. What is most noteworthy about the state of the electoral process during the postwar era is what is missing—strong political parties as a contributing factor to centralized House leadership. Partisan identification in the electorate was relatively strong from the 1950s through the mid-1960s, with about four-fifths of the electorate consistently identifying with one of the two major parties and over three-fourths voting for their party's House candidates.[19] Still, decentralized local, state and national party organizations generally played limited roles in recruitment and campaigning in congressional races. As Charles L. Clapp quotes a member in the late 1950s on the role of parties: "If we depended on the party organization to get elected, none of us would be here. Because the organization is not too helpful, it doesn't have very much influence with us."[20] Clapp noted that except for "the rare member who is the beneficiary of a strong city organization," this outlook appeared to be characteristic of most House members during this period.[21]

By the 1950s the conditions that produced high levels of party voting in Congress during the initial phase of the New Deal had given way to "a new and enduring split in the congressional Democratic party that was rooted in differences between rural conservative southern constituencies and urban liberal Northern ones."[22] Although alignments varied across issues, regionally based factions, especially in the Democratic party, had become a major factor limiting the integrative role of parties in the House.[23]

With or without the support of party organizations, however, House members who wished to remain in office were highly successful in getting reelected. In only three elections from 1950–70 did more than one in ten incumbents lose a bid for reelection.[24] With a relatively low retirement rate, the membership of the House remained highly stable; mean years of service in the chamber steadily increased from just under ten to almost twelve years between 1953 and 1969.[25]

Thus a review of the influences on the postwar House from the electoral side finds a situation in which party was an important factor in voting, but in which House candidates were left largely to their own devices in deciding to run and in seeking electoral support. The existence of the so-called incumbency effect—consistently high rates of reelection—indicated that members appeared to have adapted quite successfully to the individualized electoral process. This in turn meant that members could and did view House membership as a long-term prospect.

The Governmental Agenda. With the exception of the actual number of bills passed, virtually all indicators of the work load in the House in the period between the Eighty-first (1949–50) and Ninety-first (1969–70) Congresses showed substantial increases. The number of bills introduced doubled from around 10,000 to over 20,000. Recorded votes increased by over one-half (from 275 to 443). Probably most indicative of an increasing work load were steadily climbing figures for hours in session during each Congress and increasing frequency of committee and subcommittee meetings. The House of the 1950s averaged about 1,100 hours in session during a two-year Congress. In each of the three Congresses between 1965 and 1970, sessions began to run in excess of 1,500 hours. The number of committee and subcommittee meetings per Congress likewise rose from around 3,000 in the late 1950s to over 4,000 by 1969–70.[26]

In terms of the issues before Congress in the 1950s and 1960s, the central questions on the agenda involved whether to extend governmental activity in economic and social welfare areas that had begun during the New Deal. In the foreign policy area, the debate from the early 1950s through the late 1960s had, according to Sinclair, "largely narrowed to the details of the foreign aid program," in that "a bipartisan consensus on the containment policy and presidential supremacy . . . was firmly established."[27] A major break with the generally incremental nature of the postwar domestic agenda came in the Eighty-ninth Congress when, with the backing of large Democratic majorities, President Lyndon Johnson engineered an outpouring of federal education, employment, civil rights, poverty, and health programs.[28]

From a fiscal perspective, the issues of the postwar era arose in a period of economic growth which "tended to generate increases in federal revenues that outstripped the rise in expenditures needed to carry out existing programs. The resulting 'fiscal dividend' was available to reduce taxes or to launch new federal programs."[29] As Allen Schick has pointed out, these conditions facilitated a distributive, incremental approach to the allocation of resources: "Government was able to expand not by taking from the disposable incomes of Americans but by reaping the growth dividends of a buoyant economy. Economic growth made everybody into a winner. Government provided more benefits without raising taxes and without shifting productive resources from the private to the public sector."[30] On balance, then, the congressional agenda of the postwar period tended toward proposals for incremental expansion of federal involvement in economic and social welfare problems until the mid-1960s. At that point Great Society programs adopted by Congress represented a major expansion of federal activity in the domestic sphere.

Executive-Legislative Relations. By the 1950s the expanded presidential role that had arisen with the response of the Roosevelt White House to the Depression and Second World War had become a more or less established feature of American politics. Although neither Truman, for political reasons, nor Eisenhower, for ideological ones, followed up the Roosevelt record of dramatic expansion of federal domestic programs, the idea of the president as chief overseer and integrator of domestic policy became routinized during their administrations, and both exercised and defended broad presidential prerogatives in foreign affairs. As Fred I. Greenstein has argued, "Truman's practice of executive assertiveness entrenched the tendency of all but the most conservative policy makers to look at the President as the main framer of the agenda for public debate."[31] Eisenhower's conduct in office, though considered less than dynamic by many enamored of an activist presidency, stabilized expectations further. When the more conservative party controlled the White House "and the institutional changes and role expectations of the modern presidency were not fundamentally altered, the Great Divide had been crossed."[32] After the relative quiescence of the Eisenhower years, the active styles of John Kennedy and Lyndon Johnson further solidified the expanded presidential role.

In the area of executive resources, the buildup of the institutionalized presidency that began in the late 1930s with the creation of a formal White House staff and supporting units in the Executive Office of the President continued under Truman with the establishment of the Council of Economic Advisers and the National Security Council. In the area of domestic policy, the Bureau of the Budget emerged as an elite unit assigned the tasks of developing a coordinated budget and legislative program. Kennedy and Johnson continued the buildup of White House staff and tapped other expertise through task forces set up to develop new proposals.[33] In the area of congressional liaison, Truman for the most part continued the ad hoc approach employed by Roosevelt. Neither set up a formal organizational unit to look out for the president's interests on Capitol Hill. However, with the creation of the Office of Congressional Relations under Eisenhower, presidential liaison with the legislative branch became increasingly sophisticated and professionalized.[34]

A second aspect of the political relationship between Congress and the postwar presidency was the basic accommodation that developed with Congress. Individual cases can be cited in which the institutional rivalry built into the Constitution surfaced, but the basic role of the presidency as initiator and coordinator in the policy process seemed for the most part settled. Not until the late 1960s, when disillusionment began to surface with Johnson's Vietnam policies, were fundamental questions about institutional roles reopened to political debate.

Public Opinion on Institutional Legitimacy. As Cooper notes, the broad acceptance in American society of basic tenets of representative democracy defines one of the fixed parameters for institutional arrangements in Congress. Yet there have been important changes over time in how these basic tenets are interpreted. Apparent changes in public opinion regarding the appropriate degree of openness and participation in government, for example, have spawned recent and past reform efforts. At a deeper level, there exists in American political culture an enduring ambivalence toward governmental power and the institutions through which it is exercised. These aspects of American political culture tend to make institutional arrangements in Congress periodically vulnerable to reform movements grounded in egalitarian and participatory interpretations of the basic American commitment to representative democracy.[35]

For most Americans, though, the years from the end of World War II through the early 1960s were a period of contentment with social and governmental institutions. In survey research done in 1960, Gabriel Almond and Sidney Verba found that 85 percent of their respondents volunteered some aspect of governmental institutions when asked about things in the country they were most proud of.[36] Public opinion polls designed to measure approval of the performance of specific political institutions showed some volatility in the postwar years, but evaluations were generally positive. A review of polling data on perceptions of congressional performance for the years between 1943 and 1965 found only one point in time (late 1963) when even one-third of the respondents gave a negative evaluation.[37] Seymour Martin Lipset and William Schneider concluded in a recent study of trends in American public opinion that the early 1960s were "a high-water mark in the American public's attitudes toward their key social, political, and economic structures."[38] In summary, although a steady stream of criticism of the performance of Congress from academics and journalists may be found in the postwar period, the reform impulse in American politics for the most part lay dormant until the mid and late 1960s.

Decentralized Power in the Postwar House

Both the formal organization and informal norms and processes of the postwar House have been documented in great detail by political scientists and other observers of the institution. The objective here is to offer an outline or stylized picture of the postwar order to show its relationship to the broader political environment. This is necessary for understanding both the politics of the Mills-era Ways and Means Committee and the onset of institutional reforms in the 1970s.

With the electoral conditions conducive to centralized party control lacking, the most prominent feature of the postwar House was a decentralized power structure. Party was still an important force in the chamber in structuring voting and in organizational matters, but neither formal authority nor support existed for party leaders to direct policymaking activity. Because rules in the chamber "gave the committees immense power over the handling of legislation within their jurisdictions and committee rules and practice gave their chairmen immense power within their committees, the decline in leadership power redounded to the advantage of committees and their chairmen."[39]

The basis for the considerable autonomy of standing committees and committee leaders was in turn traceable to the need for division of labor and to certain norms that had emerged in the relatively stable internal life of the chamber. The norm of seniority automatically assigned committee leadership positions according to length of service on a committee, thereby insulating committee leaders from control by party or chamber majorities. Norms of specialization and reciprocity buttressed committee prerogatives and legitimized the partitioning of policy issues among committees.[40] As Fenno put it in an essay published in 1965, standing committees in effect maintained "treaties of reciprocity ranging from 'I will stay out of your speciality if you will stay out of mine' to 'I'll support your bill if you will support mine.'"[41]

The expansion of federal revenues due to steady economic growth, an agenda characterized by consensus on foreign policy and incremental expansion of domestic programs, and the buildup of policymaking capabilities in the White House all tended to limit the need for congressional coordination across committees and the issues they handled. The president was responsible for developing the budget and was expected to produce a legislative program to set the agenda in Congress. With a growing revenue base, new and existing programs usually did not have to compete in a zero-sum manner in which explicit trade-offs would have to be made. Until at least sometime in the 1960s, maintenance of balanced budgets in peacetime was a generally accepted norm in Congress. Most legislators were still, to use James L. Sundquist's term, "pre-Keynesians."[42] As long as the money committees protected the government's revenue base and moderated the pace of spending growth, members of other committees could be left to shape policies reflecting ideological or partisan views, constituent or group interests, or other concerns important to those involved in different policy areas.

These conditions produced a pattern of institutional control over some committees and a sort of laissez-faire approach toward others. The clearest manifestation of this pattern was in the committee assignment process in the postwar House. Nicholas Masters found that, for most committee positions, "the most impressive argument in any applicant's favor is that the assignment he seeks will give him an opportunity to provide the kind of service to his constituents that will sustain and attract voter support."[43] However, assignments to three major committees—Rules, Appropriations, and Ways and Means—were made on a much more selective basis. Party leaders were more active in the recruitment process and the successful applicant tended to be a "responsible legislator": an experienced member who "had demonstrated loyalty to the institution and acceptance of its norms."[44] In addition, members were sought who were not highly vulnerable to constituency pressures or electoral competition, allowing them "to make controversial decisions on major policy questions without constant fear of reprisals at the polls."[45] Finally, geographic balance was much more important on the money committees, than on most other committees, where the tendency to accommodate members' constituency needs often produced highly unrepresentative memberships.[46]

Fenno's comparative study of House committees also concluded that the money committees held special status in the postwar House. He found that members held "a fairly well developed set of prescriptions concerning the behavior of the money committees," and that "basically, House members want their two money committees to be *influential* committees—that is to make independent policy judgments (particularly vis-a-vis the executive branch) and have those judgments supported in the parent chamber. To this end the House prescribes and/or acquiesces in rules and customs allowing the two committees a special degree of procedural autonomy."[47]

It is clear, then, that Ways and Means played a special role in the postwar House and, to an extent that was unusual when compared to most other committees, that the tax committee was subject to both formal and informal institutional constraints. However, as the political conditions that characterized the postwar years began to change markedly in the late 1960s and early 1970s, new demands by both members and outsiders began to undermine the institutional foundations of the postwar order.

The Onset of a Reform Era

By the late 1960s the political stability of the postwar years had given way to a period of unrest in which many became critical of American social and political institutions. Political reforms were enacted that were unmatched in scope and importance since the Progressive era. As the environmental factors that shaped the postwar order began to change, many of the institutional arrangements that had shaped the politics of the Mills-era Ways and Means Committee also began to break down.

Public Opinion on Institutional Legitimacy. The 1960s and 1970s were a period of turmoil in American society. Americans experienced, among other things, a seemingly unending series of assassinations of public figures, growing opposition to American involvement in Vietnam and ultimate withdrawal under conditions many saw as the nation's first defeat in war, unrest and violence in cities and on college campuses, the Watergate affair and the resignations of both a president and vice-president after revelations of extensive misconduct in office, and a growing sense that the economic prosperity of the postwar years had been purchased at considerable cost to the natural environment and could no longer be taken for granted.

Not too surprisingly, public confidence in political institutions and leaders was shaken. There also occurred a reawakening of conflicts in American political culture between acceptance of institutional hierarchies and egalitarian notions of democratic legitimacy. During the 1960s and 1970s, these tensions became infused with new arguments for greater openness and participation in government. As Samuel H. Beer has observed, the new emphasis on participatory democracy

> had, and continues to have, a profound effect on American politics.
> . . . It would be difficult to find today a program involving regula-
> tion or delivery of services in such fields as health, education, welfare
> and the environment that does not provide for "community input."
> In a more diffuse, but more important way the participatory idea
> has affected attitudes toward the whole process of representative gov-
> ernment. . . . Many forces, ideal and material, have been reshaping
> American attitudes toward political action. But the idea of participa-
> tory democracy . . . has given a sharp new twist to the democratic
> values of the American political tradition and to any future public
> philosophy.[48]

It is difficult to judge the extent to which new ideas about partici-patory democracy influenced mass opinion. But an unmistakable trend emerged in measures of public trust and confidence in political leaders and institutions. In the mid-1960s public opinion surveys began to find sharp increases in the number of people who questioned the competence of gov-ernment and similarly sharp decreases in those expressing confidence in public officials and institutions. To cite only a few examples, in 1964 only 29 percent of the respondents in a national sample agreed with the state-ment that government is "pretty much run by a few big interests looking out for themselves." By 1974, 66 percent agreed with this statement. An-swers to other questions concerning honesty of government officials and the amount of money wasted by government showed similar patterns of growing cynicism.[49] The part of the population expressing a great deal of confidence in the people running either the executive branch or Congress declined from around 40 percent in 1966 to average between 10 and 20 percent during the mid and late 1970s.[50] When asked to rate the job Congress had done in the preceding year as either excellent, pretty good, only fair, or poor, responses of excellent or pretty good dropped from a high of around 60 percent in the mid-1960s to fluctuate in the 30 to 40 percent range in the 1970s.[51]

It is not clear just what these patterns meant in terms of mass support for institutional reforms. The loss in confidence was not confined to political institutions, suggesting that something broader was at work. According to opinion polls, confidence in the medical profession, education, the military, organized religion, major companies, the press, and organized labor all declined significantly during the same period.[52] Occasional polls in the 1960s and 1970s did find majority support for some specific reforms in national political institutions: national primaries and direct popular elections for choosing presidents, public financing of campaigns, extension of House members' terms to four years, and limitation of both House members and senators to twelve years in office.[53] But high levels of underlying support for the American political system showed little change.

Whatever its meaning, the apparent loss of public confidence in political institutions did not go unnoticed by political elites. Advocates of congressional reform often cited polling data on declining confidence as evidence of the need for institutional change.[54] Even among many of those who did not embrace the new participatory democratic ideas, the result was a climate of uncertainty, a sense that something needed to be done to restore public confidence. As Roger H. Davidson and Walter J. Oleszek described the situation in Congress, by 1973 the idea of reform had become "an issue akin to motherhood."[55] No longer did members operate in the "atmosphere of self-satisfaction" that had perplexed some earlier critics.[56]

Electoral Politics. In some respects, the congressional electoral process also witnessed important changes in the late 1960s and 1970s. Campaign finance reform in the 1970s produced a rapid proliferation of political action committees (PACs), which became an important source of money for financing campaigns. As technological sophistication increased so did campaign costs, with widespread use of mass media and direct mail techniques, often under the direction of paid professional consultants. Although national party organizations—especially that of the Republicans—had begun to provide increased financial and technical support to candidates, the role of party organizations in congressional elections was not undergoing any fundamental change. As Gary Jacobson has pointed out recently, "most congressional candidates remain largely on their own."[57] If anything, congressional elections were becoming more candidate centered by the 1970s. An erosion of partisanship in the electorate encouraged candidates to downplay party ties. Also, in keeping with the changes in public opinion already noted, public attitudes toward political parties became increasingly negative during the late 1960s and 1970s. As the authors of *The Changing American Voter* concluded regarding the shifts in the electorate from the 1950s to the early 1970s, "Citizens are less likely to identify with a party, to feel positively about a party, or to be guided in their voting behavior by partisan cues."[58]

In terms of the electoral bases of the two parties, most analysts describe the late 1960s and the 1970s as a period of party "dealignment." Events and issues tended to break down party attachments and cut across existing party alignments in the electorate. Although party coalitions in the electorate were becoming more fluid as measured by presidential voting and party identification, an important long-term shift was also taking place in the electoral bases of the two parties in the House. Republican inroads in the South steadily reduced the proportion of the House Democratic party elected from that traditionally conservative region. The percentage of House Democrats elected from the South (following Congressional Quarterly's definition as the eleven states of the old Confederacy, Kentucky, and Oklahoma) had declined from a high point of 52 percent in 1953–54 to only 33 percent by 1974.[59] This represented a major shift in the factional balance in the party as southern conservatives declined in number.

The state of electoral politics in the late 1960s and early 1970s indicates that the already limited electoral incentives for House members to view their fates as shared with other partisans in Congress or in the White House were growing weaker. Although the majority party was becoming somewhat more ideologically homogeneous with the declining strength of southern conservatives, most members remained minimally dependent on party organizations for winning and holding office, and negative attitudes of voters toward parties encouraged an independent stance. Thus, with minimal party control over recruitment, the fraying of partisan coalitions in the electorate, and a proliferation of interests organizing to participate directly in electoral politics through PACs, the electoral conditions that allowed for strong party leadership in the past were absent.

Also significant for internal House politics, the anti-institutional tone of the period reverberated through the electoral system, adding a new influence in the process of congressional recruitment. "It's really easy to . . . support Common Cause type issues of opening up the institutions and letting the sun shine in," explained Connecticut Democrat Anthony Toby Moffett (who was first elected in 1972), "because there's not a district in this country where you can lose by being young, independent and aggressive with regard to process things like getting rid of old committee chairmen."[60]

The Governmental Agenda. During the late 1960s and early 1970s, most indicators of the congressional work load continued to increase beyond the levels of the postwar period. Between the Ninety-first Congress

(1969–70) and the Ninety-fourth (1975–76), committee and subcommittee meetings increased from around 5,000 to almost 7,000, and hours in session approached 1,800 (compared to an average of less than 1,400 hours for Congresses in the 1960s). As in the earlier period, the one exception to the pattern of an increasing work load was the actual number of bills passed, which continued a downward trend from the 1960s. But if fewer bills were being passed, they were getting considerably longer; the total pages of statutes enacted by Congress continued to rise.[61]

Although these data indicate that the level of activity on Capitol Hill continued to increase, by the end of the Johnson administration political and economic conditions had become less conducive to further expansion of the scope of the governmental agenda. Agreement on the desirability of an expanding federal role to redress social and economic ills—what some have termed a liberal public philosophy—began to break down as critics questioned the effectiveness of many Great Society initiatives and costs of domestic programs soared. Nonetheless, as economic growth slowed a new set of issues came to the fore during the 1970s—including energy shortages and environmental protection—which brought demands for new federal government activity in response. Finally, although new diplomatic overtures to the Soviets and the Chinese were initiated during the Nixon administration, these came in a context where, as a result of the American defeat in Vietnam, political support had deteriorated for the active containment policy that set the terms for the foreign policy debate in the postwar years. Fundamental questions about what American foreign policy should be and how it should be made were an important part of the governmental agenda in the late 1960s and 1970s.

Of major importance for the roles of Ways and Means and the other money committees, during the late 1960s the decentralized incrementalism of the postwar years began to break down as a system of fiscal control.[62] From 1955 to 1963 federal nondefense expenditures grew at an incremental pace (about 2 percent a year), with most of the growth attributable to increases in Social Security benefits and a new federal highway program. Modest growth continued in the start-up years of Great Society programs, but much larger increases in the rate of growth began to appear once these programs were under way. While defense spending fell from 9.1 to 6.0 percent of GNP in the decade from 1963 to 1973, nondefense domestic spending grew from 9.9 to 13.2 percent. Just over half of this increase on the domestic side was due to Great Society programs enacted in the mid-1960s.[63] In conjunction with the costs of the Vietnam War and reduced revenues from tax cuts in 1964, 1969, and 1971, accelerating growth in domestic spending eliminated any "fiscal dividend" from economic growth. Continuing increases in domestic spending more than offset reduced defense outlays as withdrawal from Vietnam proceeded. Except for a small surplus that occurred in 1969 after Congress enacted a tax increase, growing budget deficits became the norm in the late 1960s and early 1970s, with deficits reaching $45.1 billion in 1975 and $66.5 billion in 1976.

The result, in fiscal terms, was a different agenda from that characteristic of most of the postwar years. As a Brookings Institution study described the situation in 1972:

> In the past the problem in peacetime was how to deal with the resources channeled into the government by economic growth. For the immediate future at least, the problem appears to be one of trying to find enough resources to finance the growing demand for public services. Paradoxically, the growing absolute affluence of society is now accompanied by a relative squeeze on the resources of the federal government. . . . the problem of setting priorities in the public sector is becoming more, rather than less, acute despite the continuing rise in national income.[64]

So new energy, environmental, and economic problems emerged in the 1970s in the context of an agenda in which rapid increases in federal spending were sharpening the debate on priorities in domestic policy and the controversy over Vietnam had undermined the postwar consensus on foreign policy.

Executive-Legislative Relations. Two developments were of particular importance in presidential-congressional relations during the Nixon and Ford administrations that spanned the late 1960s and early 1970s. The first was a breakdown in the basic accommodation between the two branches that had developed during the postwar years. Serious questioning of institutional roles began with congressional criticism of executive conduct of foreign policy in the 1960s. Foreign policy continued to be a source of controversy in the 1970s, and Nixon's assertive use of the resources of the institutionalized presidency to attempt to check expansion in domestic programs brought tensions to a peak. The second important feature of presidential relations was divided party control of the two branches throughout the period. Democrats, who controlled Congress, and Republicans, who controlled the White House, frequently had sharp differences over how to deal with the fiscal situation and problems such as fuel shortages. Even with the weakening of party attachments in the electorate, the divided government of these years imparted sharp partisan conflict to many issues in Congress. Thus a decline in the generally cooperative relationship between the presidency and the legislative branch arose in part from policy differences that existed between the two presidents of this period and Democratic majorities in Congress, but also from Richard Nixon's willingness to challenge congressional prerogatives through actions such as impoundments of appropriated funds. As A. James Reichley describes the view that developed in the Washington community, "Nixon seemed to be changing the rules."[65]

Faced with divided government and a conflictual relationship with the president, Congress began to focus attention on rebuilding congressional capabilities to avoid reliance (or dependence) on executive resources.

Challenges to the Postwar Order

Many of the major features of the political environment that had shaped the institutional arrangements in the postwar House of Representatives were undergoing change by the late 1960s and early 1970s. Established political practices such as the use of seniority to assign leadership positions or conducting business behind closed doors no longer seemed legitimate by the standards of the new participatory politics. Declining public confidence in government encouraged an adversarial posture toward existing institutional arrangements. A new electoral environment was emerging in which party ties were weakening further, campaigns were becoming more technologically sophisticated and expensive, and involvement of organized groups was expanding rapidly. A major shift in the factional balance in the majority party was taking place. The congressional agenda created more demands on members' time and involved unwieldy new problems and conflictual issues of foreign policy and domestic priorities in a restrictive fiscal situation. Divided party control and challenges to congressional authority posed by Richard Nixon increased partisanship in Congress and undercut a more or less comfortable institutional relationship with the presidency. The convergence of these factors, coupled with relatively high turnover due to retirements by members who became disaffected with House service under these conditions, resulted in major institutional changes in the House during the 1970s. For the operation of the Ways and Means Committee the two most important developments were the emergence of a new procedural majority in the House Democratic caucus and the attempts by members of both houses of Congress to respond to the breakdown in fiscal control.

The New Procedural Majority. During the 1970s organizational and procedural reforms in the House were enacted in a number of different ways. Some involved statutes passed by both chambers of Congress. Others took the form of resolutions approved on the floor of the House. But one of the most important mechanisms for bringing about structural change was the party organization, especially the House Democratic caucus. The revitalization of the Democratic caucus in the late 1960s represented the emergence of a new *procedural* majority in the House to which the previously autonomous standing committees and their leadership would have to be accountable. "Procedural majorities," as Charles O. Jones defined the concept, "are those necessary to organize the House for business and maintain that organization."[66] With the revival of the House Democratic caucus as an active forum for deciding questions of organization and procedures, prerogatives of standing committees and committee leaders were subject to change not only through the loss of support of a procedural majority of the entire chamber, but also by discontent within a numerically smaller majority of the majority party.

Revitalization of the Democratic caucus was part of a program of structural reform developed within the liberal wing of the House Democratic party in the 1960s. The origins of this reform movement went back even earlier, to frustrations among Democratic activists in the 1950s over a "perceived conservative institutional bias" in the House.[67] The practice of assigning committee chairmanships by seniority had consistently placed a disproportionate share of committee leadership positions in the hands of southern Democrats. Liberals in the House chafed under the influence of southern chairmen who were seen as insufficiently responsive to the agenda of the national Democratic party.

In 1959 the Democratic Study Group (DSG) was organized to further liberal policy objectives. Growing out of a core group of Democrats who had previously worked together on an informal basis, the DSG, with the support of a professional staff, became active in disseminating information and coordinating legislative strategy, as well as developing plans for institutional change to reduce the seniority-based influence of conservative committee leaders.[68] The DSG reformers scored their first major victory in 1961 with the expansion of the Rules Committee from twelve to fifteen members. After the 1964 election DSG leaders developed a series of reform proposals designed to reduce further the ability of committee-based minorities to block new legislative initiatives. These proposals included a return to the lapsed practice of formal caucus approval of Democratic committee assignments, adjustment of party ratios on committees, creation of a party policy committee, creation of a joint committee to study congressional organization, and procedural changes to allow legislation supported by House majorities to bypass the Rules Committee if that committee failed to schedule floor debate or send bills to conference with the Senate. The liberal bloc had also indicated that it would press for removal of committee seniority from Democrats who openly supported Republican Barry Goldwater in the 1964 election. Through informal agreements with the Democratic leadership, caucus action to strip two southern Democratic Goldwater supporters of seniority, and floor action on the Rules Committee measures and joint committee proposal, the reformers (backed by a 295-seat Democratic majority) were successful in enacting their program in 1965.[69]

Support within Congress for further reform waned during the remaining years of the decade. The House took no action in 1967 on a Senate-passed plan (developed by the Joint Committee on the Organization of

Congress) that included provisions to limit the ability of chairmen to thwart committee majorities. Still, important precedents were set in the use of the party caucus as an instrument for change.

In the 1970s the House began to experience new forces for institutional change—especially the demands of members who were products of the new participatory politics. The initial reforms of the decade were adopted on the House floor as the Legislative Reorganization Act of 1970. The act came about as a result of cooperation between liberal Democrats and a group of Republican reformers. Both groups supported changes to open committee and floor procedures to greater public scrutiny and ensure that adequate time was allowed to review committee actions and debate floor amendments.[70] In addition to taking an active role in the passage of this measure, the leaders of the Democratic Study Group had been instrumental in gaining approval in 1969 for holding regular caucus meetings. With this groundwork in place, the reform movement in the Democratic caucus gained critical momentum from new Democratic members elected in 1970, 1972, and 1974. "These elections successively reduced the South's share of the Democratic delegation in Congress, and brought younger, liberal, and reform oriented members who had little stake in the existing distribution of power."[71]

After being revived as part of this long-term campaign by House liberals to reduce what they saw as a conservative institutional bias, the Democratic caucus in the early 1970s became the base for a new procedural majority that sought change for a variety of ends. But a common element in the currents channeled through the caucus was discontent with standing committee autonomy and the seniority system that allowed committee chairmen to act independently of the desires of party or chamber majorities. Given the broad legislative jurisdiction of the Ways and Means Committee, its control over committee assignments, its senior membership, and its ethos of responding cautiously to new demands for change, tension between the revitalized Caucus and the committee was all but guaranteed.

The Attempt to Reestablish Fiscal Control. The second source of major institutional changes affecting the Ways and Means Committee was the congressional response to the deterioration of fiscal control that began to occur in the 1960s. Conflicts over priorities and the expansion of entitlements and other spending mechanisms produced what political scientist Allen Schick has described as a "seven year budget war" from 1966 to 1973, as conflicts developed within Congress and between Congress and the president over how to bring federal spending under control.[72] The result was that, for the first time since the demise of a short-lived budget mechanism set up by the 1946 Legislative Reorganization Act, Congress began seriously to consider steps to achieve a more integrated budget process.

Challenges to congressional spending authority from the Nixon administration highlighted the deterioration of informal controls in Congress that had begun to appear during the Johnson years. Despite the apparent support among many legislators for some form of spending control, the inability to agree on spending priorities encouraged a Republican president to enforce restraint by refusing to spend funds appropriated for programs, some of which remained popular with congressional Democrats. The resulting partisan conflict and the broader institutional concern over further loss of control over spending to the executive branch encouraged consideration of ways to coordinate congressional spending and revenue decisions.

Dennis Ippolito reports that more than 250 bills and resolutions calling for budget reform were introduced at the peak of the conflicts with Nixon over the budget.[73] The most important of these was the proposal adopted in 1972 to establish a Joint Study Committee on Budget Control. For the first time in decades, Congress during the early 1970s began to move toward creating an integrative mechanism to coordinate the heretofore highly decentralized process of making revenue and spending decisions. Like the revival of the Democratic caucus, this signaled serious discontent with the postwar institutional order that had defined the role of the Ways and Means Committee during the Mills era.

Conclusion

By 1975 the Ways and Means Committee bore little resemblance to the body whose politics had been so carefully documented by Manley and Fenno. Wilbur Mills had stepped down as chairman in the face of certain removal by a hostile Democratic caucus; authority to make Democratic committee assignments had been shifted to a party body; legislative subcommittees had been reestablished; freshman legislators and outspoken reformers had gained seats on a committee that numbered thirty-seven rather than twenty-five members; major bills were being drafted in open sessions under the glare of publicity and a number were defeated or heavily amended on the House floor. The sequence of events through which the developments outlined in this chapter became translated into the reforms that helped produce such dramatic changes in the politics of the Ways and Means Committee is examined in detail in the chapter that follows.

Chapter 3

Open Season on Ways and Means

In an article entitled "Waning Institution?" *Wall Street Journal* reporter Albert R. Hunt wrote in July 1973 that "the House Ways and Means Committee is being shaken by a subtle upheaval."[1] Citing increased infighting on the committee and rules changes that threatened the long established practice of shielding Ways and Means bills from amendments on the House floor, Hunt noted that the cautious, consensus-oriented approach that had been characteristic of Ways and Means decisionmaking under Mills's leadership appeared to be breaking down. In the context of the broader political developments reviewed in the previous chapter, this chapter examines how this "subtle upheaval" became by 1974 an open revolt against the institutional prerogatives and established mode of operation of the Ways and Means Committee.

The early 1970s were a transitional period for the committee. Some of the characteristics portrayed in the Manley and Fenno studies were still visible, but new conflicts had begun to appear within the committee and between the committee and the parent chamber. The first section of the chapter looks at committee politics during this transitional period, which included the demise of Chairman Wilbur D. Mills as a committee and House leader. The chapter then traces the sequence of events through which discontent in the House became channeled into a series of direct assaults on the power and autonomy of the Ways and Means Committee, the most successful of which were mounted from the House Democratic caucus. Finally, the chapter looks briefly at the budget reforms that were also enacted during the mid-1970s. The new budget process had a relatively limited impact on the politics of the Ways and Means Committee in the initial postreform years, but the new process created possibilities for some major changes in House decisionmaking which were realized in the deficit-driven politics of the 1980s.

The Ways and Means Committee in Transition

Increasing internal conflict in the early 1970s was one sign that the complex of norms and incentives that had influenced the politics of the Ways and Means Committee during the late 1950s and 1960s had begun to break down even before major structural changes took place. During 1973, Hunt and other journalists reported committee members' impressions that conflicts within the panel over policy issues were becoming sharper.[2] Joseph K. Unekis and Leroy N. Rieselbach have shown that bipartisanship (agreement among a majority of both parties) declined precipitously in committee voting from the Ninety-second Congress (1971–72) to the Ninety-third (1973–74). In the Ninety-second Congress 34 percent of recorded votes produced opposing party majorities; almost two-thirds (64 percent) were bipartisan. Over the next two years this pattern was almost reversed as 55 percent of committee votes were partisan and only 36 percent bipartisan. In terms of ideological influences, voting alignments corresponding to divisions of members rated above and below fifty by Americans for Constitutional Action increased substantially over the same period, from 44 to 63 percent. Partisanship in committee *voting* had not been that unusual during the Mills years, but the increased polarization at the *deliberative* stage of committee work noted by committee members and others during the early 1970s was new. Also suggesting that a consensual deliberative style was breaking down, the actual number of committee votes more than doubled from the Ninety-second Congress to the Ninety-third (from thirty-two to seventy-five).[3]

Although political forces external to the committee were also clearly at work, the rise in internal conflict paralleled some important changes in the committee's membership during the early 1970s. First, four of the seven Democrats appointed to Ways and Means between 1969 and 1974 were outspoken liberals who appeared to place policy goals above established committee norms of restrained partisanship and consensus seeking. James C. Corman of California, William J. Green of Pennsylvania, Sam Gibbons of Florida (all appointed in 1969), and Joseph E. Karth of Minnesota (appointed in 1972) were frequently described by journalists and committee colleagues as less prone than most senior members to compromise on issues.[4] Speaking of this group, committee Republican Barber B. Conable, Jr., of New York commented in 1974: "They understand consensus and they know how to obstruct it. They've stretched the tent."[5] Consensual norms were also strained in some instances by junior Republicans such as Bill Archer of Texas (appointed in 1973), who proved to be an aggressive and unyielding defender of oil industry tax incentives during his first term on the committee.[6]

Of course, the potential for sharp ideological and partisan conflict had, as Manley and Fenno emphasized, always been built into the committee due to the involvement of party leaders in recruitment and in policy coalitions on the issues within its jurisdiction. Even during the heyday of the Mills era, leadership on the Ways and Means Committee involved striking a balance between protecting committee prestige and pursuing partisan policy goals. With a shared interest in maintaining committee prestige, Mills and ranking Republican John W. Byrnes brought a great deal of political and substantive expertise to the task of containing partisan and ideological conflict on the committee.[7] Thus Byrnes's retirement from the House in 1972 further complicated the task of maintaining moderate partisanship on the committee. Herman T. Schneebeli of Pennsylvania, Byrnes's successor, lacked the stature among fellow Republicans and the close ties to Mills of his predecessor, making minority support for committee compromises less certain. "It'll be some time before anybody can fill John Byrnes' shoes," Mills commented in 1973.[8] Due to back problems, Mills himself was also away from the committee for extended periods during 1973 and 1974, leaving a less assertive member, Al Ullman of Oregon, to serve as acting chairman. Thus, along with changes in the committee's political environment, changes in both leadership and membership during the early 1970s appear to have contributed to the erosion of a consensual deliberative style and the pattern of restrained partisanship.

New strains in House-committee relations also began to appear. As the Ninety-third Congress (1973–74) progressed, the committee came under increasing criticism for moving too slowly and failing to produce major legislation in the areas of national health insurance and tax reform, both of which were top agenda items for many House Democrats in the early 1970s. Despite the allocation of considerable time and effort to these issues, by the end of 1974 the Ways and Means Committee had failed to get legislation in either area to the House floor.

The goal of enacting some form of expanded health insurance coverage had the backing of the Nixon administration (and of President Ford after Nixon's August 1974 resignation), House Democratic leaders, and Democratic clientele groups including organized labor. But differences remained among House liberals and conservatives over whether the coverage should be privately or publicly administered, and whether participation should be voluntary or compulsory.[9] The Ways and Means Committee had begun reviewing national health insurance proposals in April 1974—including a compromise plan cosponsored by Mills and Senator Edward Kennedy—but was evenly divided on competing approaches when an August 1974 markup reached the basic issue of how a new program would be administered. When broader agreement could not be reached on the issue, Mills abruptly adjourned a committee markup session on August 21. According to one account, Mills told the committee he "had never worked harder to reach a consensus than . . . on national health insurance." He then explained, "We don't have that consensus, and I will not go to the House floor with a Committee bill approved by a thirteen to twelve vote."[10] Mills also stated his intention to set aside the health insurance issue until the committee completed work on tax reform legislation.[11] But in returning to the controversial tax issues the committee had been wrestling with for over a year, Mills jumped from the frying pan into the fire.

After coming up empty-handed in the area of health legislation in August 1974, Mills faced an even more difficult political challenge in attempting to produce a passable tax reform bill while also protecting his committee's traditional control over deliberations on tax policy. The Ways and Means Committee had begun hearings on tax reform legislation in February 1973. But before any legislative action could be taken, work on taxes had to be suspended in May so the panel could review a major trade proposal from the Nixon administration (a situation not lost at the time on those who argued that the committee simply had more jurisdiction than it could handle—especially when Mills refused to delegate legislative work to subcommittees). With Ullman serving as acting chairman, the committee worked primarily on trade and pension legislation through October, leaving insufficient time to complete a tax reform bill in 1973. While Mills was convalescing from back surgery, Ullman remained in the chair as the committee again took up tax revision legislation in early 1974.

Against a backdrop of energy shortages and escalating oil company profits, the committee first took up provisions involving taxation of the oil industry. The central issue to be resolved was the status of the percentage depletion allowance that had been allowed to oil producers since the 1920s. Liberal Democrats had criticized the provision for decades as an unjustified tax loophole; conservatives and oil state representatives argued that the depletion allowance and other tax incentives were needed to encourage new exploration and development. After the committee (with Ullman at the helm) had gone through almost a month of inconclusive deliberations in early 1974 on what to do about the depletion allowance and a windfall profits tax proposed by the Nixon administration, Mills returned to the committee chair in mid-March.

Working with ranking Republican Herman Schneebeli, Mills broke the impasse on oil taxes by developing a provision to phase out the depletion allowance over a three-year period. The committee subsequently reported a compromise bill on April 30 by a 20-4 margin. Although neither tax reformers (who sought immediate repeal of the depletion allowance and further tightening of other oil provisions) nor industry advocates were entirely happy with the bill, it first appeared that Mills had regained his old form in fashioning a compromise acceptable to most committee members. Said one industry representative of Mills's direction of committee deliberations on the depletion issue: "It was a beautiful thing to watch even if we don't like what he did."[12] James S. Byrne, of the tax reform group Tax Analysts and Advocates, likewise conceded to the *National Journal,* "Mills pulled a rabbit out of his hat, didn't he."[13] But Mills's political success proved short-lived as committee members impatient with the chairman's consensus-oriented style rejected the compromise bill and sought intervention by the Democratic caucus to open the bill to stricter oil tax amendments on the House floor.

After the committee voted to report the Oil and Gas Energy Tax Act on April 30, Mills concluded an informal agreement among committee members to request a closed rule to govern debate on the bill.[14] After Democrats Sam Gibbons of Florida and Charles A. Vanik of Ohio expressed interest in offering floor amendments that would go further than the committee bill in tightening up oil industry preferences, Mills indicated that, the formal request for a closed rule notwithstanding, he would endorse making a limited number of amendments in order when the matter came before the Rules Committee. Mills proved unable to maintain control of the politics of the bill, however, as first William J. Green (D-Penn.) and then Vanik requested that the Democratic caucus meet to consider requiring floor votes on amendments to effect immediate repeal of the depletion allowance and eliminate tax credits for oil companies' foreign tax payments. Under the rule adopted by House Democrats in 1973 (see the discussion of Democratic caucus reforms below), at the request of fifty Democratic members a caucus meeting could be called to consider amendments to a bill for which the reporting committee was requesting a closed rule. By a majority vote of the caucus, the Democratic members of the Rules Committee could then be instructed to allow floor consideration of a specific amendment. When the caucus assembled in May 1974 to consider the Green and Vanik amendments, both were approved by voice votes.

Mills's response was first to deny the responsibility of the Ways and Means Committee to act in accordance with the caucus decision, then to circumvent the decision by withdrawing his committee's request for a rule when the Rules Committee met to consider the issue on June 6. "The caucus has nothing to do with my committee. The caucus can't bind the Ways and Means Committee," Mills contended after the appeals by Green and Vanik succeeded.[15] The Ways and Means chairman's interpretation may have been technically correct (the Democratic Study Group issued an opinion stating that the caucus procedure applied only to the Rules Committee), but it proved politically disastrous as Mills ultimately failed to get a tax reform bill to the House floor and further undermined support for his committee's authority and procedural autonomy in the House.[16]

Upon withdrawing the committee's request for a closed rule for the energy tax bill, Mills first indicated that he would take the bill directly to the floor as allowed for certain types of "privileged" legislation (including revenue bills) under House rules. It seems unlikely that Mills, long a defender of the idea that major tax bills should not be subjected to the uncertainties of floor amendments, was seriously considering such a move, which would have placed no restrictions at all on germane floor amendments.

Whatever the chairman's intentions, a committee meeting held on June 10 found little support on the Ways and Means Committee for taking the bill directly to the floor, and the oil taxation measure was temporarily shelved the following day when Speaker Albert announced that the legislative schedule would not allow it to come up again until later in the summer.

In early August Mills took a new tack on resolving the controversy, proposing that the committee develop a new bill by combining revised oil tax provisions (including a quicker phaseout of the depletion allowance) with some other tax reform measures on which the committee had been working. Although committee members Green and Vanik accused the chairman of attempting to kill the oil tax legislation through the maneuver, a majority of Ways and Means members endorsed the new strategy and work on the bill proceeded during the fall of 1974. However, by the time the new bill was reported in late November 1974, there was sharp disagreement in the committee over the bill's provisions and little support in the House for taking up a major tax bill.[17] Resentment of Mills's earlier evasion of the caucus undercut support for the committee's efforts, and with the substantial Democratic gains that had been registered in the November election, many Democrats favored holding off on tax legislation until the next Congress when it was assumed a stronger tax reform measure could be passed. On December 12 the Rules Committee formally rejected the request to send the revised tax measure to the floor for a vote, killing the bill.

Thus, as the Ninety-third Congress came to an end, neither tax nor health care legislation had reached the House floor. Instead, the Ways and Means Committee's unsuccessful maneuvering on health and tax legislation in 1974 fueled reform forces that sought to restructure the committee, and marked the final episode in Wilbur Mills's career as a congressional leader.

The Fall of Wilbur Mills

At the same time his efforts to pass a tax reform bill were collapsing at the close of the Ninety-third Congress, Mills's long and influential career as a congressional leader effectively ended on December 3, 1974, when he entered Bethesda Naval Hospital after a second public incident involving an Argentine dancer. After a number of his committee colleagues and other House members made it clear that his behavior would lead to his removal as Ways and Means chairman, while hospitalized Mills agreed to give up the position which he had held since 1958.[18] Although Mills's departure as chairman came swiftly in late 1974, both his reputation for reading and anticipating political currents in the House and support for his cautious, consensus-oriented leadership style had begun to slip noticeably in the years before his personal conduct foreclosed the possibility of continuing as Ways and Means chairman.

Some traced the onset of a decline in Mills's influence to a long-shot bid for the presidency in 1972. One Ways and Means member, for example, commented in 1974: "Since his run for the Presidency, Mills has acted more and more like a politician."[19] Not only did Mills's candidacy itself raise doubts about his political judgment, but his election-year conversion to support for revenue sharing and a huge Social Security benefit increase that had not gone through the normal committee review process also raised questions among Mills's colleagues, given his long history of professing concerns with fiscal responsibility.[20] Whatever the cause of the chairman's newfound enthusiasm for rapid expansion of Social Security benefits, as Martha Derthick points out, the endorsement of a big benefit increase in 1972 meant that the "cautious, consensus-building style that had marked Mills's leadership for fourteen years was suddenly cast to the winds."[21]

Mills's reputation for mastery of House politics had also been tarnished in 1970 and again in 1973 by floor defeats on major legislation. In May 1970 Mills suffered what Derthick termed "an extraordinary defeat" on a motion to recommit a Social Security bill that had been reported by the Ways and Means Committee. Although Mills had consistently opposed the idea, the House voted 233-144 to make a major change in the program—indexation of Social Security benefits for inflation—before accepting the committee bill.[22] Mills again misjudged House sentiment when he brought a conference agreement on a bill containing debt ceiling and Social Security provisions to the House floor in June 1973. After the agreement was rejected by a 185-190 vote, Mills had to bring a revised version to the floor the next day, conceding his embarrassment at having been wrong the first time about what the chamber would accept.[23]

Rumblings also began to be heard in the early 1970s against the way the Ways and Means Committee operated under Mills—especially the resistance to creation of subcommittees, which kept the chairman directly in charge of all of the issues in the committee's vast jurisdiction. When Mills announced in July 1973 that he might retire from Congress because of chronic back pain, the next ranking Democrat, Al Ullman of Oregon, observed regarding the chairman's close-to-the-vest style and resistance to delegating responsibility: "Even if Wilbur decides to stay in Congress he's going to have to revise his operating scheme because times have changed and the needs of the House have changed."[24] And while Mills was away from the committee in 1973 and early 1974, Ullman in fact ran the committee in a more open and decentralized fashion. Ullman tended to be much more direct in expressing his own opinions, but rather than seeking to incorporate minority members' views or frame bipartisan compromises, as Mills had, he also worked primarily with committee Democrats in assembling major legislation.[25] Ullman also broke with longstanding committee practice by creating temporary subcommittees during Mills's absence.[26]

Mills's much publicized involvement with an Argentine stripper and problems in maintaining his reputation for keen political judgment may have been due in part to alcoholism. Mills later acknowledged he had begun drinking heavily in 1969, and that the problem had worsened with his back ailment in 1973.[27] But Mills's erratic personal behavior was only part of the reason for his decline as a leader. By the mid-1970s the political climate in the House was such that Mills's centralized, consensus-oriented leadership regime and the committee's autonomy and extensive authority would likely have come under attack even if the Arkansas Democrat had spent all of his evenings in 1974 home studying the tax code.[28] That Mills did not read correctly the sea change that was occurring in the House of the mid-1970s is suggested by his provocative response to the caucus action on tax legislation in 1974 and by his claim the previous year that the Ways and Means Committee had few critics inside Congress. "Most of the problems," he contended, were "caused by Common Cause and Nader's people."[29] Public interest group types were indeed among Mills's sharpest critics, but the underlying political changes that were undermining Mills's influence ran considerably deeper.

House Reform and the Ways and Means Committee

With the final demise of its old leadership, the forces of reform hit the Committee on Ways and Means with full force in 1974. A series of structural changes approved by the Democratic caucus in December 1974 transformed the organization of the committee and recast the institutional environment within which its members would work in the future. Earlier work by Catherine E. Rudder examining the effects of reform on congressional policymaking in the tax area provides a starting point for considering the impact of House reform on the Ways and Means Committee.[30] The following reforms, according to Rudder, had the greatest impact on the committee's operation:

1. Secret ballot selection of committee chairmen instead of complete reliance on the seniority system.

2. Modification of the closed rule under which Ways and Means bills could be considered on the House floor without amendment.

3. Open committee proceedings, including House-Senate conferences, except when a majority of the committee agrees by a roll call vote to close a meeting.

4. Enlargement of the Ways and Means Committee by one-third.

5. Transfer of House Democratic committee assignments from Ways and Means to the Steering and Policy Committee.

6. Creation of Ways and Means subcommittees.[31]

Rudder and others have also emphasized the importance of the congressional budget process set up by the Budget and Impoundment Control Act of 1974 as a new factor in Ways and Means Committee politics.[32] In interviews conducted by the author, senior Ways and Means members and staff whose service on the committee predated the reforms cited largely these same reforms as most important. But also cited were the buildup in partisan committee staff and the introduction of regular partisan committee caucuses that occurred after Mills's departure in 1974. With the exception of the budget reforms, virtually all of these changes originated in the House Democratic caucus. Some were directly implemented by the caucus through changes in party rules; others were formulated there and then enacted by the House or Congress as a whole.[33] Thus the transformation of the Ways and Means Committee from one of the most highly regarded committees in the House to a "bastille" that needed to be pulled down to bring in a new order reached its completion primarily through actions of the new procedural majority in the Democratic caucus.

The Democratic Caucus Reforms

According to Fenno, during the 1960s the procedural autonomy of the Ways and Means Committee in the parent chamber and the restrained partisanship inside the committee were accepted by most House members as means to developing responsible policies and protecting institutional prerogatives of the House.[34] By the mid-1970s, in part because of the failure of the committee to make headway on issues such as national health insurance and tax reform, these characteristics were seen by many in the Democratic caucus as major *obstacles* to responsible policymaking and to the proper functioning of the House. In addition to showing discontent with the committee arising from frustrated policy goals, the Ways and Means reforms originating from the majority party caucus also reflected the goals of the new participatory politics, in light of which the traditional justifications for maintaining committee autonomy appeared simply as props for an illegitimate concentration of power in the hands of a small group of senior members.

The changes in the Ways and Means Committee initiated by the Democratic caucus were only part of an extensive series of changes in House committee and party structures and procedures implemented by Democratic reformers during the first half of the 1970s. Within the caucus, the primary mechanism for developing proposals for structural reform was the Committee on Organization, Study, and Review, which was created by a resolution adopted in March 1970. The idea for an official party unit to review the seniority system and other organizational issues had been the brainchild of Democratic Study Group staffer Richard Conlon, and the motion to create the committee had been introduced by DSG chairman Donald Fraser of Minnesota.[35] Julia Butler Hansen of Washington was named to chair the committee (hence it became known as the Hansen committee), and the membership was carefully chosen to be representative of the caucus with respect to seniority, region, and ideological outlook.[36]

Following recommendations drafted by the Hansen committee, the caucus first began to move against the seniority system and the autonomy of standing committees in 1971 and 1973 by adopting new rules requiring election of committee chairmen and limiting control of chairmen over committee organization and procedures.[37] The first direct attacks on the prerogatives of Ways and Means came in 1973 when the caucus voted through DSG-sponsored proposals to modify the use of the closed rule and add three elected party leaders (the Speaker, majority leader, and caucus chairman) to the Committee on Committees, which had for over half a century included only Ways and Means Democrats. Under the new closed rule reform (first invoked by dissatisfied Ways and Means members on energy tax legislation in 1974), the caucus could vote to instruct the Rules Committee to allow floor consideration of specific amendments on bills for which a closed rule had been requested.[38] In an action also reportedly directed in part at Ways and Means, the caucus acted in 1973 to strengthen procedures designed to encourage open committee meetings. Under the new rule, meetings would be open to the public unless a roll call vote was taken to meet behind closed doors on a particular issue.[39]

In January 1973 the full House voted to create an additional mechanism for considering reform proposals, a bipartisan Select Committee on Committees. Chaired by longtime reform advocate Richard Bolling of Missouri, the Select Committee was given a mandate to review committee organization and jurisdictional alignments. In March 1974 the Bolling committee reported a reform plan that proposed the most extensive redefinition of committee jurisdictions since the Legislative Reorganization Act of 1946. But in this case the Democratic caucus again assumed a dominant role in defining how reform would proceed by developing an alternative proposal which won out over the Bolling plan in a vote of the House in October 1974.

The creation of the Bolling committee in early 1973 reflected agreement among leaders in both parties that changes were needed to rationalize committee jurisdictions and redistribute more evenly the legislative work load of the House. These goals inevitably focused attention on the Ways and Means Committee, given its extensive jurisdiction and evident problems in managing its legislative responsibilities during the early 1970s. As Roger H. Davidson and Walter J. Oleszek (both of whom served as Bolling committee staffers) noted in their detailed account of the politics of committee reform: "The Ways and Means Committee's excessive power had been from the beginning a major target of reorganization. Speaker Albert and Minority Leader Ford certainly had Wilbur Mills's domain in mind when they proposed the reform effort, and the subject frequently found its way into the committee's hearings."[40] Bolling himself remarked in July 1973 that the jurisdiction of Ways and Means was "so vast that it can't possibly be handled by a committee that doesn't even have subcommittees."[41] As the Bolling panel worked to restructure committee jurisdictions in 1973 and 1974, a provision to shift responsibility for most trade issues and nontax aspects of unemployment and health programs from Ways and Means to other standing committees became a centerpiece of the Select Committee plan.[42]

The Select Committee formally reported its reform proposal (H. Res. 988) on March 19, 1974. Along with the changes proposed in the jurisdiction of the Ways and Means Committee, the plan also included controversial provisions to redistribute the responsibilities of the Education and Labor Committee among two new panels, consolidate most energy and environmental issues within a single committee, and limit members to service on only one of the fifteen major committees that would exist after these and other jurisdictional changes were in place. Together with other committee members of both parties, Mills had expressed opposition to the Ways and Means changes and actively sought to mobilize opposition to the Bolling plan after it was reported.[43] Probably more important for the final outcome, a broad array of other members, staff, and interest groups (including organized labor, environmentalists, and Ralph Nader's Congress Watch) also offered active opposition to the plan.[44]

On May 9 the Democratic caucus voted 111-95 to refer the Select Committee proposal to the Committee on Organization, Study, and Review (the Hansen committee) with instructions to report back by July "any recommendations deemed appropriate."[45] A revised plan reported by the Hansen committee in July 1974 eliminated most of the contentious jurisdictional changes that had been proposed by the Select Committee as well as the limitation of members to a single major committee assignment. In the case of the Ways and Means Committee, the Hansen plan proposed relatively limited jurisdictional reductions—shifting general revenue sharing, work incentive programs, renegotiation of currency agreements, and health programs supported by general revenues to other committees—but restored full responsibility for trade, unemployment, and Medicare. However, also included in the Hansen committee proposal was a new provision tailored to apply specifically to Ways and Means. All committees larger than fifteen members would be required to establish at least four subcommittees. Hansen committee member Wayne L. Hays (D-Ohio) later explained that the subcommittee requirement was included because Ways and Means "simply has not produced."[46] As directed by the caucus, the Rules Committee on September 25 sent both plans to the floor for debate under an open rule.

After six days of debate on the House floor, an amended version of the Hansen committee plan was approved on October 8. Although other aspects of the two major proposals (and a third plan introduced by Bolling committee ranking Republican David T. Martin of Nebraska) were debated at length, the proposed subcommittee reform for Ways and Means received very little attention. Over the six days of debate neither Mills nor anyone else on the committee spoke against the change. Congresswoman Hansen did state early in the debate that the creation of subcommittees would allow the committee to undertake a heavier work load, making the wholesale transfer of health programs contemplated by the Bolling plan unnecessary.[47] But other references to the change came almost in passing. Expressing disappointment over the lack of new health insurance and tax reform legislation, freshman Democrat William Lehman of Texas observed: "It is no secret to which committee this recommendation particularly applies."[48] A supporter of the more extensive changes in the Bolling plan, Republican Peter Frelinghuysen of New Jersey, remarked: "I do not think I am exaggerating when I suggest that there is at least occasionally some constipation of results so far as the Ways and Means Committee is concerned. This is not only because they have no subcommittees but because they physically do not have the time to engage their full attention on such widely disparate responsibilities."[49]

By adopting the Hansen plan over the proposal of the Select Committee on Committees in October 1974, the House rejected what would have been a major reduction in the jurisdiction of the Ways and Means Committee in favor of more limited jurisdictional changes and a requirement that subcommittees be created. But it became clear by the actions taken by the Democratic caucus the following month (both the Hansen and Bolling plans had included provisions for early organizational caucuses to allow a quicker start on legislative business) that the rejection of the Bolling plan reflected more the broad range of opposition to a major committee realignment than any vote of confidence in the Ways and Means Committee.

As the Ways and Means Committee struggled in late 1974 to salvage some type of tax reform legislation after Chairman Mills's confrontation with the Democratic caucus, the outcome of the November election created a strong impetus for a major assault against the committee in the Democratic caucus that would be convened in early December to deal with organizational matters. Not only were seventy-five new Democratic members elected, tipping the political balance in the caucus decisively in favor of liberals who had long sought to rein in Ways and Means, but many of these new members had naturally embraced the anti-institutional reformist orientation of the time. Also, during the election Common Cause had pressed House candidates for public commitments to work for procedural reform.

Shortly after the election the public interest lobby announced that 146 of the 221 Democrats elected to the Ninety-fourth Congress had already pledged to support removing authority for making House committee assignments from Ways and Means Democrats.[50] On November 21 Speaker Carl Albert publicly endorsed this change along with expansion of the committee to make it "more representative of the House."[51] During the weeks after the election the AFL-CIO, United Auto Workers, Americans for Democratic Action, and Ralph Nader's Congress Watch each wrote Democratic House members to endorse restructuring the committee.[52] Accurately foreshadowing the mood of the caucus that was to be convened in early December, one liberal Democrat declared to the *Wall Street Journal* during the last week in November of 1974, "It's open season on Ways and Means."[53]

Following an agenda developed by the DSG, on December 2, the first day of the organizational caucus, House Democrats approved by a 146-122 margin a proposal to transfer committee assignment responsibilities from Ways and Means Democrats to the Steering and Policy Committee—a larger group composed of party leaders, regional representatives elected by the caucus, and a number of additional members appointed by the Speaker.[54] On the following day the caucus decided by voice vote to enlarge the size of the Ways and Means Committee from twenty-five to thirty-seven members. Other caucus actions directed at Ways and Means included a permanent increase in the majority/minority ratio on the committee from 3:2 to 2:1 and strengthening the previously enacted subcommittee reform to require creation of a minimum of five rather four subcommittees. (In a final blow to the committee, previously enacted seniority reforms requiring chairmen to submit to caucus election also came into play when Mills stepped down as Ways and Means chairman in the face of almost certain removal.) Buoyed by success in enacting these and other changes, the reform-oriented caucus went on in January 1975 to take the unprecedented step of removing three senior committee chairmen: Wright Patman of Banking and Currency, W. R. Poage of Agriculture, and F. Edward Hebert of Armed Services.

While the Bolling committee was careful to maintain extensive records of its work on committee reform, there is remarkably little in the public record related to the restructuring of the Ways and Means Committee undertaken by the Democratic caucus in December 1974. In contrast to the revolt against Speaker Cannon in 1910, we have almost nothing in the way of public debate that offers a bill of particulars in support of change, because the procedural majority that enacted the reforms worked behind closed doors in the Democratic caucus. Even so, it seems clear from other evidence that the primary rallying points for the sweeping changes enacted in 1974 were impatience among Democratic liberals with the committee's cautious approach to new policy initiatives and increased demands for openness and broader participation in House decisionmaking. Wilbur Mills's embarrassing personal behavior and subsequent loss of support in the House probably made the assault on the committee easier than it otherwise might have been, but the convergence of forces for change in late 1974 would have presented a major challenge to the existing pattern of House-committee relations in any event.

The consensual deliberative style and norm of restrained partisanship that developed on Ways and Means under Mills's leadership allowed almost all members an opportunity to be influential in committee decisions. The result, as Manley emphasized, was a more moderate or conservative tendency in policy outcomes than would have been the case had the Democratic majority on the committee strictly controlled its decisions. Fifteen years after Manley wrote, a senior Republican made this same point in explaining why the committee had run afoul of the Democratic caucus in the 1970s. "It was great being part of a consensus committee," he mused when asked about the Mills years.

> Wilbur Mills worried about the least Republican vote as much as he worried about a Democratic vote. If he couldn't bring a bill to the floor with a 23 to 2 vote [in committee] he felt he'd failed. He wanted to stretch the tent so we all could get in it. And that's why the Committee had come to have a life of its own, why it tended to be more conservative than the Democratic party wanted.

"If I were a liberal Democrat," he concluded, "I'd be upset to see the Ways and Means Committee bringing out conservative bills too."

Liberal Democrats in the House had long been arguing that standing committees and their leaders should be more accountable to party majorities. Although some proponents of this view (especially Richard Bolling) were influenced by notions of responsible party government, most found it attractive for the simple fact that the liberals' status as a working majority was much more likely in the party caucus than in committees or on the House floor where alliances between conservative Democrats and Republicans could come into play.[55] For this reason, making the standing committees more responsive to the party caucus was one of the central goals of the ongoing efforts at structural reform by the liberal Democratic Study Group.

The basic orientation of the Ways and Means Committee under Mills —seeking broad consensus in order to win comfortable majorities on the House floor—was anathema to liberal Democrats who sought a more active party apparatus in the House as a means for policy activism. Because many of the most important items on the liberal agenda fell within the jurisdiction of Ways and Means, the committee's cautious decisionmaking style naturally became a source of discontent. This frustration was articulated in an interview with a public interest group lobbyist who was closely allied with liberal House reformers during the 1970s. Looking back, he was little impressed with the Ways and Means Committee as it operated under Mills. He explained that

> Mills's way of being responsible to the House involved finding the lowest common denominator on visible issues. Mills wouldn't want to bring a bill to the floor unless he had a count of 235 to 250. Christ, you *never* can get a count of 235. . . . Mills prevented dealing with basic problems until they almost got out of hand. He was not a leader who tried to figure out how to put things together. . . . He was trying to take temperatures rather than initiate things.

Fenno reported encountering similar sentiments among some Democrats even in the 1960s. Said one Democratic leader of Mills: "He always takes three times longer bringing out a bill than we think he should. Nothing ever comes out of that Committee on time." Said another: "I think they (House Democrats) feel Ways and Means is more conservative than the whole House. . . . They have no problem with the mechanics of what Ways and Means does, but the policy—that's another matter. It's more conservative."[56] As the factional balance in the House Democratic party shifted toward the liberal wing during the 1970s, the gap between the consensus approach that had developed under Mills and the policy activism sought by many liberals was a major reason why the revitalized Democratic caucus spelled trouble for Ways and Means.

In addition to this long-simmering discontent over policy outcomes, Ways and Means also began to come under fire during the 1970s for "the mechanics" of how it operated. Restricting participation in policy formulation for major economic and social welfare issues to a carefully selected group of senior members clashed with the new participatory ethic in the House. Said one member who joined the committee after it was expanded in 1974: "This committee operated in secret for so long and played it so safe, it became a joke."[57] In part, demands for broader participation in issues handled by Ways and Means were also the product of frustration among liberals over policy outcomes. A common theme among liberal reformers was that majorities in fact might have existed in the House for new policy initiatives—including tax reform and national health insurance—but they were stymied by institutional arrangements that gave advantages to supporters and beneficiaries of the status quo. Charles A. Vanik (D-Ohio), the member who introduced the caucus measure to expand the size of Ways and Means, afterward explained the desirability of such a change in these terms: "In the past, the committee has operated as a brake, preventing legislation from coming to the floor and burying the impetus for change such as tax reform."[58]

One member who was a senior Ways and Means Democrat at the time of the 1974 reforms endorsed the idea that ideological forces were at work in the caucus moves to restructure the committee, but also pointed beyond liberal discontent to a broader movement as the driving force:

> [Some critics] said the Committee was too small, too clubby, too much hand-picked to represent the conservative segments of the House. . . . But this whole movement wasn't really a liberal movement, it was a movement to break down the old power structure in the House, which isn't necessarily a liberal objective. The guiding motive was to make way for easier access to power for the newer members.

This view lends support to the contention by Davidson and Oleszek that "reform politics in the 1960s and early 1970s were mainly attempts to give more legislators a piece of the action."[59] According to one account, the overwhelming support from newly elected Democrats for the caucus resolution stripping the committee assignment function from Ways and Means Democrats is a good case in point. Based on interviews with key participants in the Democratic caucus reforms, Burton Sheppard reports that freshmen members, naturally concerned with winning assignments to important committees, "were encouraged by veteran reformers to believe that they could expect more favorable treatment from the Steering and Policy Committee."[60]

In this way a number of motivations converged to produce the caucus reforms. Structural changes were sought in order to achieve policy objectives as well as to "open up" the process to broader participation and redistribute power. In terms of Fenno's prereform observations on the Ways and Means Committee's institutional environment, members of the Democratic caucus in the 1970s rejected the idea that the policy responsibilities of the tax committee required an unusual amount of power and procedural autonomy, because many had come to view committee autonomy as an obstacle to needed policy changes and/or inconsistent with the goal of achieving a more participatory legislative process. The result was changes that reduced the committee's procedural autonomy in the House (increased size, open meeting reforms, and changes in committee recruitment, discussed in the following chapter) and increased the authority of the majority party organization over recruitment and decisionmaking (transfer of committee assignments to Steering and Policy, closed rule reform, and seniority reforms).

The New Budget Process

Members of Congress also decided in 1974 to restructure the entire framework for making money decisions. Problems with the existing informal, decentralized budget process and the Nixon challenges to congressional spending authority ultimately led to the passage of the Congressional

Budget and Impoundment Control Act of 1974. Unlike the Democratic caucus reforms, few changes in Ways and Means Committee politics during the mid-1970s can be attributed to the budget reforms. At the time the process was set up, its impact was limited by the fact that no real consensus existed within the House on budgetary objectives. Under the political and economic conditions that developed in the 1980s, however, the budget process has become at times an important influence on committee politics.

The development and operation of the congressional budget process have been described in detail elsewhere by Allen Schick and others.[61] The objective of the discussion of the budget process here is to complete the account of 1970s reforms affecting the Ways and Means Committee by offering a brief description of the budget process as it was set up in 1974 and as it has evolved during the 1980s.

The 1974 budget act mandated both organizational and procedural changes. The organizational changes included the creation of a standing Committee on the Budget in each house and the establishment of a new support agency, the Congressional Budget Office (CBO). The new standing committees in the House and Senate were assigned similar responsibilities, but were structured somewhat differently. Both committees are responsible for formulating and reporting budget resolutions that specify overall spending (authority and outlays) and revenue levels, as well as the deficit or surplus and overall public debt for the upcoming fiscal year. However, only the Senate committee was set up on an equal organizational footing with other standing committees. The greater importance of formal structure in policymaking in the House usually makes its members more hesitant than senators in embracing proposals that redistribute power among standing committees. Representatives who have built careers around existing arrangements simply have more to lose in jurisdictional shifts (a point amply demonstrated by the fate of the jurisdictional changes proposed by the Bolling committee in 1974).[62]

This concern with the authority of House committees was reflected in the structure of the House Budget Committee. The interests of the existing money committees were protected by a provision requiring that part of the budget panel's membership would be drawn from the Ways and Means and Appropriations committees. The potential for the new committee to emerge as an independent power base in the House was also circumscribed by limiting the time individual members can serve on the Budget Committee (presently the limit is no more than six years out of ten). In this way incentives for members to build up the House committee's power were balanced against the fact that careers of any length would have to be spent elsewhere in the committee system. Commented one Ways and Means member who also served on the House Budget Committee:

I was very sensitive to the relationship with Ways and Means. Know-
ing my tenure on Budget was temporary and my tenure on Ways and
Means was permanent, I did not want to get the Budget Committee
in the role of writing tax legislation.

A new timetable for budget-related decisions and the use of concurrent
resolutions to set overall revenue and spending levels were the most important procedural innovations affecting the Ways and Means Committee contained in the 1974 act.[63] As the process was originally set up, each year two
budget resolutions were to be developed. The first, to be adopted by May
15, was to set targets for revenues and spending, with the latter broken out
by functional areas (defense, agriculture, health, etc.). The second, to be
adopted on September 15 after all tax and spending measures had been
enacted, was to set binding totals for revenues and expenditures. Provision
was also made for a reconciliation process, through which spending and
revenue levels could be brought into line with totals specified in the second
resolution.

During the 1970s the budget process resulted in the generation of a
great deal of new information but had limited impact, serving primarily to
accommodate the existing system of decentralized control over tax and
spending decisions by the standing committees. Indeed, it would be hard to
imagine the same House of Representatives that revolted against the autonomy and power of the Ways and Means Committee during the mid-
1970s acquiescing in the creation of an even more powerful, highly centralized budget process.[64]

A number of features of the budget process also limited its impact on
the tax policy area that is of central importance to the role of the Ways and
Means Committee in the House. First, the budget resolutions provide a
relatively blunt tool for influencing tax policy. Unlike the treatment of
spending authority and outlays, which are broken out into a number of
functional categories, revenue figures can be mandated only at the level of
aggregate totals. Thus, while changes in total revenues can be mandated
under the budget act, specific tax policy changes cannot.[65] The other major
revenue feature of the process involves "tax expenditures"—special provisions that provide taxpayers with exemptions of some type from the basic
structure of the tax code. The 1974 act produced "an outpouring of data on
tax expenditures" by requiring that the president, the budget committees,
and CBO assemble and report information on these tax provisions, but no
mechanism was created to deal directly with tax expenditures through the
budget process.[66]

But if the impact of the budget process on tax and spending decisions was limited in the 1970s, changing economic and political conditions
worked to transform the process from one that worked primarily to accommodate the actions of the standing committees on tax and spending issues

to one that has allowed for a more "top-down" or centralized approach to budgetary decisionmaking. Due to concerns over rising deficit levels in 1980, the budget committees moved to incorporate the reconciliation procedure in the first budget resolution. When tied to reconciliation, the first budget resolution became capable of being used as a centralized mechanism for directing both spending and revenue decisions. Under the reconciliation process, each chamber may instruct its standing committees to report out legislation affecting spending or revenues by a specified amount on or before a specific date. These changes may then be submitted to the entire chamber for approval as a package. This process has been especially important in controlling expenditures in entitlement programs in which benefit levels are mandated under existing law.

The use of the reconciliation procedure by the new Reagan administration to enact budget cuts in 1981 and the fiscal pressures created by the massive deficits that followed the enactment of the Reagan economic program and the onset of recession in 1982 reinforced the shift toward more centralized budgeting in Congress.[67] Thus the budget process after 1980 has allowed for a more centralized, integrative approach to budget decisionmaking *when congressional majorities will support it*. As John W. Ellwood has observed, "The reconciliation process . . . has shifted power from committees and subcommittees to the budget committees, to the party leadership, and to each chamber as a whole."[68]

A second important development in the budget process during the 1980s was the enactment of the Balanced Budget and Emergency Deficit Control Act of 1985—better known as "Gramm-Rudman-Hollings."[69] The Gramm-Rudman-Hollings law as enacted in late 1985 (and reenacted in 1987 to remedy constitutional flaws) streamlined the schedule for enacting budget resolutions and established maximum annual deficit levels to be enforced through a process of automatic spending cuts known as sequestration.[70] As revised, the act requires successive annual reductions in deficit levels leading to a balanced budget by 1993. Because the deficit targets set for the initial two years (see Table 3-1) did not prove to create severe constraints on spending or revenue decisions in Congress, this change in the budget process had limited effects on committee politics during the most recent period covered by this study. (Gramm-Rudman-Hollings has been important in structuring budget debates in some years since 1986.)[71] The earlier change in the use of the reconciliation process, on the other hand, has had a major impact on the Ways and Means Committee as well as other standing committees during the 1980s.

Because its jurisdiction includes both revenue bills and a number of major entitlement programs (Social Security, Medicare, Unemployment Compensation), the Ways and Means Committee has been one of the most important targets of the reconciliation process in the 1980s. Almost all of the major deficit reduction proposals that have been debated during this

Table 3-1
Maximum Deficit Amounts under Gramm-Rudman-Hollings (in billions of dollars)

Fiscal Year	Original Version	Revised Version
1986	171.9	
1987	144	
1988	108	144
1989	72	136
1990	36	100
1991	0	64
1992		28
1993		0

period have included revenue increases and/or cuts in entitlement programs as major components. Ways and Means members differ in their assessments of the independent effects of the budget process on the committee's policy decisions, but most stated that it had become an important factor in committee decisionmaking during the 1980s.

Most Ways and Means members interviewed indicated that they do feel obligated as a committee to comply with the mandates of the budget process. As one member put it: "We do feel obligated to meet the revenue figures. We are sometimes resentful when the Budget committee mandates something—especially on the spending side—but we try to meet those goals." Members differed on the question of whether the budget process has shifted power away from the committee to the budget committees or the floor. One member described the reconciliation process as having functioned as a "prod for the committee to act." Another concluded that "it has caused us to do some things we wouldn't otherwise do on the spending side." Still another member questioned the independent influence of the budget process on committee decisionmaking. "We respond to what the House wants," he contended. "We would do it [make policy changes] with or without the Budget committee."

In addition to challenging the Ways and Means Committee's autonomy in deciding the revenue and spending issues within its jurisdiction, the budget process during the 1980s has structured the committee's deliberations by creating time constraints when the panel has been required to report legislation under reconciliation instructions. Referring to this aspect of the budget process, one Ways and Means member commented: "It has had a profound impact because we spend a lot of time responding to the process." A senior committee staffer expressed frustrations with the time constraints under which the committee has sometimes had to work to meet deadlines established through the budget process:

> The budget process can mandate that certain things happen by artificially set dates. When you start bumping up against those dates, very often the quality of your work suffers. . . . so corners have to be cut. You don't have time to think things out.

A final significant change traceable to the new budget process that has affected the Ways and Means Committee has been the emergence during the 1980s of a more active role for the Senate in initiating changes in tax and spending policies. Although the Constitution gives the House of Representatives authority to initiate all new revenue legislation (Article I, section 7), under the budget process each house is responsible for developing a budget resolution and "each budget committee puts together its budget resolution *de novo* with respect to the other chamber."[72] Hence, as Schick has pointed out, on tax and spending questions "the Senate is no longer in a reactive role vis-a-vis the House."[73] The budget process now makes it possible for the Senate effectively to initiate changes in revenue policy through the reconciliation mechanism—as occurred with a major tax increase enacted in 1982 (see Chapter 6). Prior to the 1980s this initiating function had almost always been performed by Ways and Means.

Budget resolutions have become an important feature of congressional policymaking during the 1980s because they have been used at times as a mechanism to set and enforce spending and revenue figures rather than simply to accommodate decisions of the standing committees. In the context of the large deficits that have existed since 1981, the requirement of enacting a budget resolution has repeatedly spawned deliberations on proposals incorporating changes in both tax and spending policies. Consideration of proposals of this scope was extremely difficult in the decentralized congressional process that existed before the budget reforms; enacting them was even more so.

The budget reforms contributed two important features to the new institutional context that emerged from the breakdown of the postwar order in the House: first, a new set of organizational units (the House and Senate budget committees, CBO) with authority and resources for getting involved in the jurisdictions of the existing standing committees—with the tax and spending jurisdiction of Ways and Means a major case in point; and second, a procedure (reconciliation) with the potential—if congressional majorities would support it—for allowing integration of tax and spending decisions. As will be shown in the analysis of tax policymaking in Chapters 6 and 7, attempts (sometimes successful, sometimes not) to use the budget process to enact deficit reduction packages including both spending and tax components became a regular feature of congressional politics in the

1980s. These developments signaled an important shift in congressional politics with major consequences for Ways and Means as well as other House committees.

Conclusion

The institutional context within which the Ways and Means Committee functioned after 1974 was much different from the one that had been described in the Manley and Fenno studies. An active procedural majority had undertaken an extensive reform program through the authority of the Democratic caucus. With Democratic liberals seeking a more party-oriented House to advance new policy initiatives, and broad acceptance among new members of the tenets of the new participatory politics, the old rationale for insulating the tax committee (or, for that matter, any committee) from external influences was no longer tenable. Although the committee maintained most of its legislative jurisdiction, Ways and Means Democrats lost the power of making Democratic committee assignments that they had exercised for over half a century, and new procedures allowed broader access and much greater influence by the majority party in committee politics. Finally, although the short-term impact of the budget reforms was relatively limited, new procedures and organizational units were put in place that made possible a more comprehensive budget politics in place of the decentralized tax and spending decisions that were formerly the exclusive province of the various standing committees.

The decline of the postwar institutional order in the House spelled the end of the conditions that had allowed the Ways and Means Committee to dominate House deliberations on tax, trade and social welfare issues within its jurisdiction through a process of restricted participation and consensus-oriented coalition building. Although, as the next chapters will show, some continuities remained in the operation of the committee and in House-committee relations, new influences were introduced into committee politics by the reforms. Moreover, the transfer of authority to the majority party apparatus and the budget process allowed for a variety of new possibilities for conducting deliberations that had formerly been dominated by the Ways and Means Committee.

Chapter 4

The Committee on Ways and Means in the Postreform House

When asked by the *National Journal* in late 1974 about the effects of House reforms on the Ways and Means Committee, John Manley commented: "The committee is going to have to spend a great deal of time redefining itself. Everything important about the committee when I looked at it in 1969 [in *The Politics of Finance*] is changed. . . . But whether or not these are lasting changes is quite an open question."[1]

This chapter addresses the question of the permanence and scope of reform-era changes by providing an overview of the institutional context within which the Ways and Means Committee has operated in the aftermath of the 1970s reforms. The perspectives on congressional politics developed by David R. Mayhew and Richard F. Fenno, Jr., provide the focus for the first part of the chapter, which examines change in the institutional factors identified by each as important influences on committee members' behavior. The chapter then examines how reform-era changes have affected two characteristics of the committee that directly relate to capabilities for performing deliberative functions for the House: the regional and ideological balance of its membership and the availability of information and staff support in the policy areas within its jurisdiction.

Some of the institutional patterns that had influenced Ways and Means Committee politics during the prereform years survived the upheavals of the mid-1970s or reemerged when reform forces began to wane later in the decade. Others, including the committee's distinctive prestige and power in the postwar House, were permanently altered by reform-era changes. A brief statement of the two purposive theories that serve as the framework for assessing the effects of institutional change on Ways and Means Committee politics provides the starting point for the chapter.

The Electoral Connection Model

David R. Mayhew's *Congress: The Electoral Connection* has become one of the most influential recent works on congressional politics by offering a clear statement of the case for viewing members of Congress as rational actors who seek to maximize their individual chances for reelection. And of importance for the present study, this influential model of congressional politics suggests that reform-era institutional changes in the House should produce certain predictable effects on the behavior of members.

The basic premise of the Mayhew model is the assumption that members of Congress are concerned above all else with maintaining electoral support and winning reelection. Institutional incentives to follow party leadership are weak, and each individual member can do relatively little to affect the success or failure of party objectives. Therefore, the logic of this model suggests, members devote little if any attention to their responsibilities as national legislators, and instead focus primarily on bolstering their own electoral fortunes through nonsubstantive "advertising," posturing on issues of importance to constituents (position taking), and claiming credit for constituency services and tangible benefits distributed by government.[2] The result, Mayhew argues, "is that congressional policy-making activities produce a number of specifiable and predictable policy effects."[3] These effects include: *delay*, especially on issues where few electoral benefits are expected; *particularism*, formulating legislation to provide benefits for local constituencies; *servicing the organized*, special responsiveness to clientele groups with resources to influence electoral outcomes; and *symbolism*, for in most policy areas, Mayhew argues, "the electoral payment is for positions rather than effects."[4]

Of course, over the long run a membership whose activities are motivated primarily by the quest for particularistic benefits or opportunities to serve electorally active clientele groups could be expected to produce seriously flawed policies. This would especially be the case in tax and spending decisions where uncontrolled distribution of benefits (special tax breaks or spending targeted at specific groups or localities) for electoral and credit-claiming purposes would inevitably conflict with fiscal responsibility in policymaking. Only "selective incentives"—specifically, internal power and prestige—keep some members at work on the broader responsibilities of the institution for national policymaking.[5] Especially important at the time Mayhew was writing (the early 1970s) were what he called the "control committees" in the House of Representatives: Rules, Appropriations, and Ways and Means. In restraining the distribution of particularized benefits in tax and spending decisions, these committees were "like governors on what can all too easily become a runaway engine."[6] It was primarily the selective incentives of institutional power and prestige associated with top leadership positions and membership on control committees, according to Mayhew, that explained why Congress had in fact managed to avoid some of the adverse policy effects of the electoral connection in the prereform years.

For assessing the consequences of the 1970s reform era for the politics of the Ways and Means Committee, Mayhew's theory suggests a focus on the effects of reforms on committee prestige in the House. As the discussion below will show, the reforms of the 1970s resulted in a loss in the institutional power and prestige associated with membership on the Ways and Means Committee. The transformation of a control committee into a committee more like other House committees should, if Mayhew's theory is correct, produce more of the "specifiable and predictable policy effects" that normally result from the electoral connection. With a decline in the prestige associated with Ways and Means membership and conscious attempts by reformers to reduce its members' power, the cautious policy-making style of the prereform "control" committee would be expected to change in the direction of less carefully crafted decisions that reflect greater attention to servicing clientele groups and more distribution of particularized benefits to members' constituencies. The traditional concern shown by Ways and Means members for careful consideration of broad policy effects should be much less in evidence as committee members, no longer accorded as much power and prestige for taking the long view, come to see their committee positions more as a means of access to particularized benefits and as a platform for position taking.

Fenno on Committee Politics: Members' Goals and Environmental Constraints

In a comparative study of congressional committees published in the early 1970s, *Congressmen in Committees*, Richard F. Fenno, Jr., set forth a different type of purposive framework, one that suggests the possibility of different patterns in Ways and Means Committee members' behavior in the aftermath of the 1970s reforms.[7] A major difference between Fenno's model of committee behavior and the electoral connection model is that Fenno's approach offers a more complex view of members' motivations, sacrificing parsimony for what Fenno argues to be a more realistic conceptualization of members' goals. The pursuit of reelection is incorporated in this explanatory framework, but so are the assumptions that members seek prestige or influence in the House and seek to enact good public policies, that is, those consistent with their views of the public interest.[8]

Fenno proposes that different committees are seen by members as offering opportunities to pursue different goals: some may be seen as beneficial primarily for building electoral support through constituency service, some as allowing opportunities to participate in debates on the important policy issues of the day, and some in conferring prestige and power. Thus one factor that helps explain the behavior of committee members is the mix of goals its members seek to pursue—which may or may not be primarily reelection. The second major factor is the committee's political environment. "The members of each committee," Fenno states, "will develop strategies for accommodating the achievement of their individual goals to the satisfaction of key environmental expectations."[9] These environmental constraints are defined by the institutional context in the parent House and by the policy environment, in more specific terms, by the extent of involvement of executive officials, clientele groups, and party leaders in the issues that fall within the committee's jurisdiction. If committee members are in basic agreement on goals, according to Fenno's model, they will develop a set of strategic premises (decision rules) and organizational arrangements for achieving their goals within the constraints defined by the committee's environment. Committee decisionmaking processes and decisions flow in turn from these strategic premises.

As Fenno's analytical framework is more complex than the electoral connection model, the potential sources of change in committee behavior it suggests are more complex and the propositions that may be derived about the effects of institutional change necessarily less precise.[10] Along with changes affecting the prestige of the committee, other aspects of recruitment patterns could also be important if changes in goal orientations of committee members follow. Changes in the institutional context in the House that embodied new expectations about committee behavior or that affected the ability of executive officials, clientele groups, or party leaders to influence the satisfaction of committee members' goals might also be important in redefining environmental constraints.

Fenno's analysis of the prereform Ways and Means Committee paralleled Mayhew's in citing the importance of the committee's prestige, yet Fenno's theory suggests possibilities for the behavior of the postreform committee other than the increased tendency toward "runaway" policymaking one would anticipate from the electoral connection model. Viewed through Fenno's analytical framework, evidence on the effects of the 1970s reforms on members' goals and environmental constraints suggests that the more likely effect of the reforms is the emergence of a more partisan, ideological committee decisionmaking process, that is, one in which members' efforts to advance their views of good public policy rather than the intensified pursuit of constituency and clientele benefits become the dominant new feature of committee politics.

The evidence about the postreform institutional context from which these propositions are derived follows. The discussion focuses first on the institutional factor emphasized in the electoral connection model, committee prestige.

Reform, Committee Prestige, and the Pull of the Electoral Connection

Measures that have been used to gauge committee prestige or attractiveness show that the Ways and Means Committee remained an attractive committee for House members during the 1970s and into the 1980s. It continued to be one of the top panels in terms of drawing senior members from other committees and in holding members once they obtained a seat. Nonetheless, these measures and interview data on committee recruitment show that the Ways and Means Committee's high status in the House underwent a significant decline during the 1970s.

Malcolm Jewell and Chu Chi-Hung have shown that for the period from the Eighty-eighth through the Ninety-second Congresses (1963–71), Ways and Means drew more members who had accumulated high levels of seniority than any other committee in the House.[11] Other panels that drew the most senior members from other committees during this period were the Rules and Appropriations committees. An update of this study, analyzing committee transfers from the Ninety-third through the Ninety-seventh Congresses (1973–81), found that significant changes in these patterns had occurred during the reform era.[12] Ways and Means remained among the top three House committees in attraction of senior members, but it had slipped in rank from a distant first to second (behind Rules) on the index used by both studies.[13] Looking at this measure alone it is hard to say what this change means in terms of the prestige associated with the committee, except that fewer senior members were switching committees to go on Ways and Means during the period covered by the second study than during the first.

The author of the more recent study, Bruce A. Ray, points out that the decline in committee transfers among senior members is consistent with changes in the committee assignment process and reforms in committee structure during the 1970s. First, more freshmen during this period were receiving seats on desirable committees to begin with, leaving them less reason to switch as senior members. In addition, the redistribution of power to the subcommittee level and the accessibility of subcommittee leadership positions to members with modest amounts of seniority meant that members with some seniority on less prestigious committees were becoming more and more hesitant to give up a subcommittee leadership position (or the imminent likelihood of attaining one) in order to start over on the seniority ladder of a new committee. What this suggests is that a "flatter" committee hierarchy has emerged in the reformed House. Some committees—especially Rules, Appropriations, and Ways and Means—are still more prestigious than others, but the accessibility of leadership positions elsewhere has significantly dimmed the luster of the "prestige committees" for many House members today.

The pattern suggested by these studies of committee attractiveness was confirmed in interviews with Ways and Means members. Said one Democrat who obtained a seat in the early 1980s at the beginning of his second term in the House:

> I would never have thought I wanted to get on Ways and Means if
> the position from my region had remained filled for . . . six years. I
> would have moved up on Energy and Commerce and I would have
> stayed on Energy and Commerce because I would have started devel-
> oping seniority. But if I had a choice of any committee *during the first
> six years* I would pick Ways and Means [emphasis mine].

A very similar comment was offered by a Republican who joined the committee at the beginning of his third House term: "I wanted to move up. . . .
I felt that the time had come; if I ever was going to make a move, this was
the time to do it. Otherwise I would be so senior on my other committees I
wouldn't want to give that up the next time an opening came around." The
mean seniority of the forty members who joined the committee during the
Mills era (1958–74) was 7.7 years, while the mean seniority of the fifty-two
new committee members over the 1975 to 1986 period fell to 3.5 years.[14]

That Ways and Means remained a desirable committee assignment is
indicated also by the continuity in membership on the committee. Over the
five Congresses studied by Jewell and Chu, only one member who remained in the House left the committee—Hale Boggs, who left to become
majority leader in 1971.[15] A review of the forty-four departures from the
committee from 1973–86 indicates that Ways and Means members are no
more likely to transfer to other committees in the postreform House than
before. All forty-four involved members who left the House.

Ways and Means is still a desirable assignment, but membership no
longer confers the degree of institutional status it did in the prereform
House. A number of changes in the 1970s contributed to this erosion in
committee prestige. One senior committee member emphasized the loss of
the Democratic committee assignment function when describing the effects
of the 1970s reforms on the committee:

> The committee no longer has the reputation and power that it once
> had. You no longer see senior members of the Democratic party
> struggling to get on the Ways and Means Committee. . . . Now that
> the political [committee assignment] function has been cut away they
> have more power as senior members of other committees than they
> would have as a rank-and-file member of Ways and Means.

Along with the proliferation of subcommittee leadership positions on other
committees, other possible causes of reduced prestige would include the
problems experienced at times by Mills's successors in building majorities in
the committee and on the House floor, and the enlargement of the committee from twenty-five to thirty-seven members.[16]

Given the importance of prestige as an incentive for members of "control committees" in the electoral connection model, a loss of committee
prestige would be expected to result over time in significant changes in
Ways and Means Committee members' behavior. Members of Congress, it

should be recalled, are viewed in this model as single-minded seekers of reelection who pay little attention to broader societal interests or overall policy effects of congressional actions. Instead, they respond to electoral incentives that encourage advertising, credit claiming, and position taking, with the result that certain recognizable patterns—including particularism and servicing of organized interests that control resources that might affect electoral outcomes—normally are present in members' behavior. The policy effects of the electoral connection were limited in the prereform House primarily by institutional arrangements that conferred prestige within the House on members who were willing to invest time and effort in attending to the broader legislative responsibilities of the House.

Noting the prestige associated with leadership positions and membership on three "control committees" (Appropriations, Rules, and Ways and Means) in the prereform House, Mayhew concluded: "What happens is that prestige and power within the Congress itself are accorded to upholders of the institution; the Capitol Hill pecking order is geared to the needs of institutional maintenance. Members are paid in internal currency for engaging in institutionally protective activities that are beyond or even against their own electoral interests."[17]

By expanding the Ways and Means Committee and reducing its power and autonomy, the 1970s reforms in effect reduced the "payments" that would be made to individual Ways and Means members for attending to institutional prerogatives and fiscal policy effects of committee decisions. In addition, House reforms resulted in a major devaluation of the "currency" of institutional prestige by creating such a large number of subcommittee leadership positions that the relative attractiveness of serving on one of the control committees was reduced considerably for many members. A number of observers have also argued that, although even harder to document than changes over time in committee prestige, *external* incentives—especially those associated with a highly individualized electoral environment and the increased importance of the news media—have become more important for many members of Congress in recent years.[18] If so, such a shift would also tend to lower the value of the internal "currency" of prestige in the House.

Any policy effects from a weakening of prestige incentives should be pronounced for members involved in money decisions. These, according to Mayhew, are especially vulnerable to the pull of the electoral connection. Tax and spending decisions offer excellent opportunities for channeling benefits to local constituencies and clientele groups, and members of Congress have "little or no electoral reason" to be concerned about overall fiscal or macroeconomic effects of distributing benefits in this way.[19]

Therefore, when viewed from the perspective of the electoral connection model, the institutional changes of the 1970s reform era should produce an increased tendency on the part of Ways and Means members to exploit the opportunities for position taking, credit claiming, and distributing benefits to individual constituencies and organized groups that are offered by the issues within their committee's jurisdiction. In other words, more pork barreling and clientele servicing and less attention to broader fiscal objectives should be visible in deliberations and policy outcomes on the postreform committee if the electoral connection model captures accurately the essential dynamics of House politics.

Reform, Members' Goals, and Environmental Constraints

In contrast to the emphasis in the electoral connection model on committee prestige as the primary institutional factor influencing the behavior of Ways and Means members, Fenno's theory suggests a number of other factors to be examined in considering the effects of reform-era institutional changes on committee politics. For Fenno, committee members' behavior is the product of the interplay between members' goals and the environmental constraints that affect achievement of those goals. Prior to the reforms, support in the parent chamber for powerful money committees and acceptance by House members of a high degree of procedural autonomy helped to define the panel's environmental constraints, as did a distinctive recruitment process. A committee consensus on the goal of prestige or influence also existed. The previous chapter documented the erosion of support in the parent chamber for committee autonomy. Structural changes that reduced the committee's procedural autonomy in the House also increased the importance of clientele groups and the majority party organization in the committee's environment.

The primary difference between Fenno's theoretical framework and the electoral connection model is that the former admits a broader range of possibilities for postreform committee behavior, depending on the particular configuration of members' goals and environmental constraints that emerges in the wake of the reforms. When the effects of the 1970s reform era are viewed from the perspective of this second purposive theory of congressional politics, a closer survey of recruitment patterns and the committee's political environment is needed to determine the specific changes that may have occurred in members' goals and in the institutional environment in which they are pursued. A look at committee recruitment over the postreform years provides a point of departure for this more detailed exploration of postreform institutional change.

Committee Selection: Democrats

Prior to the 1970s reforms, committee assignments for House Democrats were made by the Democratic members on Ways and Means; the only exception was the Ways and Means Committee itself, where vacancies were filled by caucus election.[20] Since 1974 committee assignments have been made by the Democratic Steering and Policy Committee subject to approval by the caucus. The only exception in the new system is the Rules Committee, whose members are nominated by the Speaker, also subject to caucus approval.

The shift in the assignment power from the Ways and Means Democrats to the larger group that makes up the Steering and Policy Committee brought broader participation in assignment decisions, a more open process, and a formal role for party leaders. However, after examining actual assignment decisions in three Congresses after the 1974 reforms (the Ninety-fifth, Ninety-sixth, and Ninety-seventh), Steven S. Smith and Bruce A. Ray concluded that "there are few detectable differences between the pre- and postreform periods in the factors that shape assignment outcomes."[21] As before the reforms, the process functions less as an instrument of political control than as "a routine effort to accommodate the requests of as many members as possible."[22] One change with important implications for Democratic recruitment for Ways and Means is noted, however: "Freshmen expectations about the quality and quantity of assignments to which they are entitled have risen."[23] As Smith and Ray point out, in contrast to the 1950s and 1960s, by the late 1970s freshman requests for and assignments to top committees were no longer considered extraordinary.

The appointment of freshman members to top committees marked a significant change in the institutional environment for committee politics in the House. Those who made Democratic committee assignments in the postwar House were not expected to be quite as accommodative of junior members' requests for the two money committees and the Rules Committee as for most other panels. In describing how the committee assignment process changed after 1974, one senior Ways and Means Democrat remarked: "Well, they threw all those basic rules out the window." This turns out to be something of an overstatement, but it accurately conveys the point that within the general pattern of continuity in the committee assignment process, some important changes have occurred in the selection process for Ways and Means members. Three aspects of committee recruitment merit attention in examining the effects of reform-era institutional changes on members' goals and environmental constraints: who influences the committee assignment decision, what criteria are used in selecting Ways and Means members, and how the goal orientations of members who are selected compare with the patterns that were present on the prereform committee.

Interviews with fourteen of the thirty-six Democrats who were appointed between 1975 and 1986 show that most who were successful in obtaining a seat on Ways and Means waged an active personal campaign focused on building majority support in the Steering and Policy Commit-

tee. Thirteen of these fourteen were, to use Fenno's term, self-starters;[24] only one was sought out by others and encouraged to take a seat on the committee. In addition to personal lobbying efforts directed at the membership of the Steering and Policy Committee, three other factors were most often mentioned as important by those who sought a nomination for a Ways and Means seat: support within the state delegation, support of the party leadership, and after 1980, support of the chairman of Ways and Means.

A tradition of maintaining "state seats" for states with large Democratic delegations survived the reform era more or less unscathed. From 1975 through 1986, 75 percent of the Democratic vacancies created by departures of committee members have been filled—either immediately or within one Congress—by a member from the same state.[25] A state claim was specifically cited by seven Democrats as a key factor in gaining a seat. Almost all of the Democratic members indicated that they began their effort to win a Ways and Means seat by lining up support within the state delegation in order to become their state's "designee" for an open seat. With the backing of the state delegation, members usually then asserted state or regional claims for representation on Ways and Means when soliciting support from members of Steering and Policy.

For most of the members who joined the committee after 1974 the support of the party leadership—now formally represented on the Steering and Policy Committee and responsible for appointing a sizable portion of its members—was also seen as very important in gaining the nomination. All but two of the Democrats who went on Ways and Means during this period described the support of the party leadership, especially that of the Speaker, as important.

A member who went on in the late 1970s described his "campaign" as follows:

> I had first to be elected in my own state delegation, so that required a
> lobbying effort inside the state delegation. . . . I then had to go talk
> to all the people involved with the Steering and Policy Committee.
> And then after that there were key powers in the House you needed
> to go to: the majority leader and the Speaker.

Recalling a difficult decision to vote with Speaker O'Neill and the Democratic leadership on President Carter's 1977 energy package, the same Democrat explained that the Speaker "was very, very helpful to me as a result of that particular vote."

If the Speaker's support has been helpful, it has not been essential. Some members won nomination by the Steering and Policy Committee without the Speaker's support. One explained that he did not have the Speaker's support but was still able to mount a successful bid by "contacting every single member of Steering and Policy personally," and enlisting the active support of personal acquaintances and the representative from his region on the Steering and Policy Committee. Concerning his ultimate success without the support of the top party leadership, he explained: "I had a lot of Democrats who would go with me simply because I had fought in the trenches in Steering and Policy and had won." The requirement that assignments be approved by the Democratic caucus also allows the possibility of challenging Steering and Policy nominations in the caucus. A number of caucus challenges of Ways and Means nominations have been attempted since 1975, but only one (mounted in 1979 by Wyche Fowler of Georgia) has been successful.[26]

Those who were appointed to the committee after 1980 added Ways and Means chairman Dan Rostenkowski of Illinois to the list of influential participants in the selection process. (Al Ullman of Oregon, who served as Ways and Means chairman from 1975–80, by all accounts took little or no part in assignments to the committee.) Rostenkowski, who became Ways and Means chairman in 1981, had served on the Steering and Policy Committee since 1979 and was ensured a continuing role in the committee assignment process when House Democrats began in the Ninety-seventh Congress (1981) to maintain ex officio positions on Steering and Policy for chairmen of the Ways and Means, Rules, Appropriations, and Budget committees.

All of the seven Democrats interviewed who went on the Ways and Means Committee after 1980 mentioned Chairman Rostenkowski as an important participant in the selection process. As one Democrat explained:

> If the Speaker and a lot of other people support someone, [Rostenkowski] is probably going to go along unless he finds something very offensive about the guy. But if he for some reason didn't like the guy, that member wouldn't get on. He [Rostenkowski] would talk to the Speaker and find someone else to fill the position.

Explaining that he "spoke with the chairman, the Speaker, and the majority leader" about getting on the committee, a second member stated:

> Probably of the three, the chairman is the most important to be supportive of your candidacy. He likes to know who those members are who are desiring to become members of the Ways and Means Committee. So it's very important to have the support of the chairman of Ways and Means.

In addition to these junior Democrats, a number of Republicans and more senior Democrats also commented on the current chairman's role in recruitment, agreeing that Rostenkowski takes an active interest in Ways and Means assignments (see Chapter 5).

Despite the 1974 reform that moved the committee assignment function to the Steering and Policy Committee, the Democratic recruitment process for Ways and Means remains in many ways similar to prereform patterns that Manley traced as far back as the 1930s. Party leaders are influential in assignments, claims by state delegations to retain "state seats" play a major role in the process, and, after 1980 at least, the chairman of the committee takes an active interest in screening prospective members.[27]

But other aspects of committee recruitment did change during the 1970s. In the 1950s and 1960s, those influential in the committee recruitment process generally limited Ways and Means appointments to senior members, with considerations of party loyalty, electoral security, and a "responsible" legislative style also important. This unusual care in committee selection, Fenno concluded, was an important environmental constraint and the most important way in which House members sought to ensure that this powerful committee would remain responsive to the parent chamber.[28] Ironically, the view that these selection practices had in fact produced an unrepresentative and unresponsive committee had been an important contributing factor in the revolt against the committee in the Democratic caucus. Not unexpectedly, the aftermath of the 1974 caucus reforms brought some significant changes in these informal selection criteria for Ways and Means members.

Even so, when asked what those influential in making committee assignments were looking for in candidates for openings on Ways and Means, Democrats interviewed in the mid to late 1980s mentioned characteristics remarkably similar to those found by prereform studies. A member appointed in 1981 commented that three considerations seemed to be most important:

> One, [they wanted] somebody who was reasonably loyal to the
> Democratic party; two, somebody from a reasonably safe seat; and
> three, someone who from a stylistic point of view was collegial—who
> could get along with his neighbors and wouldn't grandstand.

What is conspicuously absent here is the expectation that a member acquire substantial legislative experience in the House before seeking appointment. Only two Democratic members even mentioned seniority as an important factor in obtaining a seat.

The diminished importance of seniority in Ways and Means recruitment is readily apparent when Democratic appointments during the Mills era (1958–74) are compared with those after 1974. During the Mills era the mean seniority for those appointed to Ways and Means was nine years.[29] No freshmen and only two second-term members were among the twenty-three Democratic members appointed while Mills was chairman. Consistent with the demands of junior members for greater access to top committee positions, mean seniority for new Ways and Means Democrats between 1975 and 1986 dropped to 3.1 years, with appointments of freshmen and second-term members becoming more the rule than the exception between 1975 and 1980. As shown in Table 4-1, almost two-thirds of the thirty-six appointees had served one term or less in the House; one-fourth have been freshmen. However, no freshmen have won appointment since 1979.

While the postreform years have witnessed greater success of junior members in Ways and Means recruitment, the selection process still tends to favor party regulars. The ability of the committee to protect most of its vast jurisdiction during the 1970s apparently gave party leaders more than ample incentive to remain active in the recruitment process and steer selections toward party loyalists.

One member who was appointed in the early 1980s observed that this was especially true after the Democratic-controlled House approved presidential budget and tax initiatives early in the Reagan administration:

> There was a lot of sensitivity [on Steering and Policy] in 1981 and 1983, when the Republican party was riding roughshod over us, that people going on the [Ways and Means] committee generally be good Democratic votes, that they not be mavericks or be from unsafe districts where they couldn't afford to hew the Democratic line.

Of the fourteen Democrats interviewed who were appointed after 1975, eight mentioned party loyalty or a willingness to work with the Democratic leadership as an important reason for their success in obtaining a seat on Ways and Means.

Congressional Quarterly party unity scores, which show the percentage of times a member votes with his or her party on the votes on which party majorities oppose one another, provide a rough indication of who the party regulars are in the House. As Table 4-2 shows, the majority of Ways and Means appointees since 1975 continue to fall in this category: eighteen of the twenty-seven who had served a full year in the House before they went on the committee had higher support scores than the party average for that session. Eight of the nine members who were newly elected freshmen or had not served a full year before their appointment also voted with their party more frequently than the average Democrat during their first full year in the House.

Five of the fourteen Democrats who joined the committee after 1975 mentioned their electoral margins as an important factor in committee recruitment. A sizable electoral margin, as the member quoted above indicated, is viewed as important because it should allow a committee member greater freedom to "hew the Democratic line" on difficult votes. Said a second member,

Table 4-1

Seniority of Democratic Ways and Means Appointees, 1975–1986

Year	Member	Years in House before Appointment
1975	Otis G. Pike (N.Y.)	14
	J. J. Pickle (Tex.)	12
	Henry Helstocki (N.J.)	10
	Charles B. Rangel (N.Y.)	4
	William R. Cotter (Conn.)	4
	Fortney H. Stark (Calif.)	2
	James R. Jones (Okla.)	2
	Richard F. Vander Veen (Mich.)	1
	Andrew Jacobs (Ind.)	8[1]
	Abner J. Mikva (Ill.)	4[2]
	Martha Keys (Kans.)	Fr[3]
	Joseph L. Fisher (Va.)	Fr
	Harold E. Ford (Tenn.)	Fr
1977	Ken Holland (S.C.)	2
	William M. Brodhead (Mich.)	2
	Ed Jenkins (Ga.)	Fr
	Richard A. Gephardt (Mo.)	Fr
	Jim Guy Tucker (Ark.)	Fr
	Raymond F. Lederer (Pa.)	Fr
1979	Thomas J. Downey (N.Y.)	4
	Cecil Heftel (Hawaii)	2
	Wyche Fowler, Jr. (Ga.)	2
	Frank J. Guarini (N.J.)	Fr
	James M. Shannon (Mass.)	Fr
	Marty Russo (Ill.)	4
1981	Don J. Pease (Ohio)	4
	Kent Hance (Tex.)	2
	Robert T. Matsui (Calif.)	2
	Don Bailey (Pa.)	2
	Beryl Anthony, Jr. (Ark.)	2
1983	Ronnie G. Flippo (Ala.)	6
	Byron L. Dorgan (N.D.)	2
	Barbara B. Kennelly (Conn.)	1
1985	Brian J. Donnelly (Mass.)	6
	William J. Coyne (Pa.)	4
1986	Michael A. Andrews (Tex.)	3

Source: *Congressional Directory.*

1. Initially elected to the House in 1964. Served four terms before being defeated in 1972, then reelected in 1974.
2. Initially elected to the House in 1968. Served two terms before being defeated in 1972, then reelected in 1974.
3. Fr = Freshman.

Table 4-2
Party Unity Scores of Democratic Ways and Means Appointees,
1975–1986

Member	Party Unity, Year Preceding Appointment[1]	Mean Party Unity, Year Preceding Appointment for All Democrats[1]	+/−
Otis G. Pike (N.Y.)	73	72	+1
Richard F. Vander Veen (Mich.)	90	72	+18
J. J. Pickle (Tex.)	60	72	−12
Henry Helstocki (N.J.)	90	72	+18
Charles B. Rangel (N.Y.)	92	72	+20
William R. Cotter (Conn.)	87	72	+15
Fortney H. Stark (Calif.)	91	72	+19
James R. Jones (Okla.)	37	72	−35
Andrew Jacobs (Ind.)	77	70[2]	+7
Abner J. Mikva (Ill.)	80	70[2]	+10
Martha Keys (Kans.)	(89)	(75)	+14
Joseph L. Fisher (Va.)	(93)	(75)	+18
Harold E. Ford (Tenn.)	(84)	(75)	+9
Ken Holland (S.C.)	61	75	−14
William M. Brodhead (Mich.)	94	75	+19
Ed Jenkins (Ga.)	(48)	(74)	−26
Richard A. Gephardt (Mo.)	(76)	(74)	+2
Jim Guy Tucker (Ark.)	(87)	(74)	+13
Raymond F. Lederer (Pa.)	(85)	(74)	+11
Thomas J. Downey (N.Y.)	87	71	+16
Cecil Heftel (Hawaii)	73	71	+2
Wyche Fowler, Jr. (Ga.)	67	71	−4
Frank J. Guarini (N.J.)	(85)	(75)	+10
James M. Shannon (Mass.)	(94)	(75)	+19
Marty Russo (Ill.)	53	71	−18
Don J. Pease (Ohio)	84	78	+6
Kent Hance (Tex.)	58	78	−20
Robert T. Matsui (Calif.)	96	78	+18
Don Bailey (Pa.)	86	78	+8
Beryl Anthony, Jr. (Ark.)	70	78	−8
Ronnie G. Flippo (Ala.)	69	77	−8
Byron L. Dorgan (N.D.)	83	77	+6
Barbara B. Kennelly (Conn.)	92	77	+15
Brian J. Donnelly (Mass.)	92	81	+11
William J. Coyne (Pa.)	94	81	+13
Michael A. Andrews (Tex.)	79	86	−7

Source: *Congressional Quarterly Almanacs*, and Ornstein et al., *Vital Statistics*, p. 209.

1. All scores are normalized to eliminate the effects of missed votes. Party unity = (unity) / (unity + opposition). Scores in parentheses are for freshman appointments and indicate scores for the year of appointment.
2. Scores for Mikva and Jacobs are for 1972. See notes for Table 4-1.

I think [Steering and Policy Committee] members look to see if you are in a position to take a vote that may not be politically popular. If you are in a district that's highly marginal, where every big vote could be critical in your reelection, that detracts from your ability to campaign for the [Ways and Means] committee [with Steering and Policy members].[30]

Catherine E. Rudder has argued that assignment of electorally vulnerable members to Ways and Means has been an important factor in opening congressional tax policymaking in the reformed House to particularistic interest group and district demands.[31] Table 4-3 indicates that assignment of Democratic members from marginal districts was commonplace during the late 1970s but has not occurred after 1980. From 1975 through 1986 one-fourth of the Democrats assigned to Ways and Means had won less than 60 percent of the vote in the election prior to appointment, with all of the appointments of members from marginal districts occurring between 1975 and 1980. This compares with a rate of assignment of members from marginal seats of about one-fifth (five of twenty-three) during the Mills years.

A responsible legislative style—a willingness to compromise and work with others—was mentioned by five of the fourteen Democrats who obtained seats after 1975 as an important factor in their success. Those likely to win a seat were described as "all-American guys," "consensus types," "players"; those likely to have problems were "mavericks," "bomb-throwers," "ideologues."[32] Whether the cases of the five members who brought up legislative style in interviews are typical of the thirty-six appointees who have gone on the committee since the reforms is another question—especially in the case of the members added to the committee immediately after it was expanded in 1974. It would be difficult, for example, to fit Fortney H. (Pete) Stark of California into the "responsible legislator" mold at the time he went on the committee in 1975. According to one Democrat who was a senior member of Ways and Means at the time, Stark was well known as an individual who was "very flamboyant in his opposition to the power structure" in the House.[33] Other Democrats who were assigned to the committee in the immediate aftermath of the reforms, such as Andrew Jacobs of Indiana—described by one Ways and Means colleague as "a free spirit" and generally considered a bit on the eccentric side—also fail to fit the mold of the insider or consensus type. One senior Republican contended that the choice of Democratic members with independent streaks had become much more of a rarity after Chairman Dan Rostenkowski began to take an active role in the recruitment process. Lending at least some support to this view, four of the five Democrats who mentioned the importance of legislative style in getting on the committee joined after Rostenkowski became Ways and Means chairman in 1981.

Table 4-3
Electoral Marginality and Democratic Appointments to Ways and Means,
1975–1986

Year	Number of Appointments	Number of Marginals[1]	Percent Marginal
1975–76	13	6	46
1977–78	6	1	17
1979–80	6	2	33
1981–82	5	0	0
1983–84	3	0	0
1985–86	3	0	0
Total	36	9	25

Source: Reports of election results in *Congressional Quarterly Weekly Report*.

1. Members who won with less than 60 percent of the vote in the election prior to appointment.

Overall, recruitment of Democratic committee members shows a good bit of continuity in terms of who is involved in the selection of Ways and Means members and in the characteristics of members who are successful in winning a seat. Party leaders and state delegations appear to have been important in most cases, as does the chairman of Ways and Means after 1980. Democratic members now get on Ways and Means earlier in their careers, but most continue to be relatively strong partisans. Finally, a general pattern appears of a more "open" selection process for committee Democrats during the mid and late 1970s, followed by a somewhat more restrictive process after 1980, when fewer freshmen, fewer appointees from marginal districts, and perhaps fewer members with highly independent or conflictual legislative styles have been assigned to Ways and Means. These patterns indicate that expectations of responsiveness to regional concerns and especially to *partisan* goals remain part of the committee's institutional environment in the postreform House.

Committee Selection: Republicans

In contrast to the Democratic committee selection process, relatively little attention has been paid by students of Congress to how Republicans have assigned House committee positions in recent years. This may be in part because the pattern on the minority side has shown greater continuity. No major changes in assignment procedures were instituted by House Republicans during the 1970s. Assignments continued to be made by the

Executive Committee of the party's Committee on Committees, with appointments subject to approval by the full membership of the committee. In the case of Ways and Means, the factors mentioned as important by minority members who have been assigned to the committee since 1975 appear very similar to those that were important during the 1950s and 1960s.

As on the Democratic side, during the prereform years party leaders, state delegations, and the party's senior member on Ways and Means were important participants in selecting Republican committee members.[34] Interviews with seven of the sixteen Republicans who have been appointed between 1975 and 1986 did not produce evidence of much involvement by the ranking Republican in committee assignments, but the continued importance of party leaders and state delegations in the process was very much in evidence. All of those interviewed agreed that the Committee on Committees would normally recognize the claim to a "state seat" on Ways and Means from states with large GOP delegations. Those from the larger state delegations emphasized that the choice of a designee by their delegation was the major hurdle involved in obtaining a committee position.

Thus, as on the Democratic side, the "same state" rule has continued to be a major influence on Republican recruitment to Ways and Means. Between 1975 and 1986, eight of the thirteen Republican openings created by departures from the committee (62 percent) were filled by a member from the same state. A Ways and Means Republican who also held a post on the Committee on Committees explained that the body "has traditionally given seats on Ways and Means to representatives of the largest states." He also pointed out that although states with smaller delegations could not lay claim to a seat, an attempt was made in assigning the remaining Republican positions "to ensure that there was some kind of reasonable regional representation."

For Republicans from the smaller state delegations, an active personal campaign for support from the minority leadership and members of the Committee on Committees is more important. As a Republican member (from a small state) put it, "There are two ways you can get on this committee. One, you can come from a big state and be anointed, . . . or two, you can fight like cats and dogs for the seats that are not big state seats." This member and others stressed that in the latter case Minority Leader Robert Michel was almost always an important figure in building a winning coalition in the Committee on Committees. Also mentioned as important were personal acquaintances on the party selection committee—in two cases members mentioned personal ties developed through party groups such as the Chowder and Marching Society.

A review of the characteristics of the Republicans appointed to Ways and Means reveals continuity here as well. Attention to seniority, party loyalty, electoral marginality, and legislative style had been characteristic of both parties' selection processes for Ways and Means during the 1950s and 1960s. In the Republican case, however, relatively little of the "opening up" of recruitment that occurred on the Democratic side during the 1970s is to be found.

As Tables 4-4 and 4-5 illustrate, those recruited to Ways and Means on the Republican side continued to be members from relatively safe seats who had accumulated at least modest amounts of seniority. Little mention was made of seniority in interviews, perhaps because Republicans take for granted that some seniority is necessary in order to make a successful bid for Ways and Means; the last time a freshman was appointed to the committee was in 1967.[35] One member who did mention seniority related his experience as a freshman congressman in the early 1970s:

> When I was elected to Congress, I came down here and saw my leader, Gerald Ford, and I told him I wanted to be on the Ways and Means Committee. He laughed. I was assigned to the Banking Committee.

Said a second Republican member of his experience in trying to win a Ways and Means seat as a freshman in 1981:

> One of the first calls I made after being elected in 1980 was to [Ways and Means ranking Republican] Barber Conable saying I wanted to be on the Ways and Means Committee. He sort of chuckled and said "Good luck."

Both members later won Ways and Means appointments after serving two terms in the House.

Comparing minority assignments after 1974 to those during the Mills years shows that Republicans have been only slightly more likely to assign junior members and actually slightly less likely to assign members from competitive districts to Ways and Means. Between 1958 and 1974, mean seniority for the seventeen committee appointees was 5.9 years, with only one freshman and three second-term members gaining seats. Mean seniority dropped for the sixteen assignments made between 1975 and 1986 but was still 4.4 years, with no freshmen but five second-termers in the group. With a failure to win 60 percent of the vote as the indicator of a marginal seat, the rate of appointments of Republican members from marginal seats has been even lower in the more recent period (35 percent for the Mills era; 31.3 percent for the postreform years). One member who joined the committee in the 1980s stated simply: "You can't get on this committee on the Republican side unless you come from a safe district."

Republican appointments to Ways and Means also continued to be drawn primarily from party loyalists. This suggests an ongoing concern on the minority side similar to that found for the Democrats. Ways and Means members are chosen in part to represent their party's positions on the issues

Table 4-4
Seniority of Republican Ways and Means Appointees, 1975–1986

Year	Member	Years in House Before Appointment
1975	Guy Vander Jagt (Mich.)	9
	William A. Steiger (Wis.)	8
	Phillip M. Crane (Ill.)	6
	Bill Frenzel (Minn.)	4
	James G. Martin (N.C.)	2
	L. A. (Skip) Bafalis (Fla.)	2
	William M. Ketchum (Calif.)	2
1977	Richard T. Schulze (Pa.)	2
	Willis T. Gradison (Ohio)	2
1978	John H. Rousselot (Calif.)	9[1]
1979	W. Henson Moore (La.)	4
1983	Carroll A. Campbell (S.C.)	4
	William M. Thomas (Calif.)	4
1985	Raymond J. McGrath (N.Y.)	4
	Hal Daub (Nebr.)	4
	Judd Gregg (N.H.)	4

Source: *Congressional Directory.*

1. Includes seven years continuous service prior to appointment and service during the Eighty-seventh Congress (1961–62).

dealt with by the committee. One member emphasized this fact in discussing regional patterns in recruitment: "The reason you never see very many New England people in the Republican party getting on committees like Ways and Means . . . is because most of the New England members are moderate to liberal." "So," he explained, "they don't get picked because they aren't trusted," meaning trusted to represent the party's conservative positions on committee issues. Congressional Quarterly party unity scores indicate that, like their Democratic counterparts, most Republican appointees were party regulars. As Table 4-6 illustrates, in the year prior to appointment twelve of the sixteen GOP appointees had party unity scores exceeding the mean for the party as a whole.

Few Republican members mentioned legislative style as a factor in winning a seat. One member who did suggested that it was an advantage to be viewed as a constructive legislator (a "player") but that this was of

Table 4-5
Electoral Marginality and Republican Appointments to Ways and Means,
1975–1986

Year	Number of Appointments	Number of Marginals[1]	Percent Marginal
1975–76	7	4	57
1977–78	3	1	33
1979–80	1	0	0
1983–84	2	0	0
1985–86	3	0	0
Total	16	5	31

Source: Reports of election results in *Congressional Quarterly Weekly Report*.

1. Members who won with less than 60 percent of the vote in the election prior to appointment.

limited importance in many cases because of the role of large state delegations in the process:

> Almost without exception . . . with the large states the Committee [on Committees] takes who the state offers. So you have to deal with the dynamics inside the state. So you wind up getting a Bill Archer who is generally considered not a player, fairly ideological, or a Phil Crane. So at times it's just circumstance; they were the one in line at the time.

Committee Selection: Conclusion. Even though committee assignment procedures have been restructured for the Democrats, recruitment for Ways and Means positions after 1974 looks surprisingly similar to the patterns described by Manley and Fenno in the prereform House. Party leaders continue to take a special interest in Ways and Means appointments, and within constraints defined by demands for regional representation, Ways and Means seats are reserved primarily for party loyalists. This is not to say change has not occurred. During the 1970s recruitment on the Democratic side was opened to freshman members, those from competitive districts, and those with more independent or even combative legislative styles. For Republicans, the pattern in Ways and Means recruitment is one of greater continuity, with a modest decline in the seniority of appointees the only readily apparent reflection of the reform-era upheavals in the House.

When these recruitment patterns are viewed from the perspective of Fenno's model of committee politics, the parent chamber still plays a major

Table 4-6
Party Unity Scores of Republican Ways and Means Appointees, 1975–1986

Member	Party Unity, Year Preceding Appointment[1]	Mean Party Unity, Year Preceding Appointment for All Republicans[1]	+/-
Guy Vander Jagt (Mich.)	70	71	-1
William A. Steiger (Wis.)	63	71	-8
Phillip M. Crane (Ill.)	95	71	+24
Bill Frenzel (Minn.)	51	71	-20
James G. Martin (N.C.)	88	71	+17
L. A. (Skip) Bafalis (Fla.)	77	71	+6
William M. Ketchum (Calif.)	91	71	+20
Richard T. Schulze (Pa.)	86	75	+11
Willis T. Gradison (Ohio)	76	75	+1
John H. Rousselot (Calif.)	95	77	+18
W. Henson Moore (La.)	86	77	+9
Carroll A. Campbell (S.C.)	88	76	+12
William M. Thomas (Calif.)	90	76	+14
Raymond J. McGrath (N.Y.)	70	77	-7
Hal Daub (Nebr.)	86	77	+9
Judd Gregg (N.H.)	85	77	+8

Source: *Congressional Quarterly Almanacs*, and Ornstein et al., *Vital Statistics*, p. 209.

1. All scores are normalized to eliminate the effects of missed votes. Party unity = (unity)/(unity + opposition).

role in defining the committee's environmental constraints through the committee selection process. If an extraordinary degree of procedural autonomy is no longer considered necessary to protect the chamber's revenue prerogatives as during the Mills era, expectations of responsiveness to the parent chamber are still reflected in attention to regional balance. And the leadership of the two parties in the House remains active in Ways and Means recruitment; committee members are still expected to be especially responsive to partisan objectives. To use Manley's phrase, partisanship is still being "built into" the Ways and Means Committee through special attention to partisan considerations in the recruitment process.[36] In this respect continuity exists with the prereform house. But when turning from these aspects of the committee's institutional environment to interview data on members' goals, evidence of change following the 1970s reforms is more striking.

Members' Goals

Steven S. Smith and Christopher J. Deering have observed in their comparative study of postreform committee politics that institutional reforms may "restructure committee members' opportunities to pursue their objectives."[37] If opportunities on a particular committee for acquiring prestige or influence, advancing one's views of good public policy, or servicing constituents change, it follows that members with different priorities or interests may be attracted to serve on a committee. Given that patterns in committee politics, according to Fenno's model, are determined by the interplay of committee members' goals with the environmental constraints within which committees operate, any shifts in members' goals would be of central importance for understanding the behavior of the postreform Ways and Means Committee.

A devaluation of the internal prestige associated with Ways and Means membership in the wake of the reforms has already been noted. Because of the 1974 rule change requiring creation of subcommittees, the committee also may have become more attractive to policy-oriented members. "The creation of subcommittees and the availability of subcommittee staff to more members," Smith and Deering point out, "gave them the tools to pursue their own policy interests."[38] In 1975 the committee set up subcommittees on Social Security, Trade, Public Assistance, Unemployment Compensation, Health, and Oversight. In 1977 the Public Assistance and Unemployment Compensation panels were merged and a new Miscellaneous Revenues subcommittee was created to deal with minor tax measures (this subcommittee was renamed Select Revenues in 1979). Major tax issues remained the responsibility of the full committee.

When this new committee structure is considered together with the other organizational changes mandated by the Democratic caucus and the high turnover that has occurred in the postreform years, it should be no surprise that significant differences in committee members' goals appear when members who joined the committee after 1975 are compared with those of the prereform years. According to interview findings reported by Manley and Fenno, most who sought positions on Ways and Means prior to the reforms wanted to serve on the committee primarily because of its prestige and influence in the House. Only a few of those interviewed in the 1960s cited either specific policy interests or constituency or electoral benefits as the primary reason for seeking a Ways and Means seat.[39]

Interviews with twenty-one of the fifty-two members who have joined the committee between 1975 and 1986 suggest that a significant shift in this pattern of members' goals has occurred. Just under half (nine of twenty-one) mentioned influence or prestige as the primary consideration when asked why they sought a position on Ways and Means. But an equal number cited policy interests alone or some combination of policy and constituency interests as reasons for joining the committee. The remainder cited combinations of prestige, policy, and/or constituency interests as equally important (see Table 4-7).

That prestige or influence remains the single most frequent explanation for the decision to seek a seat on Ways and Means confirms other evidence suggesting that the postreform committee is still seen as a desirable appointment by House members. As a committee Democrat who was elected to the House after the reforms commented:

> If I had a choice of any committee, I would pick Ways and Means.
> It's the most active, the most prestigious and important committee in the House of Representatives. It's *the* committee of Congress.

A number of other members from both parties concurred. They described Ways and Means as "a gold mine I never thought I'd achieve," and as the committee with "the best jurisdiction—the lion's share of the action in Congress." These responses resemble those reported by Manley and Fenno in the 1960s. But it is important to keep in mind that the members who made these types of comments in the earlier period were willing to give up substantial seniority on other committees to join Ways and Means—in effect *to vote with their feet* in favor of committee prestige in a way that postreform House members are not.

Two prestige-oriented members emphasized the importance of the committee as a result of the budget politics of the 1980s. Said one, a Republican, about the decision to go after a Ways and Means seat:

> First of all it's a prestigious committee. I wanted to move up. Also I was tired of being on committees that served little function. It is frustrating to be on authorizing committees with the present process where the Appropriations Committee goes first.

Unlike the prereform committee, however, an equal number of those interviewed cited policy interests or some combination of policy and constituency interests as the primary reasons for joining the committee—a significant change from the pattern that had existed in the 1960s.[40] As one Democrat explained: "Tax policy, municipal finance, health care were all issues that had interested me for a long time and are substantively more of a challenge to me than any of the other committees in Congress." Said another: "I have an interest in taxation . . . based on my education in the accounting field. When I came to Congress one of the basic interests I had

Table 4-7
Ways and Means Members' Goals, Members Appointed 1975–1986[1]

Reason for Seeking a Seat	Number
Prestige/influence	9
Policy interests[2]	6
Policy and constituency interests	3
Prestige/influence and constituency interests	2
Prestige/influence and policy interests	1
Total	21

Source: Personal interviews conducted by the author. The twenty-one individuals interviewed who joined the committee between 1975 and 1986 included fourteen Democrats and seven Republicans.

1. The table shows the distribution of responses to the question: Why did you want to get on the Ways and Means Committee?
2. This total includes one member who did not actively seek a seat on Ways and Means, but was persuaded to take an opening by others. He is included in this category because he explained that his initial interest in seeking a committee assignment was to participate in deciding certain policy issues handled by another committee.

was in tax reform." A Republican member also cited policy interests in explaining why he sought a Ways and Means seat rather than a position on another traditionally prestigious committee, Appropriations:

> They say if you are going to serve in Congress and make a career and stay here forever, go to the Appropriations Committee. It's a very comfortable committee and it's powerful because you get to hand out the money. I didn't come up here to hand out money. I came here to make things happen that ought to happen and the Ways and Means Committee is the committee that sets the rules for private enterprise in this country—trade, tax law, whatever. My interest is in dealing with the private sector.

None of those interviewed cited constituency interests or concern with reelection alone as determinative in the decision to seek a Ways and Means seat, but three mentioned constituency-related motivations in combination with policy interests, and two mentioned constituency concerns along with committee power. Said a Democrat: "I felt it was one of the most powerful committees in the House and if I could get on it early enough, it would be good for me *and* my district." A Republican commented: "It is such an influential committee that it gives you credibility with the opinion makers in the district."[41]

A number of those who cited both policy and constituency interests were more specific in noting areas within the committee's jurisdiction that directly affected their constituencies. A Democrat from the Midwest stressed the importance of trade and social welfare policy for his economically depressed district. A Republican also emphasized the importance for his district of trade issues handled by the committee. Part of the reason for transferring to Ways and Means, he explained, was because the trade policies it shapes are "life blood to my [district's] private sector." An urban Democrat wanted a Ways and Means seat in order to participate in the making of tax policy, but also considered Ways and Means a desirable position because "it has jurisdiction over Social Security, Medicare, and a variety of other services that are very important to my constituents."

Prior to the reforms a broad consensus on the committee in support of the goal of maintaining committee prestige, together with expectations in the House that the committee remain responsive to the chamber while asserting the institution's revenue power, resulted in a set of strategic premises that stressed fiscal responsibility and writing bills that would pass the House, with pursuit of partisan goals a secondary objective. Interviews with twenty-one members who joined the committee between 1975 and 1986 show that the consensus on the goal of maintaining prestige was undermined by an influx of members who placed equal importance on policy goals and, to a lesser extent, constituency interests. Fenno's model suggests that these changes in members' goals as well as changes in environmental constraints should affect strategic premises of committee members and in turn affect committee decisionmaking processes and outcomes.

Postreform Environmental Constraints

Some preliminary observations about postreform environmental constraints have already been made in the discussion of recruitment. Party leaders retain a significant role in committee recruitment and continue to emphasize the appointment of members who will, all other things being equal, hew the party line. Partisan influences tied to recruitment are reinforced for committee Democrats by institutional reforms that increased the authority of the Democratic caucus and by organizational changes inside the committee, including a buildup in partisan staff, reestablishment of partisan committee caucuses, and the increased majority/minority ratio that came with the 1974 expansion. These characteristics of the committee's institutional environment suggest that partisan goals would become a more important factor in postreform committee politics.

A final factor that should be noted regarding institutional change is the increased importance of clientele groups in the committee environment after the reforms due to appointments of Democratic members from marginal districts and new rules that encouraged more open deliberations and weakened the closed rule that had been used to prohibit amendments to committee bills. Fenno observed of the prereform committee: "Ways and Means is supported by its parent chamber . . . in espousing a set of attitudes and procedures that give it some counterweights in coping with clientele pressure."[42] Some of these counterweights have been reestablished over the postreform years (see Chapters 6 and 7), but many were weakened substantially during the reform era.

Strategic Premises after the Reforms: Wandering in the Desert

In Fenno's explanatory framework, if committee members agree on goals they will develop strategies or strategic premises for achieving those goals within the constraints defined by the committee's environment. The basic consensus on goals found by Fenno among Ways and Means members during the 1960s had been strained during the early 1970s and had broken down in the aftermath of the 1974 reforms. If members in the earlier period placed first priority on maintaining committee prestige, and hence usually moderated partisan and ideological conflicts in order to review legislation carefully and enhance prospects for floor success, many who joined the committee during the mid-1970s and after held different goals and different views about how the committee should operate. As a senior Republican told Catherine Rudder in 1975:

> Take Stark [a new member] and Corman [an old member]. There's not so much difference in their philosophy but in their approach. Mills would try to build a consensus . . . and Corman would help to work toward a consensus. That's not true anymore with the many new faces with strong philosophical views. It's pulling the committee apart.[43]

On the matter of making sure that committee bills pass on the House floor, a number of Ways and Means members publicly repudiated this strategic premise in the period immediately following the reforms. Democrat Sam Gibbons of Florida, for example, stated of a tax bill in 1975: "I say get a good bill, take it to the floor and if they beat it, let them beat it. If it's not a good bill, the hell with it."[44] Al Ullman, who had become chairman in 1975, also publicly rejected the notion that the committee should focus on the objective of winning on the House floor. "If you follow the Mills philosophy," Ullman observed in a 1976 *Fortune* profile of the post-Mills committee, "you'd wait until the controversy had run its course and then you'd try to do something. But I haven't done that. I don't worry about being defeated on the floor."[45] In interviews for this study most committee members stated that they do not like to see committee bills defeated on the House floor, but a broad consensus in support of submerging other goals to this one did not appear to exist.

Some members did express concern with protecting the committee's record of success on the floor. Said one Republican who joined the committee after it was expanded in 1974:

> We look around at the other committees and we see the Education
> and Labor Committee, the Banking Committee as kind of jokes.
> Their bills traditionally get kicked to pieces on the floor. . . . Most of
> the time we try to present a balanced piece of legislation. We take it as
> a great affront if a bill is amended.

Others were more ambivalent. "I tend to think that's basically irrelevant," one member commented in regard to the prospect of having a committee bill defeated on the floor. "It's just a pain in the neck. The House has a way of disciplining its agents if it is not pleased with the result." A junior Republican offered a similar response. In a case where the committee reports a controversial bill, he observed, "to beat that legislation, to overturn it or send it back [to committee] is just part of the system working." A third member, a Democrat, viewed the importance of committee defeats in terms of the specific policy questions involved. When asked about the significance of losing on the House floor, he responded:

> Well, there were some bills that I thought were more important than
> others. Some of them, it hurt me a lot whenever I would lose energy
> tax credits because I feel so strongly that that's the way to do it. . . .
> but as to whether or not I felt any overwhelming personal attachment
> to whether the capital gains rate was 20 percent or 18 percent, not
> really. The tax code is not the stuff of widows and the homeless and
> the death penalty.

Overall, six of the twenty-one members interviewed who joined the committee after the 1974 reforms directly indicated that they were unconcerned with the effects of floor defeats on the prestige or reputation of the committee.

The actual patterns in committee success on the House floor over the postreform period (1975–86) are shown in Table 4-8. Of the 346 recorded floor votes on Ways and Means bills over this twelve-year period, the position taken by a majority of committee members prevailed on 303, or 87.6 percent. In comparison to the 93 percent success rate found by Manley for the prereform committee (1933–64), this represents a noticeable decline during the postreform years.[46]

In comparison to the Mills-era committee, members who have joined the panel since the mid-1970s reforms have a different mix of goals and thus differing views about how the Ways and Means Committee should operate. More policy-oriented members were appointed to the committee, and institutional changes made the majority party leadership and organization much more important in the committee's environment. What Fenno's

Table 4-8

Ways and Means Committee Floor Success on Recorded Votes, 1975–1986

Congress	Total Recorded Votes[1]	Total Committee Wins[1]	Percent Wins
94th (1975–76)	100	85	85.0
95th (1977–78)	87	73	83.9
96th (1979–80)	63	57	90.5
97th (1981–82)	20	17	85.0
98th (1983–84)	49	47	95.9
99th (1985–86)	27	24	88.9
Overall (1975–86)	346	303	87.6

Source: Compiled by the author from Ways and Means Committee Legislative Calendars and *Congressional Quarterly Almanacs*.

1. Excluding multiply referred bills.

model suggests, then, is a shift in committee politics to a pattern in which prosecution of policy partisanship becomes the dominant goal for a substantial portion of Ways and Means members, while others remain oriented toward attaining prestige in the House. Under these conditions the establishment of a new consensus on strategic premises will be problematic. Increased openness in committee deliberations also suggests the possibility of greater influence for clientele groups in the committee's environment than before the reforms, but the limited number of members who cited constituency service as an important goal, together with the reestablishment of some procedural autonomy during the 1980s (see Chapter 6), would suggest that increased pursuit of policy goals and partisanship rather than increased clientelism or particularism would be the most prominent change in Ways and Means politics after the reforms.

In addition to those that have been reviewed, one additional factor merits consideration in attempting to trace through the interplay of members' goals and environmental constraints in the postreform House. In discussing how the committee has operated since the reforms, a number of senior members stressed the importance of committee leadership. Explaining that Al Ullman (who chaired the committee from 1975 to 1980) had not attempted to reassert any strong direction in committee politics after the reforms, one senior committee member described the Ullman years as "this time of wandering in the desert." Other senior members described the period under Ullman as "transitional," "a growing period," or even as "chaos."

In contrast to Ullman, after assuming the chair in 1981 Dan Rostenkowski actively attempted to rebuild support for prestige-oriented strategic premises. Explained one committee Democrat:

> [Rostenkowski] . . . does a very good job in communicating to members the specialness of the Ways and Means Committee. It is a special committee. It is the most powerful committee. And he's like a good general in telling his troops they are the elite and they ought to act like it.

Two other committee members, a Republican and a Democrat respectively, described Rostenkowski's approach in terms that clearly invite comparison to the strategic premises of the prereform committee:

> His main objective is to have a committee that is respected. He is very interested in having the respect of the committee's marketplace —the House floor and the people who deal with the committee. He wants respect for the committee and the product. . . . I think he is more interested in respect than the substance.

> He wants to win and does everything he can to make sure legislation can pass. He prefers to get bipartisan support when he can because that will enhance the chances of passing legislation.

Because of the importance of leadership in the unsettled conditions that followed the 1970s reforms, the very different leadership styles of the two chairmen who have served since the mid-1970s will be examined in more detail in the chapter that follows.

Purposive Theories and the Effects of Reform

Whether one looks at the effects of reform from the perspective of Mayhew's electoral connection model or of Fenno's scheme of members' goals and environmental constraints, institutional changes in the House during the 1970s altered key factors that had been identified as important for understanding the behavior of the Ways and Means Committee during the 1950s and 1960s. But the principal consequences of institutional change each theory suggests are different: more attention to particularistic concerns and clientele groups in the former case, an increase in partisan and policy conflict with limited responsiveness to particularistic interests in the latter. As a means of testing these competing propositions, postreform committee politics in the area of tax policymaking are examined in detail in Chapters 6 and 7.

The Ways and Means Committee and Deliberation in the Postreform House

Along with an examination of the effects of reform-era institutional changes on the behavior of members of the Ways and Means Committee, a second objective of this part of the study is to assess the effects of reform-era changes on the problem of deliberation in the parent legislature. As was outlined in Chapter 1, this problem arises from the responsibilities of legislators for representing diverse interests and opinions on the one hand, and for making authoritative rules for the entire political community on the other. Effective legislative deliberation requires that members have access to information about issues on the congressional agenda, that they have time to engage in discussion to discover grounds for agreement, and that they have an institutional setting in which the range of views represented in the legislative body will be present. The final section in this chapter focuses on two of these conditions in relation to the postreform Ways and Means Committee—the extent to which it has been a representative subgroup of the House, and the availability of information and staff support in the policy areas in the committee's jurisdiction.

One line of criticism of the Ways and Means Committee during the early 1970s was that the committee was no longer representative of majority views in the House. An important question concerning the role of the committee as a deliberative body in the postreform House is representativeness of the panel in terms of regional and ideological balance. A committee that maintains a membership representative of regional interests as well as ideological views in the parent legislature is better situated to anticipate and incorporate the range of views that must be reconciled in deliberations within the chamber.

Because Ways and Means Democrats were responsible for representing different regions in the committee assignment process that existed prior to 1974, a formal system of geographic representation existed on the prereform committee. Concerns with regional representation for those seeking committee assignments were reinforced by the importance of the tax, trade, and social welfare issues in the committee's jurisdiction. The importance of these issues also produced expectations for regional representation on the Republican side. Being drawn disproportionately from the ranks of party regulars, Ways and Means members tended on average to be more liberal than their fellow partisans in the case of the Democrats, and more conservative in the case of the Republicans. Still, the conservative southern wing of the Democratic party was represented on the committee, and as a group, the membership of Ways and Means closely reflected ideological voting patterns in the House during the late 1950s and 1960s.[47]

As the preceding discussion of recruitment has shown, regional considerations continue to play an important role in recruitment for both parties. Recruitment practices during the postreform years have continued to produce at least a rough regional balance on Ways and Means (see Table 4-9). Using the index of representation developed by George Goodwin shows that the regional makeup of Ways and Means in the postreform House appears similar to that found by Goodwin for the Eightieth through the Ninetieth Congresses (1947–68). Some disparities in regional representation exist, but the same basic pattern of broad regional representation occurs after as well as before the reform era.

If regional representation is one rough indicator of the extent to which the Ways and Means Committee is representative of the House at large, an equally important dimension to consider is the ideological complexion of the committee. Conservative coalition support scores compiled by Congressional Quarterly provide a workable means of gauging changes in the ideological cast of the membership of Ways and Means. Based upon the percentage of votes on which a member votes with majorities of Republicans and southern Democrats against a majority of non-southern Democrats, this score gives a rough indication of ideological outlook, as well as propensity to vote with ideologically based cross-party coalitions. Conservative coalition support scores are strongly correlated with the often-cited liberal/conservative ratings of members of Congress by Americans for Democratic Action and Americans for Constitutional Action.[48] In addition, an analysis of conservative coalition activity from the 1930s through the early 1980s has shown that this voting bloc has been most active in issues involving government management of the economy, suggesting that the ideological divisions involved are consistently important in the policy areas handled by Ways and Means.[49] Reflecting the liberal/conservative debate that emerged from the New Deal period, the conservative coalition has tended to oppose expanded involvement by the federal government in regulation of the economy and expansion of social welfare programs. Thus conservative coalition support scores are useful for evaluating the ideological makeup of the Ways and Means Committee, even though this inevitably involves simplification of the complex ideological forces at work in policymaking in the House.

As Table 4-10 shows, if conservative coalition support scores are taken as an indicator of ideology, the postreform committee has generally been representative of the House. As before the reforms, Democrats on Ways and Means tend to be somewhat more liberal, and Republicans more con-

Table 4-9

Regional Representation on the Ways and Means Committee, Postwar House and Postreform House

	North	South	Midwest	West
Postwar era (1947–68)	.81	1.13	1.10	.91
94th Congress (1975–76)	.71	1.26	1.26	.62
95th Congress (1977–78)	.71	1.36	1.17	.62
96th Congress (1979–80)	.83	1.30	.90	.79
97th Congress (1981–82)	.74	1.35	1.13	.65
98th Congress (1983–84)	.81	1.35	1.10	.58
99th Congress (1985–86)	1.06	1.19	1.02	.58

Source: Goodwin, *Little Legislatures*, pp. 108–9; *Congressional Directory*.

Note: The index shown in the table is calculated by dividing the percentage of committee members from a region by the percentage of House members from that region. From a proportional standpoint, a score of less than 1.0 means that the region is underrepresented in relation to its numbers in the House. A score of greater than 1.0 means that a region is overrepresented in these terms. Goodwin, *Little Legislatures*, p. 109.

North = Maine, Vermont, New Hampshire, New York, Massachusetts, Rhode Island, Connecticut, Pennsylvania, West Virginia, Maryland, Delaware, New Jersey.

South = Texas, Oklahoma, Louisiana, Mississippi, Tennessee, Kentucky, Virginia, North Carolina, South Carolina, Alabama, Georgia, Florida, Arkansas.

Midwest = North Dakota, South Dakota, Nebraska, Kansas, Minnesota, Iowa, Missouri, Wisconsin, Illinois, Indiana, Michigan, Ohio.

West = Montana, Wyoming, Idaho, Washington, Oregon, California, Nevada, Arizona, New Mexico, Colorado, Utah, Alaska, Hawaii.

servative, than the House average for their respective parties. Taken together, though, the mean conservative coalition support scores for all committee members tend to reflect fairly closely those for the entire House. Figure 4-1 illustrates the long-term continuity of this pattern from the Mills era to the present.

Recruitment patterns for the Ways and Means Committee have continued to produce a committee that is, by and large, representative of the

Table 4-10

Mean Conservative Coalition Support Scores, Ways and Means Members, Parties, and Entire House, 1975–1986

Year	Democrats W&M	Democrats House	Republicans W&M	Republicans House	Overall W&M	Overall House
1975	34	37	84	81	50	51
1976	37	39	85	80	53	53
1977	39	38	86	82	54	51
1978	40	39	84	79	53	52
1979	33	41	90	85	52	57
1980	36	41	84	81	54	56
1981	45	45	87	82	60	61
1982	41	41	87	81	56	59
1983	36	39	85	81	55	55
1984	36	38	88	84	55	56
1985	34	36	87	84	53	56
1986	39	41	86	83	55	59
Mean, 1975–86	38	40	86	82	54	56

Source: Calculated from scores reported in *Congressional Quarterly Almanacs*, and Ornstein et al., *Vital Statistics*, pp. 211, 214. All scores are normalized to eliminate the effects of missed votes. Conservative coalition support = (support)/(support + opposition).

regional and ideological makeup of the House. The continued maintenance of a representative committee in relation to the House membership at large suggests that the capabilities of the Ways and Means Committee for performing as an effective deliberative body for the parent House were by no means totally dismantled after 1974. Although the reduced procedural autonomy of the committee made it less able to dominate House deliberations on the policy issues within its jurisdiction than during the Mills era, the committee remained, if not a microcosm of the House, at least a group on which most ideological and regional blocs would have some representation.

A final feature of the postreform House that is important for the role of the Ways and Means Committee as a deliberative body is the availability of information and staff support on the economic and social welfare issues within its jurisdiction. During the Mills era, the staff of the Ways and Means Committee itself was small, but committee members also had direct access to the nonpartisan professional staff of the Joint Committee on Taxation. Changes during the 1970s created broader access to information for more members both inside and outside the committee.

Figure 4-1
Mean Conservative Coalition Support Scores, Ways and Means Members,
Parties, and Entire House, 1959–1986

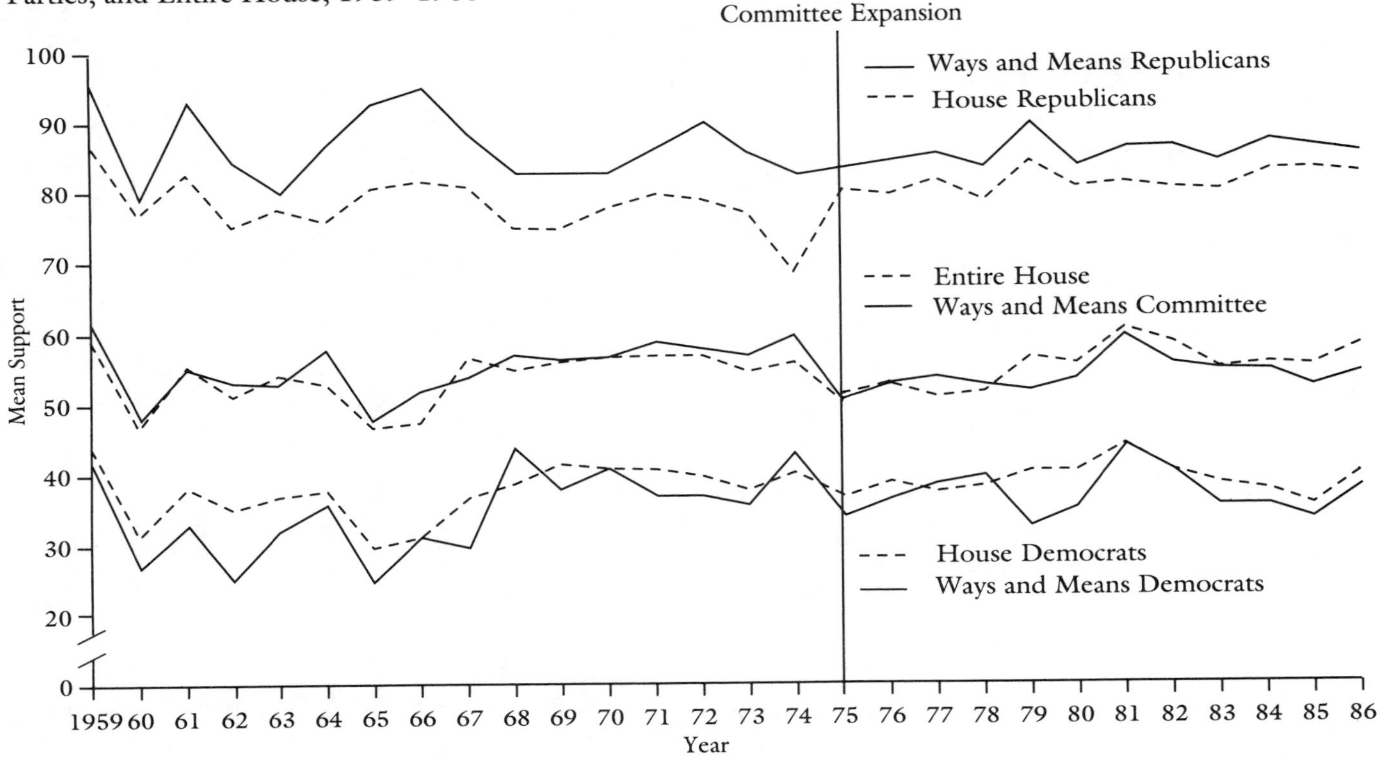

Source: See Table 4-10.

Prior to the reform era, expertise in the House on tax policy resided primarily in the Joint Tax Committee staff. As Rudder has pointed out, this arrangement also meant that noncommittee members had very limited access to expertise in the tax area: "House members who wanted to challenge the work of the committee did not have tax experts to explain proposals and suggest alternatives. The staff of the Joint Committee on Taxation . . . was not available to noncommittee members and was answerable primarily to senior committee members, especially Mills. Individual members, on or off the tax committee, did not typically have staff aides to assist on the legislation."[50]

Because of reforms that increased allocations for staff on all House committees, and the need to staff the new subcommittees that were set up on Ways and Means in 1975, committee staff increased threefold during the 1970s as both the majority and minority established sizable professional staffs. Staff increases somewhat diffused access to expertise within the committee and made the committee less dependent on the executive branch for information, but also reinforced the tendencies toward greater partisanship.[51] Although it expanded substantially in the 1970s along with the Ways and Means Committee staff (see Table 4-11), the studiously nonpartisan staff of the Joint Committee on Taxation began to lose some of its traditional influence over the formulation of tax policy on Ways and Means as members on both sides of the aisle gained access to tax experts who were more responsive to partisan policy objectives.[52]

One senior Ways and Means member described the eclipse of the Joint Committee staff as one of the most important changes in the committee's operation in the postreform period. He explained:

> We have seen a major decline in the power of the Joint Committee on Taxation, which, although it was always only supposed to be a source of technical advice, was nevertheless a kind of grey eminence under Laurence Woodworth. Now it has its contact with the [Ways and Means] members almost entirely through the partisan staff.

With the increases in partisan staff, he observed, "Rostenkowski relies heavily on his partisan staff for advice and decisions rather than on the staff of the Joint Committee on Taxation, as Wilbur Mills always used to and Al Ullman tended to."

By creating a number of new staff units, the new budget process also contributed to a diffusion of information and staff support. By the mid-1980s the Congressional Budget Office employed over 200 staffers, while the House Budget Committee staff had grown to over 100.[53] In the opinion of one individual interviewed who served in the Tax Analysis Division of CBO, in addition to its basic job of providing macro-level estimates of budget effects of existing tax policies, CBO has played an important role in

Table 4-11
Ways and Means and Joint Tax Committee Staff, 1971–1986

Year	Ways and Means	Joint Tax Committee
1971	25 (5)[1]	31
1972	28 (5)	30
1973	29 (6)	37
1974	30 (6)	40
1975	46 (6)	47
1976	80 (11)	50
1977	88 (11)	54
1978	92 (14)	63
1979	96 (18)	64
1980	90 (18)	64
1981	86 (14)	58
1982	84 (16)	57
1983	84 (17)	61
1984	80 (17)	59
1985	85 (19)	65
1986	83 (14)	63

Source: Malbin, *Unelected Representatives*, p. 182; *Congressional Staff Directory*, 1980–86.

1. Number designated as minority staff.

getting a number of major tax issues on the congressional agenda through its studies on tax expenditures.

The House has changed, then, from an arrangement where information and staff support related to policy areas within the Ways and Means Committee's jurisdiction were controlled by senior members of the committee, to a situation where both have been more broadly diffused in the committee and in the House. New sources of information and expertise on tax policy and other issues within the committee's jurisdiction now exist, including staff units associated with the budget process, which are entirely outside committee members' control.

Conclusion

Viewed from the different theoretical perspectives of Mayhew and Fenno, institutional changes that occurred during the 1970s reform era were significant for members of the Ways and Means Committee. According to Mayhew's electoral connection model, the diminution of committee prestige suggests that Ways and Means members should become more responsive to clientele interests and local constituency demands and less attentive to fiscal concerns and institutional prerogatives. Fenno's framework, on the other hand, suggests, as a result of changes in committee members' goals and environmental constraints, less concern with limiting conflict in order to win support on the House floor and increased emphasis by committee members on the pursuit of policy goals—especially partisan policy goals. Even with institutional changes that increased the importance of clientele groups in the committee's environment, patterns in members' goals suggest only a limited increase in responsiveness to clientele groups.

Even with the upheavals of the 1970s in Congress, a good bit of continuity has been present in some aspects of House-committee relations. One constant, which is significant for the role of the panel as a deliberative body for the parent legislature, is that the Ways and Means Committee remains a group that is generally representative of the parent legislature in both regional and ideological terms. On the other hand, reform-era changes have diffused expertise on the policy areas within the committee's jurisdiction through increased staffing on the committee and the creation of new staff units associated with the budget process.

As a way of testing propositions about the effects of reform derived from the Mayhew and Fenno theories, Chapters 6 and 7 examine the politics of major tax legislation on the Ways and Means Committee over the 1975–86 period. Before taking up the examination of tax politics, however, it will be useful first to look in more detail at the role of leaders and leadership on the postreform committee.

Chapter 5

Leadership

In explaining the roles played by leaders in congressional politics, most contemporary students of Congress have emphasized contextual or situational factors rather than personal qualities of individuals who hold leadership positions. Leaders are usually characterized as more or less resourceful practitioners of a "leadership style" that is defined in its essential features by the political and institutional context at the time. Leaders themselves are seen as having relatively little opportunity to act independently in defining effective leadership styles or in determining how Congress operates.

More than one would have anticipated from this view of leadership, differences in the two individuals who served as chairman of the Ways and Means Committee over the 1975–86 period, Al Ullman (D-Ore., chairman 1975–80) and Dan Rostenkowski (D-Ill., chairman 1981–present), are a significant factor in understanding the politics of the postreform committee. This chapter examines the personal and contextual factors that have shaped the leadership styles of these two chairmen and considers the influence each has had on committee politics during the postreform years. In addition, the chapter also attempts to place this case in the context of some broader questions regarding the importance of leaders and leadership in congressional politics.

Two decades ago, John F. Manley argued that understanding leadership in Congress "requires attention to individual leaders, their followers, and how the two interact."[1] As has been noted, most recent work on congressional leadership has moved away from the idea of mutual dependence of leader and context to a primary emphasis on contextual or situational factors as the major determinants of the behavior of leaders.[2] Fenno, for example, emphasized contextual factors in his discussion of leadership in *Congressmen in Committees*: "The behavior of any committee chairman must be analyzed within the context of his committee's strategic premises and, particularly, in light of individual members' goals. Whatever his personal characteristics, temperamental or ideological, this context puts limits on the kinds of behavior he can engage in and still retain his leadership, and it sets forth positive guidelines for his success and effectiveness inside the committee."[3]

However, Fenno also noted that under certain conditions—specifically, those involving tensions or ambiguities in contextual factors—personal qualities of leaders may be of greater significance in defining an effective leadership style and in determining how a committee will operate. Interestingly, the case used to make this point was Wilbur Mills, who downplayed partisan influences in the environment of Ways and Means in order to emphasize consensus building and protecting the committee's prestige and record of floor success.[4] As the discussion of changes in Ways and Means Committee members' goals and environmental constraints in the preceding chapter has shown, the postreform period was one in which a greater diversity of goals was present among committee members and in which the committee's autonomy had been reduced, making environmental influences more complex. The more complex and unsettled contextual setting faced by the chairman of Ways and Means after 1975 created both problems and opportunites for committee leadership. But in part due to personal differences, each of the two postreform chairmen has responded differently to the context he encountered.

Leadership and Contextual Factors, 1975–1986

Contextual factors that create opportunities for, and constraints on, the exercise of committee leadership, or congressional leadership generally, are of three basic types. First are institutional factors. These include both formal organization and procedures and informal, but well-established, patterns within the chamber (such as patterns of committee recruitment) that structure the expectations and behavior of its members. Second are partisan factors arising from electoral politics and conditions in the party system. Probably the most important determinant of House leadership styles over the long term is the degree of unity or factionalism in the congressional party system.[5] The role of party organizations in candidate recruitment is another potentially important factor defining the context for leadership in the House.[6] In the shorter term, the configuration of partisan control of Congress and the White House is important as well in defining opportunities and constraints for House leaders. Finally, the contextual factors important for understanding leadership in the House include agenda or issue-related factors, the particular opportunities and constraints that may be associated with different types of issues that reach the congressional agenda.[7]

Institutional Factors

By the time Al Ullman became chairman of the House Ways and Means Committee in 1975 the institutional context in the House was much different from that of the Mills era. First, the extensive structural/procedural reforms discussed in Chapter 3 had been enacted between 1970 and

1974, including changes to reduce the autonomy of standing committee chairmen by requiring caucus election and limiting their control over committee organization and procedures. Under the new procedures committee leaders were no longer assured their positions simply on the basis of seniority, and had to be attentive to concerns of rank-and-file Democrats or risk removal by the majority caucus (as occurred with three senior chairmen in 1975). The Budget and Impoundment Control Act of 1974 established a new set of organizational units and procedures and created a formal mechanism for coordination of tax and spending decisions. Finally, the reforms targeted at the Ways and Means Committee—including changes in the closed rule procedure to allow amendments to Ways and Means bills to be proposed by vote of the Democratic caucus, the requirement that subcommittees be established, and expansion of the committee's size from twenty-five to thirty-seven members—were intended specifically to bring an end to the centralized, consensus-oriented leadership regime that had developed under Wilbur Mills. Thus Ullman assumed leadership of the committee when the House was in an antileadership mood, the established ways of conducting committee business under his predecessor had been intentionally dismantled, and, as was shown in the previous chapter, no consensus was present on the committee on how to operate within the new institutional environment.

However, by the time the House reform movement had run its course in the late 1970s, members found themselves faced with the day-to-day reality of making the new organizational arrangements work. A majority of House members (58 percent) responding to a 1979 survey conducted by the House Select Committee on Committees assigned medium or high priority to strengthening the authority of committee chairmen.[8] In interviews conducted between 1981 and 1983, Steven S. Smith and Christopher J. Deering found similar concerns expressed by House members. They report that "the most common complaint . . . heard about committee leadership from committee members and staff was that chairs are no longer responsible for their committee's actions."[9] Further evidence of the emergence of a somewhat different institutional climate in which concerns with restoring decisionmaking capabilities had begun to compete with demands for openness, participation, and decentralization came in 1983, when the return by the Ways and Means Committee to the traditional practice of closing bill-writing sessions to the public excited little interest or criticism.[10] The House Budget Committee followed suit in 1985, holding its first closed markups since its creation in 1974.[11]

After 1974, therefore, the chairman of the Ways and Means Committee was working in an institutional environment in which the relationship of the committee to the parent chamber was in a state of transition, the committee had been expanded and restructured, and a broader range of views were present among committee members themselves about how the committee should function. By the 1980s, though, the reform-era demands for openness, decentralization, and participation had begun to wane perceptibly, creating an institutional context somewhat more amenable to the exercise of direction over committee politics by committee chairmen.

Partisan Factors

Aside from a continuing evolution in congressional electoral politics in the South no major changes have occurred in the organizational strengths of parties or in partisan alignments in the electorate over the 1975–86 period. Hence the most important partisan influences on House leaders have been patterns of party control of Congress and the White House, and the balance of party strength in the House. The Ullman chairmanship began in the period of divided government and interbranch conflict that marked the Ford presidency and continued through the sometimes difficult presidential-congressional relationship that existed even after Democrats regained control of the White House with Jimmy Carter's election in 1976. Throughout the 1975–80 period when Al Ullman chaired the Ways and Means Committee, Democrats maintained control of the Senate and held large majorities in the House (66.9 percent in the Ninety-fourth Congress, 67.1 percent in the Ninety-fifth, and 63.7 percent in the Ninety-sixth).

Although Democrats maintained control of the House throughout the 1981–86 period, the distinctive features of the partisan context during these years were the election and reelection of a Republican president and the presence of Republican majorities in the Senate for the first time since the mid-1950s. Democratic majorities in the House were also smaller than during the Ullman years. In the Ninety-seventh Congress (1981–82) Democrats held only a 55.9 percent majority in the chamber. As a Republican Ways and Means member pointed out, when southern Democrats voted with the Republicans during the Ninety-seventh Congress "a conservative majority controlled the House floor." After the 1982 elections House Democrats held more comfortable majorities—61.6 percent in the Ninety-eighth Congress (1983–84) and 58.2 percent in the Ninety-ninth Congress (1985–86)—but still faced opposition-party control of the Senate and the White House.

Given the importance of the presidency for shaping the congressional agenda and the natural advantages in coalition building this provides for House leaders when their party controls the White House, Ullman enjoyed some potential advantages over Rostenkowski, who served with an opposition party president throughout the 1981-86 period. However, Jimmy Carter's insensitivity to congressional politics and lack of personal and ideological ties to the House Democrats clearly mitigated some of the political advantages that might otherwise have accrued to a Democratic Ways and

Means chairman. As one senior Ways and Means Democrat commented when discussing the difficulties Ullman encountered as chair: "Al had Jimmy Carter to deal with and Carter really wasn't in step with what was going on." Still, the large Democratic majorities in the House between 1975 and 1980 offered Ullman greater opportunities than Rostenkowski for pursuing a partisan coalition-building strategy on committee bills, especially in comparison to the narrow Democratic majority that was present in the House during Rostenkowski's initial two years as chairman.

Since Ways and Means Committee politics have long reflected the politics of the parent chamber, the contextual situation faced by each leader was affected not only by the size of partisan majorities in the House, but also by the degree of unity or factionalism in the majority party. Some fairly striking increases in party unity have been visible among House Democrats during the 1980s, but these appear to reflect more short-run agenda factors than fundamental shifts in the underlying party system. Hence, these developments are treated in the section that follows.[12]

Issue-Related Factors

Issue- or agenda-related factors are of major importance in this case due to a series of shifts in the issues on the Ways and Means Committee's agenda during the 1975–86 period. First, in addition to the partisan/ideological conflicts long associated with the economic and social welfare issues within the committee's jurisdiction, the rise of energy tax issues during the 1970s introduced new regional conflicts in the committee's politics.[13] Second, by the late 1970s, the poor performance of the economy and a growing "tax revolt" had produced a shift in the economic policy agenda away from traditional liberalism's concerns with distributional equity toward a more conservative agenda focused on reducing tax burdens on the middle class and stimulating economic growth. This placed further strain on the Democratic coalition in the House as many liberals continued to stress equity, while other elements in the party sought to respond to the new agenda (see Chapter 6).

Thus, despite the large Democratic majorities in the House throughout the Ullman years, cohesive majority coalitions were far from assured in the policy areas handled by Ways and Means. As Sinclair found in her study of House voting alignments from 1925–78, "On the issues that dominated the government management [of the economy] dimension in the 1970s, the Democrats were more deeply divided than they had been at any time during the half century studied."[14] Analyses of committee voting alignments during the 1970s by Joseph K. Unekis and Leroy N. Rieselbach and by Glenn R. and Suzanne L. Parker found increased partisan polarization on Ways and Means during the Ullman years, but also found persistent factional splits among Ways and Means Democrats.[15]

The committee agenda during the 1981–86 period was dominated initially by the tax- and budget-cutting initiatives of the incoming Reagan administration, then by the deficits that followed enactment of the president's program. The tax and budget initiatives submitted by the administration in 1981 initially exacerbated divisions in the Democratic majority in the House. But after 1981 an agenda dominated by large budget deficits and attempts by the White House and the Republican Senate to reduce deficits through additional domestic budget cuts helped to produce increased partisanship in House voting and greater party unity among House Democrats on economic and fiscal policy issues.[16]

This pattern of increased unity in the majority party is reflected in the mean annual percentage of partisan votes in the House, which increased from 40.1 percent between 1975 and 1980 to 49 percent between 1981 and 1986, and in the mean annual party unity scores for House Democrats over the same periods, which increased from 74.7 percent to 81.2 percent, respectively.[17] An analysis of all Ways and Means Committee roll call votes (excluding only routine procedural motions) for this study found that the mean annual percentage of partisan votes on the committee increased from 68 percent over the 1975–80 period to 72 percent for 1981–86. An average annual index of cohesion calculated for committee Democrats on votes over these same two periods increased from 44.7 to 59.2.[18] Thus, after the initial successes of the Reagan administration in enacting its economic program, a deficit-driven agenda has helped to create a more unified Democratic coalition in the House, offering opportunities for a committee leader to assemble partisan coalitions in committee and on the House floor.

Along with encouraging greater Democratic party unity in the House, deficit politics have also created pressures for greater centralization as a means of setting priorities and reestablishing some autonomy from clientele demands. As Roger H. Davidson has pointed out, "The painful fiscal choices of the 1980s would seem to dictate a reversal of . . . [decentralizing] structural tendencies, as party leaders and the budget-making apparatus tug at the decentralization that was the legacy of the 1970s reforms."[19] The repeated use of the reconciliation mechanism of the budget process during the 1980s and the return to closed committee sessions by the Ways and Means and Budget committees during the 1980s both reflect in part the centralizing pressures of a contractive, deficit-driven agenda.

Despite the more favorable configuration of Democratic party control during most of the Ullman years, extensive structural reforms, the breakdown of a committee consensus on strategic premises, and the divisive issues that dominated the Ways and Means Committee's agenda combined to create an unsettled and difficult context for exercising leadership from the chair of the Ways and Means Committee. The configuration of partisan control and the committee agenda were even less favorable for a Democratic committee leader at the outset of Dan Rostenkowski's chairmanship, but concerns with restoring decisionmaking capabilities after the reform era, the presence of a highly contractive agenda, and the increased unity among House Democrats in the context of deficit politics each created opportunities for more active leadership and greater organizational centralization. Partly because of these contextual differences, but also because of their differing skills and views of leadership, Al Ullman and Dan Rostenkowski developed very different approaches to leading the committee.

Al Ullman: The Participatory Democrat as Chairman

Those who served under Al Ullman on the Ways and Means Committee described his leadership style as open and permissive. "Mr. Ullman operated the committee in a collegial style," said one Democrat. "He didn't try to set a strong direction." Said another Democrat: "He was more of a moderator than a chairman." Others described Ullman's approach as "very fair and non-vindictive," "low key," "laid back," and "trying to reason together." An apt characterization of Ullman's leadership style would be *the participatory democrat as chairman.*

In a 1978 interview, Ullman discussed in some detail his goals and approach as Ways and Means chairman. When asked how well the committee was working, he responded: "I'm extremely pleased with the way the committee has come together. I think the openness, the participation and the spirit of give-and-take have proven extremely effective in getting the committee to develop a mood of accomplishment."[20]

A second theme was his desire to break with the cautious approach to new policy initiatives that had been the hallmark of Wilbur Mills's leadership style:

> I see my role as altogether different than chairmen used to see theirs. They were worried about image and not losing any bills and not bringing a bill to the floor unless they had all the votes in their pocket. You can't operate that way any more. I see my role as one of leadership and trying to expand the thinking of Congress in new directions in order to meet the long-term needs of the country. We've just allowed the country to get into bad shape because of some of these very restrictive procedures in the way the leadership of Congress has operated.[21]

This statement clearly illustrates Ullman's rejection of the prestige-oriented strategic premises that had guided Mills and most members of the prereform committee. Rather than orienting his leadership style toward protecting the committee's prestige and record of floor success as Mills had, Ullman employed a set of techniques one would expect of an issue-oriented participatory democrat.

Endorse a position, then allow the committee to work its will. "When we get
to the committee process," Ullman explained, "I invite everyone to participate and accept the will of the committee." "But," he continued, "I have
another role as chairman of the committee and that is to speak out on
national issues, in a sense for the committee, and for the Congress."[22]
Ullman's normal approach in dealing with major legislation was to meet
with committee Democrats in caucus and propose a substantive position
that he believed to be the best course of action. In some cases Ullman also
set up task forces or informal working groups to formulate specific aspects
of committee bills. But having articulated his own position on the best
course of action, Ullman usually did relatively little to try to influence
committee outcomes. Instead he allowed the political forces associated with
each issue an opportunity to play themselves out in the committee's deliberative processes.

As one senior staffer contrasted Ullman's approach with that of the
current chairman:

> [Rostenkowski] . . . *thinks* in terms of putting together a majority.
> Ullman just didn't think that way. He tended to think more in terms
> of the policy issues. . . . He would express the issues involved and let
> the majority form spontaneously, form by itself.

As a Democratic member explained, "Al wouldn't call you into his office
and sit you down and talk with you until the vote was imminent." A member who was a junior Democrat at the time noted that Ullman "could be
outflanked easily" by those who held different views. Another member
noted that Ullman "let the committee do what it may. You might not know
five minutes before that someone was going to offer an amendment—even
a far-reaching one."

Encourage decentralization of organizational resources. Ullman also exercised a light hand in matters of staffing and involvement in work at the
subcommittee level. During his tenure as chairman the committee established subcommittees as required by new House rules and majority committee staff tripled in size from twenty-four in 1974 to seventy-two in 1980
(see Chapter 4, Table 4-11). According to committee members, Ullman
allowed wide discretion to subcommittee chairmen in hiring staff and rarely
attempted to intervene in decisions at the subcommittee level. Said one
Ways and Means Democrat of Ullman's attitude toward subcommittee
chairmen: "He gave them free rein, basically." The result was a great deal
of subcommittee independence. One committee staffer described subcommittees under Ullman as "fiefdoms that were outside the control of the
chairman."

Accommodate partisan coalition building. Although Ullman made no
mention of his role as a party leader in the interview quoted above, his

conduct as chairman indicates that he also pursued one other objective in leading the committee: facilitating the formation of partisan coalitions among the Democratic members of the committee. When asked about Ullman's style of leadership, a senior Ways and Means Democrat stressed that "he started having partisan caucuses and trying to make decisions *as Democrats*." A number of Republicans who served during the Ullman years likewise emphasized the emergence of a more partisan deliberative process on the committee. After 1975, one noted, "there began to be a face-off among Republicans and Democrats. Republicans were no longer part of the process." Republicans interviewed by Catherine E. Rudder in 1975 explained that they felt cut out of committee deliberations and had become more unified in opposition to the decisions arrived at by the majority.[23] Comments made to the press by Ullman and Republican Barber B. Conable, Jr., reflected the more partisan atmosphere that developed in the initial years under the new chairman. "On every important bill we've had they've always found a reason for being against it," Ullman complained of the committee minority in 1976.[24] "When Ullman asks us for votes the answer is usually no because we're given little input," Conable explained to a reporter the same year.[25]

Ullman as Leader: Context, Style, and Effectiveness

In some respects, the case for a contextual explanation of Ullman's leadership style seems a strong one. Where context appears to have been determinative is in the partisan dimension of Ullman's approach. Said a senior Democrat concerning Ullman's decision to institute partisan caucuses: "I never knew for sure why he did it. It was not that he was a particularly strong liberal Democratic partisan." A Republican also noted Ullman's limited sense of attachment to his party, suggesting that his was a more "independent" orientation characteristic of politics in Ullman's home state of Oregon.

Whatever Ullman's personal orientation toward advancing partisan goals in the House, the institutional context in the chamber after the 1970s reforms—especially the new procedures requiring election of committee chairmen by the Democratic caucus—created strong incentives for a more partisan orientation and greater attentiveness to majority party members.[26] The use of the new procedure to oust three senior committee chairmen in 1975 clearly demonstrated the risks of alienating rank-and-file Democrats. Ways and Means Republican Barber B. Conable, Jr., (N.Y.) made this point when commenting on Ullman's approach to developing energy tax legislation in 1975. "There can't be a [bipartisan] consensus," Conable observed, "because his position as chairman depends on his party, not on us."[27] As another committee Republican described Ullman's situation as chairman, "He always had to be looking over his shoulder at the Democratic caucus."

But with other aspects of Ullman's leadership style, the reform-era institutional context reinforced a personal orientation in favor of participatory decisionmaking. Ullman certainly recognized that the institutional context in the House of the mid-1970s required a permissive leadership style. "If I demanded too much," he observed in the 1978 interview, "my future would be limited by this climate we are working in."[28] Still, Ullman's comments quoted above and interviews with Ways and Means members suggest that he shared the reformers' enthusiasm for more participation and more open procedures.

Contrasting Ullman's approach with the sometimes byzantine political maneuvering of Wilbur Mills, a senior Ways and Means Democrat described Ullman as "an entirely different type of personality—very open, very direct." Another member simply characterized Ullman as "a *democratic* personality." Others noted that the chairman lacked interest in the persuading, negotiating, and cajoling that are often necessary in forging legislative coalitions. "Ullman felt uncomfortable imposing his particular views on anybody for any reason," recalled a senior committee staffer. "Al did not like to deal face to face with people," his successor Dan Rostenkowski observed. "He wouldn't call you in and say 'Listen, I need some help from you. What is it that we can put together.'"[29] In the participatory, permissive aspects of Ullman's leadership style, then, the reform-era institutional context in the House and the chairman's personal inclinations appear to have been mutually reinforcing.

Although many Ways and Means members expressed personal affection for Ullman, only one of the sixteen members interviewed who served between 1975 and 1980 (a Republican) described him as a successful or effective chairman when asked to comment on his leadership style. Others emphasized the difficult conditions Ullman faced as chairman, or criticized Ullman's performance as chairman, directly or through unfavorable comparisons with the current chairman, Dan Rostenkowski. Republicans criticized the partisan polarization that occurred during the Ullman years, but members of both parties expressed frustration with Ullman's highly permissive style of leadership. Under Ullman, one Democrat commented, "you had true democracy at work. The committee doesn't work well in that way, unfortunately." Said another Democrat: "It was chaos under Ullman. I mean I beat Ullman twice as a freshman." A Republican offered a similar assessment: "Service on the committee during that period was frustrating. There was no unity of purpose, no common direction." It is likely that Ullman's participatory leadership style enjoyed greater support among committee members during the time he was chairman than is reflected in interviews conducted during the mid-1980s when conditions in the House were different and most of those interviewed had become accustomed to working with a very different type of chairman. Still, similar criticisms of

Ullman by Ways and Means members may also be found in press accounts from the mid-1970s.[30]

Ullman's approach did provide opportunities for policy entrepreneurship and virtually unrestrained pursuit of policy goals by Democratic committee members. As one Democrat put it, "[Ullman] diffused the power which made it possible for young bucks like myself to put together coalitions." But even some who benefited individually from Ullman's permissive style questioned its effectiveness. Said another Democrat:

> Al Ullman . . . would let me as a freshman take off in any direction I wanted to go and give me the full opportunity of a hearing, not call in any chits. If I could round up sufficient support for . . . [an amendment to a committee bill] I'd pass it. And it might not be the best direction to go for the committee or for the country.

Negative evaluations of Ullman's effectiveness as a leader reflect in part the discordant contextual situation he faced as chairman.[31] It seems unlikely that *any* Ways and Means chairman could have fashioned an effective leadership style for dealing with the issues on the committee's agenda in the unsettled and antihierarchical institutional climate of the mid-1970s. As Rostenkowski commented: "We had just adopted new rules. Had I been put in the same position I would have had some of the same problems."[32] Still, Ullman's ineffectiveness also resulted partly from personal factors. The amount of criticism voiced by Ways and Means members indicates that at least later in Ullman's tenure, some would have accepted stronger direction over committee deliberations from the chair. Given his personal orientation in favor of participatory democracy, however, Ullman showed little interest in reasserting committee leadership when the extraordinary passions of the 1970s reform era began to subside.

Dan Rostenkowski: The Machine Democrat as Chairman

In the 1980 House elections Republican challengers defeated twenty-seven Democratic incumbents, one of whom was Al Ullman. With Ullman's defeat the chairmanship of the Ways and Means Committee passed to Dan Rostenkowski of Illinois, a twenty-two-year House veteran who entered politics through the Chicago Democratic organization of Mayor Richard Daley.[33] When asked to describe Rostenkowski's approach to committee leadership, Ways and Means members emphasized the assertive, centralizing character of the current chairman's leadership style.

Commenting on the contrasts between Rostenkowski and Ullman, a senior Ways and Means Democrat offered a view that was shared by most of those interviewed who have served under both leaders:

> Rostenkowski is not as strong on the substance as Ullman was, but he
> is significantly stronger on the politics. [With Rostenkowski] . . . the
> power is concentrated in the chairman and he plays hardball politics.

A second senior member described Rostenkowski as "much more interested in controlling the authority, the flow of legislation, than Mr. Ullman seemed to be."

When Ways and Means members and staff discussed Rostenkowski's leadership style, two basic objectives were consistently mentioned. First, as noted in Chapter 4, Rostenkowski has sought to protect and enhance the power and reputation of the Ways and Means Committee. "If anything characterizes him it's that he wants to win," said a senior Democrat. Another member explained: "He wants his committee to look good, to pass legislation." Said a third committee member:

> He constantly makes the argument that this is the elite committee
> in the House. [He says that] anybody who would want to serve on
> another committee if he had an opportunity to serve on Ways and
> Means doesn't know what he's talking about. He says this is the Cad-
> illac committee. . . . He is very oriented toward reputation as such.

In addition to "winning" passage of committee bills on the House floor, a number of members and staff also described Rostenkowski as a leader who seeks to maintain the committee's reputation as a responsible policymaker, as a body capable of making difficult decisions when necessary on the issues within its jurisdiction. Rostenkowski himself is quick to characterize the committee in these terms when asked about its role in the House:

> We're the best goddam committee in the House of Representatives.
> We work harder than anyone else. We take our jobs more seriously.
> We are the first ones to be criticized because we take the first bite of
> the apple.[34]

A Republican member commented on Rostenkowski's orientation toward the committee's economic policy jurisdiction: "My sense is that he feels a tremendous sense of responsibility." A senior committee staffer observed: "Rostenkowski has a sense of being a manager. . . . and we're responsible for managing Social Security, Medicare, AFDC, the tax system."

After the concern with maintaining the committee's power and reputation, a second characteristic consistently mentioned in comments on Rostenkowski's approach as chairman is his loyalty to the Democratic party as an institution. Although some members noted that Rostenkowski has a very pragmatic outlook on politics, others stressed that he remains deep down a strong party loyalist. As one senior Republican put it, "Danny is a good Democratic chairman."

In pursuing these objectives Rostenkowski has developed an assertive yet personalistic leadership style. "His attitude toward the committee," one member commented, "is like he might deal with other ward bosses in Chicago." Said another, "Rostenkowski is the ultimate expression of the Chicago view that the function of politics is control." If the term "machine" is stripped of its Progressive-era baggage and used simply to describe a type of political organization and style of politics, an appropriate characterization of Rostenkowski's leadership style is the *machine Democrat as chairman*.[35] In contrast to Ullman's leadership style, this approach employs a set of techniques that require extensive involvement in the ongoing operation of the committee, and has involved an active attempt to shape the views of committee members on how the committee should operate.

Direct involvement in committee recruitment. Rostenkowski has served on the Democratic Steering and Policy Committee since 1979, and was ensured a continuing role in that body's committee assignment function when Democrats began in the Ninety-seventh Congress (1981–82) to maintain ex officio positions for chairmen of the Ways and Means, Rules, Appropriations, and Budget committees. All of the seven Democrats interviewed who went on the Ways and Means Committee during or after 1981 mentioned the chairman as an important participant in the committee recruitment process (see above, Chapter 4). It is difficult to judge how influential Rostenkowski has actually been in determining Ways and Means appointments, but it is clear from interviews that his involvement has fostered a sense of personal loyalty to the chairman among some junior Democrats. "I wouldn't be on the committee if he had not wanted me there," volunteered one junior Democrat. Echoed a second recent appointee: "If you don't have his support, his *active* support, you can't get on that committee."

Through involvement in recruitment as well as other actions, Rostenkowski, according to some members, has built up a reservoir of personal loyalty among committee members. Discussing the chairman's ability to influence committee outcomes, one Democrat stated:

> He has the moral authority to swing several votes among people who would prefer to be in his good graces, but are not too concerned on certain issues about the outcome. There are always going to be four or five guys on that committee who might be with you or might not be with you, and the chairman's position determines that.

In discussing committee recruitment, one Ways and Means Democrat who served on the Steering and Policy Committee also pointed out that Rostenkowski has pushed actively to reestablish the older practice of restricting Ways and Means appointments to experienced members from safe districts:

> Rostenkowski is a member of the old school. He does not want fresh-
> men on the Ways and Means Committee. And he does not want any-
> one on that committee who is in trouble politically. It opens the
> door to too many compromise votes when you have a district that is
> 55 percent or so. . . . What he really wants is more stability in the
> committee.

In contrast to the Ullman years, no freshman Democrats or members from
marginal districts have been appointed to the committee since 1980 (see
Chapter 4, Tables 4-1, 4-3). This shift toward more restrictive committee
recruitment undoubtedly reflects the smaller numbers of Democratic freshmen in the House and the smaller number of committee openings during
the 1980s. But to the extent that the perceptions of these committee members are accurate, this pattern may also reflect the chairman's active involvement in the selection process.[36]

Encouragement of group solidarity. A second technique Rostenkowski
has employed as leader is encouraging strong group ties among Ways and
Means members, especially those on the majority side. "He has a different
sense of loyalty and a different sense of comradeship about the committee
than Mr. Ullman did," observed a Democrat who served under both leaders. A junior Democrat remarked enthusiastically of the relationship among
majority members: "It's almost like a fraternity atmosphere."

Attempts by the chairman to encourage group solidarity have included
informal interaction as well as a series of issue-related committee retreats
convened outside of Washington.[37] Committee members' comments in interviews suggest that Rostenkowski's involvement in recruitment and pro-
motion of group solidarity have been important in rebuilding both a sense
of group identity and some of the concern among junior members for the
committee's reputation that existed before the reforms. Note, for example,
how one junior Democrat describes Rostenkowski's influence on the
committee:

> He likes a team player. That doesn't mean you have to march in lock-
> step. But once you've tried your best to help whatever interest you
> might have or whatever issue you think is important—and you lose or
> you win—you don't embarrass the committee, you don't undermine
> the committee's work.

Early consultation, then negotiation to win firm commitments. On major
issues before the committee, Rostenkowski normally consults extensively
with committee members before proposing or endorsing a specific course
of action. As one Democratic member put it,

> Rostenkowski is constantly calling caucuses. He is meeting with us all
> the time, catching us on the floor, calling us up. The way he keeps us
> in line is that he knows what his committee members want. By the
> time he is ready to make a decision we've all played a role in it.

Members of both parties stated that Rostenkowski prefers to assemble coalitions before the committee meets to decide major issues in a markup. "He wants to know how the votes are going to come out," a Republican explained. "He doesn't like surprises even on relatively minor amendments." The key elements of Rostenkowski's approach to coalition building were summed up by a committee Democrat:

> When he's on a major piece of legislation he will have a series of conferences with the Democrats and let everyone speak their piece. He more or less sits back and listens, and then he goes to work on those he needs. . . . He works very closely with the ranking member on the Republican side—whether it be Barber Conable or John Duncan—and another member or two on the Republican side if he needs to. Then he knows where he's going. He will forge a bill. He gets solid commitments, even if he has to trade a bit. . . . Then he'll pass that bill out of committee because he will know that he has a majority of votes.

As this description indicates, Rostenkowski's normal approach to coalition building has been to solidify a base of support among committee Democrats, then bargain to attract Republican votes if possible. As was the case with Wilbur Mills, Rostenkowski's concern with reputation and "winning" on the House floor encourages the forging of bipartisan coalitions when political conditions allow. "He wants to work things out on a bipartisan basis if possible," a majority staffer noted, "because if things come out on a bipartisan basis in the committee it makes your life a lot easier when you hit the floor of the House." Thus Rostenkowski's concern with protecting committee prestige has led him to try to maintain good working relations with the minority, if not quite to embrace the norm of moderate partisanship that prevailed on the Mills-era committee.

Committee Republicans emphasized that when partisan conflict becomes unavoidable on an issue, Rostenkowski's strong partisan orientation comes into play. As one minority member explained:

> He has a genuine interest in being bipartisan. . . . In the preliminary steps of almost every issue he makes an extra effort to be bipartisan and let everybody be a player. However, when push comes to shove . . . he has a natural reaction to become extraordinarily partisan. It's almost built into his system.

Said another Republican:

> I think Rosty would rate unity a very high goal. . . . When he works with me on a trade bill I see a whole hell of a lot of him, he relies on me, and the stuff I do works. When we work on a bill where we [Democrats and Republicans] fall apart, it isn't fair to say it's an icy relationship, but the relationship dries up.

Threatening dissidents and freezing out defectors. Rostenkowski combines consultation and negotiation with the overt threat of sanctions against those who fail to support the agreements that are worked out. Especially among Democrats, one member pointed out, "once that consensus is developed, he expects you to pull together for whatever is decided." Members of both parties mentioned the chairman's willingness to threaten and punish dissident members as one source of his influence on the committee. In describing his approach to negotiating with committee members after settling on the general outlines of a bill, Rostenkowski himself once commented: "If you're against me, I might as well screw you up real good."[38]

One Democrat immediately turned to this aspect of Rostenkowski's style in explaining how the chairman had asserted greater control over the operation of the committee:

> Every member of the committee knows that they're going to have at some point a parochial problem that's going to be before the jurisdiction of the Ways and Means Committee. They know that Rostenkowski and his staff may undermine the attempt to get it on the agenda. I think that it is the threat that you are going to be frozen out when things are important to you that gives him a great deal of that power.

Commenting on the opportunities for committee members to insert minor constituency-oriented provisions in committee tax bills, a senior Republican made a similar point. "In the old days [under Ullman]," he explained, "you got one whether you deserved it or not. Now it's a tool of the chairman's diplomacy."

The most frequently cited example of Rostenkowski's willingness to retaliate against committee defectors was his treatment of Kent Hance (D-Tex.) after Hance cosponsored the Reagan administration's tax initiative that won out on the House floor over a Ways and Means Committee bill in 1981. Rostenkowski revoked authorization for Hance to travel to China with a committee group, pushed for removal of provisions of personal importance to Hance in the conference on the 1981 tax bill, and, by one account, even had the wheels removed from Hance's chair in the committee hearing room.[39]

Having witnessed or heard about cases of retaliation against defectors, individual committee members anticipate retaliation from the chairman in some form if they fail to support major committee bills. According to a committee Republican, this prospect was an important factor in his decision to support the tax reform package developed by the committee in 1985. Referring to his concern that the chairman might be able to influence the outcome at the conference stage, he explained: "There comes a certain point where you've won enough that if you abandon the bill itself, then all those issues you had in there are probably going to get stricken."

The use of the threat of sanctions places Rostenkowski's leadership style outside the highly permissive type some have associated with the contemporary Congress. Still, it is important to place the use of sanctions within the overall context of Rostenkowski's approach to leadership. One Ways and Means Democrat made precisely this point in reflecting on the chairman's influence on the committee:

> He knows how to wield power. With power you can hurt members. I've never been on the receiving end of it but I do know of cases where he has not allowed bills to come up. But no chairman, especially the chairman of the Ways and Means Committee, can maintain the kind of support he has by being a negative leader. His leadership is mainly by the force of his personality and communication. . . . people *like* him on our committee.

Control over organizational resources. A final aspect of Rostenkowski's style of leadership involves centralized control over the substantial staff resources provided for the majority members of the committee. Upon becoming chairman in 1981, Rostenkowski ended his predecessor's practice of allowing subcommittee chairmen to hire subcommittee staffs, instead allowing them only one clerical and one professional appointment as required by House rules. As a senior Democrat explained: "The chairman provides an element of control by controlling the staff on the subcommittees. All the staff view Rostenkowski as the boss, not the subcommittee chairman."

Partly because of this centralized staffing arrangement, Ways and Means subcommittees under Rostenkowski are less independent than was the case under Ullman. According to interviews, subcommittee chairmen are expected to obtain the chairman's approval for holding subcommittee hearings and markups. Although some committee members stressed that Rostenkowski prefers to defer in most cases to subcommittee chairmen, others noted that he does not simply take the laissez-faire approach toward work at the subcommittee level that Ullman often did. When a bill is being considered at the subcommittee level, a minority committee aide explained, "his staff keeps him apprised of where the thing is headed and if it starts getting screwed up his staff will tell him and he will talk to the subcommittee chairman." A subcommittee chairman offered a similar view of the chairman's role: "Unless the staff is saying that what we're doing is harebrained, as long as we are politically responsible, he gives us tremendous latitude." Noted a senior committee staffer on Rostenkowski's attitude toward bills being developed in subcommittee: "He is very much like Mills in that, if you're going to legislate, let's legislate something that's going to be law."

Rostenkowski as Leader: Context, Style, and Effectiveness

Contextual changes provide part of the explanation for the shift in Ways and Means Committee leadership from Ullman's permissive style during the 1970s to Rostenkowski's more active, centralized approach during the 1980s. After 1981, institutional, partisan, and issue-related factors have generally been more favorable to stronger leadership than was the case during the Ullman years. But the differences in the leadership styles of Ullman and Rostenkowski cannot be attributed simply or perhaps even primarily to contextual factors. In some respects, especially the emphasis on group loyalty and the willingness to threaten sanctions, Rostenkowski's leadership style is the antithesis of highly individualistic politics that have flourished in the House since the 1970s. Some of the techniques Rostenkowski has used to reestablish stronger leadership on the Ways and Means Committee during the 1980s clearly derive more from old-style machine politics than from the individualistic, participatory politics of the "New Congress" that emerged in the 1970s.

As one Ways and Means Democrat observed in discussing Rostenkowski's leadership of the committee:

> He has a very interesting set of values that is very un-eighties, if you will. He talks about [Ways and Means as] the *Cadillac* of committees and I say that you should refer to it as the *Mercedes-Benz* of committees. But he believes in these values of loyalty and stability, that there's a boss and the wise and compassionate boss checks it out with his minions before he leads them into battle. And he rewards and punishes. You know, these are all very Old Testament–type values. And they've worked very well.

Although he has shown surprising dexterity in adapting to the political environment of the 1980s (for example, the success in "going public" with the televised appeal to "Write Rosty" on the issue of tax reform),[40] Rostenkowski's leadership style bears an unmistakable imprint from his political apprenticeship in the Chicago Democratic machine. Leo Snowiss's description (written in the 1960s) of legislators selected to serve in Congress by the Chicago organization captures much of what is distinctive about Rostenkowski's political style in comparison to most contemporary House members. Members of the Chicago organization, Snowiss observed, "have been well schooled in and appreciate the value of quiet bargaining, negotiation and compromise"; they "value party cohesion as a positive good in need of little or no justification"; and they view politics "as a cooperative, organizational enterprise."[41]

Contrary to what one would anticipate from the notion that today's congressional leaders must employ highly permissive techniques of leadership, Rostenkowski is considered an effective leader by most of his fellow committee members. Five of the twenty-five members interviewed who served on Ways and Means between 1981 and 1986 offered critical comments when asked to discuss Rostenkowski's leadership style. Two (one Democrat and one Republican) criticized Rostenkowski's lack of interest in substantive as opposed to political aspects of issues before the committee; another (a Democrat) stated critically, "The chairman endeavors to have total control"; and another (a Republican) criticized the limited role allowed for minority members on some issues. One other Democrat noted that Rostenkowski had been successful in developing a sense of group loyalty on the panel, but complained: "His problem is that everybody knows that he puts personal loyalty to him ahead of individual policy views of committee members." But the remaining members (twelve Democrats and eight Republicans) each offered positive assessments of Rostenkowski's leadership.

In explaining why he considered Rostenkowski a more effective chairman than Ullman, a senior Democrat commented: "When he runs the show, he *runs* it. He's responsible for it." Said another Democrat when asked to compare Ullman and Rostenkowski:

> You're asking the person who was known as the chief rebel on the committee under Ullman but who has been pretty much of a soldier with Rostenkowski. It's not because I'm scared or not scared of either of them. It's because I appreciate the efficiency and he has given me something to follow.

Others emphasized that Rostenkowski's strong direction of committee affairs is guided by extensive consultation with committee members and, as one put it, "a strict code of fairness." "He's fair; he doesn't ride roughshod over his committee members," said a junior Democrat. A Republican offered a similar assessment in commenting on the chairman's ability to assemble committee support for the tax reform package reported by the committee in 1985:

> Danny has generally always treated the committee members fairly. He's tough. If he's against you, he's against you, and he'll beat the hell out of you. But he'll tell you up front he's going to do it. I think there was a certain amount of respect for Danny from the way he handles the committee. I think that came into play.

Minority members expressed distaste for the partisan aspects of Rostenkowski's style, but most still described him as an effective leader. One senior Republican went so far as to describe Rostenkowski as "the best chairman on the Hill." Said another: "He has begun to rebuild the pride of the Ways and Means Committee."

In a situation where reform-era institutional changes encouraged decentralization and participatory decisionmaking while other contextual factors provided opportunities for asserting stronger direction over committee politics, Rostenkowski has successfully *redefined* a stronger leadership role on the postreform Ways and Means Committee. Like Wilbur Mills, Rostenkowski has emphasized winning on the House floor and protecting committee prestige. Unlike Mills, though, Rostenkowski's style includes a strong, if pragmatic, element of partisanship. Rostenkowski has achieved some impressive legislative successes, including his role in forging a committee coalition to report comprehensive tax reform in 1985 (see Chapter 7). Interviews quoted above also suggest that he has achieved some success in reestablishing support for the prestige-oriented strategic premises that were characteristic of the committee during the Mills era. But there are fewer prestige-oriented members on the committee than before the 1970s reforms and some issues have created direct conflicts between the objectives of protecting committee prestige on the one hand and advancing partisan objectives on the other. Two examples (both of which are treated in more detail in Chapter 6) illustrate the continued interdependence of personal and contextual factors in determining an effective leadership style for the Ways and Means Committee.

In 1981, after attempts to negotiate a bipartisan tax reduction plan with the Reagan administration broke down, Rostenkowski found himself in the position of having to develop a Democratic alternative to the Reagan tax cut proposal at the high point of the new president's influence. The result was an unseemly bidding war in which Rostenkowski and the Democratic majority on Ways and Means were defeated on the House floor by the administration's proposal. In the bidding for support, both the committee bill and the administration version incorporated numerous special tax provisions that were of dubious value from a tax policy perspective. When asked in 1985 about the committee's reputation in the House, one Democrat focused on the aftereffects of the 1981 bidding war: "The '81 bill keeps coming up all the time," he noted. "It hurt our credibility." The goals of maintaining committee prestige and supporting partisan objectives came into even sharper conflict in 1982 as many House Democrats wanted the Republican-controlled Senate to take responsibility for initiating a major tax increase needed to reduce deficits resulting from the onset of recession and the enactment of the Reagan economic program. Over Rostenkowski's objection, a majority of Ways and Means Democrats supported this view, forcing the chairman to accept a strategy of ceding the initiative in formulating the 1982 revenue bill to the Senate. A majority staffer who was present at the committee caucus explained that Rostenkowski was concerned with protecting the committee's prerogatives in the tax area, but that "it was only the chairman and literally two or three others who said we should sit around the table and write a bill." Both cases illustrate well the continuing importance of the interplay of contextual factors with Rostenkowski's personal objectives and skills in determining the extent to which his leadership style "works" on the postreform committee. When the politics of the issues on the committee's agenda have created direct conflicts between goals of protecting the committee's reputation and pursuing partisan objectives of House Democrats, Rostenkowski has had problems as a leader; on issues where these goals have been compatible he has been more effective.

When Leaders Matter Most

Because of the different contexts within which committee and party leaders work, much caution is required in deriving lessons from the Ways and Means case for a more general theory of House leadership. Selective recruitment patterns, the smaller size of the group, and the narrower range of issues involved may allow leadership styles on a particular committee that would prove ineffective for the chamber as a whole or on other panels. Even so, the success of Dan Rostenkowski in establishing a centralizing, assertive leadership style on the Ways and Means Committee shows clearly that contemporary House leaders are not necessarily limited to highly permissive leadership styles. The importance of personal factors for explaining the dynamics of leadership on the postreform Ways and Means Committee also suggests the need to reconsider or at least refine the contextual emphasis that has been present in most recent work on congressional leadership.

Fred I. Greenstein proposed in *Personality and Politics* that the "likelihood of personal impact [on political phenomena] increases to the degree that the environment admits of restructuring."[42] In a later essay Greenstein argued that individual differences are most likely to manifest themselves in political situations that involve "the presence of contradictory elements" in the political environment.[43] Together with Fenno's observations noted at the beginning of the chapter on the importance of individual leaders when contextual factors are ambiguous, Greenstein's more general hypotheses suggest a basic proposition about congressional leadership that finds support in the Ways and Means case. Specifically, the characteristics of individual leaders should be of greatest importance for explaining leadership style and effectiveness during periods where contextual factors are conflictual or ambiguous, as when existing leadership regimes have broken down. Unlike periods of relative institutional stability, periods following those where existing institutional arrangements have broken down (or been intentionally dismantled) may allow unusual opportunities for individual leaders to redefine institutional forms and members' perceptions of effective leadership.[44]

At the point when Dan Rostenkowski assumed the chairmanship of the Ways and Means Committee, such a situation was present. The 1970s reforms had dismantled the underpinnings of the old Mills regime. A difficult transition occurred under Ullman's leadership, where committee politics became more partisan but also quite volatile and no new consensus on strategic premises developed. When Rostenkowski became chairman in 1981, the decentralizing reforms of the 1970s were still in place, but the organizational tendencies toward decentralization were contradicted by some committee members' frustrations with the unpredictable politics of the Ullman years and by a new policy agenda and political situation that created opportunities for more centralized leadership. Rostenkowski's political orientation and personal skills allowed him to take advantage of these conditions to reestablish a more assertive, centralized leadership style on the committee and to rebuild some support for the prestige-oriented strategic premises that had been one of the distinctive features of Ways and Means politics in the prereform years.

Conclusion

Most recent analyses of leadership in Congress have emphasized contextual determinants in explaining the behavior of leaders. None has dismissed individual leaders' traits as insignificant, but most have viewed individual leaders as more or less skillful practitioners of a contextually defined style. Personal characteristics of leaders have been an important factor in the transition of the House Ways and Means Committee during the postreform years from a participatory, permissive style of leadership to a more centralized, assertive style. The Ways and Means case suggests that, even though contextual factors remain important in determining the range of possible styles or techniques that can be effective in the House, individual leaders themselves may play an important role in determining leadership style and effectiveness during periods when contextual factors are ambiguous. The focus now turns to an analysis of the politics of the postreform Ways and Means Committee in the area of federal tax legislation.

Chapter 6

The Politics of Taxation, 1975–1984

To assess both the consequences of reform-era changes and the utility of the purposive theories of Mayhew and Fenno for understanding the effects of institutional change, this chapter and the one that follows will examine policymaking on the Ways and Means Committee in the area of federal taxation over the period from 1975 to 1986. These chapters do not pretend to offer a comprehensive account of the politics of federal taxation during this period, but instead focus primarily on two aspects of Ways and Means Committee members' behavior: partisanship and responsiveness to particularistic interests and clientele groups seeking tax benefits.[1]

The two theoretical perspectives that were employed in Chapter 4 to consider reform-era institutional changes suggest different consequences for politics and policy outcomes on the postreform Ways and Means Committee. With the reduction and devaluation of the selective incentive of institutional prestige associated with committee membership, the electoral connection model leads to the expectation that, in money decisions that offer ample opportunities for targeting benefits to electoral supporters, increased particularism and servicing of organized clientele groups should be evident. Fenno's multiple goal theoretical framework, on the other hand, suggests that changes in members' goals and environmental constraints in the aftermath of the reform era should produce new patterns in committee politics where pursuit of partisan or policy goals assumes much greater importance, with limited evidence of increased particularism or servicing of clientele groups likely.

Reformers in the 1970s dismantled many of the institutional underpinnings of the prereform pattern of restrained partisanship, limited responsiveness to clientele interests, and conservative tendencies in policy outcomes that characterized the Ways and Means Committee for most of the Mills era. After 1974 a new institutional environment existed in which the committee enjoyed considerably less procedural autonomy from rank and file House members, from clientele groups, and from the majority party caucus and its leadership. Significant changes from the Mills-era patterns in committee politics have appeared in the postreform years, but these do not fit a simple pattern of either increased policy activism and partisanship or increased particularism and responsiveness to clientele interests. The patterns that have been present in committee decisionmaking on tax issues during the 1975–86 period generally appear closer to the expectations derived from Fenno's framework, but striking evidence of responsiveness to clientele interests has also been present during this period. One reason for the variety of patterns in postreform committee politics is that committee politics over this period reflect not only reform-era institutional changes but also a series of major changes in the committee's agenda. An analysis of the politics of taxation on the postreform Ways and Means Committee indicates that both institutional *and* jurisdictional or agenda factors are important for understanding committee politics in the postreform House.[2]

The Ways and Means Committee and Tax Politics in the Mills Era

Moderate partisanship and careful deliberation on major tax policy issues were generally characteristic of decisionmaking on the Ways and Means Committee during the late 1950s and 1960s. Still, as Manley put it, partisanship had been "built into" the Ways and Means Committee by the recruitment of party regulars and by the partisan nature of the issues within the panel's jurisdiction.[3] Looking back as far as the 1930s, Manley pointed out that the behavior of the committee "veers toward conflict under certain circumstances and consensus under others."[4] Fenno found that dissenting views from minority members were not unusual in committee reports, nor were partisan divisions among committee members on floor votes. In fact, members were sharply divided along partisan lines in floor votes on six of the ten major tax bills reported by the committee between 1955 and 1966.[5]

However, as was noted in Chapter 2, when partisan conflict developed over tax policy or other issues during the Mills era it was governed by the norm of restrained partisanship. Members of both parties usually participated in the deliberations through which committee bills took form, with partisanship usually emerging only in the final stages of committee work and in votes on the House floor. The norm of restrained partisanship was reinforced by Mills's accommodative style of leadership and by the small size of the committee, reliance on the nonpartisan Joint Tax Committee staff, and the absence of partisan committee caucuses.

Along with restrained partisanship, a second distinctive characteristic of tax decisionmaking on Ways and Means during the prereform years was limited responsiveness to constituency interests and clientele groups. This tendency toward selective responsiveness to clientele interests was most evident in comparing the Ways and Means Committee to its Senate counterpart. Lacking the procedural autonomy and responsible ethos of the Ways and Means Committee, Senate Finance Committee members according to Fenno saw their primary role as providing "remedial assistance to clientele groups who appeal[ed] to them for redress from House decisions."[6]

In most cases during the Mills era, the Ways and Means Committee initiated congressional action on revenue bills and set the basic outlines for major policy changes. With very few exceptions, Ways and Means tax bills were submitted to the full House under closed rules and passed unamended.[7] Senate action normally involved revising House-passed legislation, often in response to clientele and constituency-group demands for tax relief that were unsuccessful in the more restrictive deliberative process in the House. Policy outcomes in the House tended to be more oriented toward maintaining federal revenues; those in the Senate tended to bear a greater imprint of clientele interests seeking reduced tax burdens.[8]

The Ways and Means Committee and Tax Politics in the Postreform House

Focusing on policymaking on major tax issues over the 1975–86 period, partisanship in Ways and Means Committee decisionmaking is examined both in the conduct of committee deliberations and in final committee votes. Changes over time in responsiveness to clientele interests are examined through interview data, secondary accounts, and some comparisons with policy outcomes in the Senate. Major tax legislation reported by the Ways and Means Committee between 1975 and 1984 will be examined in this chapter, with the special case of the Tax Reform Act of 1986 and the overall patterns in tax legislation taken up in Chapter 7. The analysis of tax politics on the postreform committee is divided into three periods, with each defined by a distinctive set of jurisdictional or agenda-related influences on committee politics.

The End of a Liberal Era in Economic Policy, 1975–1977

Between 1975 and 1977 the Ways and Means Committee reported out five major tax bills: two tax cuts intended to stimulate the economy (1975 and 1977); two tax bills dealing with energy production and conservation (1975 and 1977); and a long-promised tax reform package (1975). Of these five tax measures, only the 1975 tax cut (H.R. 2166) witnessed anything like the moderate partisanship of the Mills era. None offered clear evidence of the increase in particularism and clientelism suggested by the electoral connection model. Instead, the prevalent pattern in committee tax politics between 1975 and 1977 was one in which policy outcomes could fairly be characterized as liberal on the economic policy continuum, thoroughgoing partisanship was present in both committee deliberations and final votes, and expanded participation in tax policy deliberations occurred with involvement by the Democratic caucus and noncommittee members on the House floor.[9]

The first major item on the agenda of the newly reformed Ways and Means Committee that met in January of 1975 was a proposal from President Ford for a $16 billion, one-year tax cut to stimulate a flagging economy. Many House Democrats were also anticipating action on tax issues that had been left unresolved from the previous year. As discussed in Chapter 3, during Wilbur Mills's final two years as chairman the Ways and Means Committee had worked unsuccessfully to develop a major tax reform proposal and to restructure taxes on the oil industry. Along with these issues left over from the previous Congress, the committee also took action in 1975 to enact a series of energy tax measures designed to encourage conservation and help alleviate fuel shortages.

In response to the tax cut proposed by President Ford in January 1975, the committee expanded the proposed one-year cut from $16 billion to approximately $20 billion.[10] The need for economic stimulus was acknowledged by Ways and Means members of both parties and the bill was reported in February by a 29-6 vote, with only five Republicans and a single Democrat opposed. Minority members supported some provisions of the bill in committee deliberations but attempted unsuccessfully to substitute their own plan that incorporated a smaller tax reduction tipped more toward the middle class than the cuts in the committee bill. The most controversial aspect of the deliberations on the tax cut proved to be the attempt by liberal Ways and Means Democrats to attach to the bill an amendment providing for immediate repeal of the percentage depletion allowance on most income from oil and natural gas production. With Chairman Ullman arguing that the controversial amendment might slow passage of the tax cut, the committee rejected the amendment by a 23-12 margin before voting final approval of the package.

Under the closed rule reform enacted in 1973, if fifty Democrats would sign a petition requesting caucus consideration, the Democratic caucus (by majority vote) could instruct the Rules Committee to allow a floor vote on a specific amendment to a bill. The new procedure had been invoked on a Ways and Means bill in 1974 to allow floor votes on oil industry tax provisions, but had proven ineffective due to the procedural maneuverings of Wilbur Mills (see Chapter 3). After William J. Green of Pennsylvania and six other Ways and Means Democrats collected the required fifty signatures, the caucus voted 153 to 98 to have a floor vote on two amendments related to the oil depletion issue (one to terminate the allowance and one to maintain the allowance only for small producers). The House approved the tax cut measure reported by Ways and Means by a large margin (317-97), but before doing so also voted 248-163 to accept the caucus-mandated amendment to repeal the depletion allowance, thereby overruling the Ways and Means Committee. The Senate expanded the size of the 1975 cut from $20 to $27 billion, but this figure was scaled back in conference prior to final passage.

The Ways and Means Committee was much more polarized along

partisan lines in developing energy and tax revision legislation later in 1975. In May the committee reported an energy tax bill (H.R. 6860) as an alternative to an energy plan the Ford White House had proposed in January. Committee deliberations broke down almost entirely along partisan lines, as the Ways and Means bill was developed primarily through task forces and caucuses which included only Democratic members.[11] Second-ranking Republican Barber B. Conable, Jr., explained to Congressional Quarterly at the time that Chairman Ullman "can't afford to deal with the Republicans on this" because of pressure from the majority caucus to develop a Democratic alternative.[12] The committee reported a conservation-oriented bill by a 19-16 vote, but did so in the face of united opposition from Republicans, who sought more incentives for energy production in the bill, and from seven disaffected Democrats as well.

Submitted to the House by a divided Ways and Means Committee under what was termed an "orderly open rule," the energy tax bill ultimately passed by a 291-130 vote, but was heavily amended on the floor. All of the major components of the Ways and Means bill—a gasoline tax to discourage consumption, strict oil import quotas, a "gas guzzler" tax on inefficient automobiles—were either defeated or substantially weakened.[13] As Catherine E. Rudder has shown, on a number of sections of the bill a majority of Ways and Means members even joined in support of amendments to revise their own committee's work product.[14] The bill had little support in the Senate and never reached the floor of the other chamber for a vote.

In November 1975 Ways and Means approved a third tax bill, some parts of which were formulated through a similarly partisan deliberative process. The bill (H.R. 10612), which extended the 1975 tax cuts and reduced or eliminated a number of tax preferences, was voted out of committee by a 20-17 margin. Here again, Republicans voted en bloc in opposition to most parts of the bill—in this case because the committee majority refused to incorporate a spending ceiling that President Ford had requested in conjunction with the tax cuts.[15] Opposition to the bill also developed on the majority side when some committee Democrats who had sought to eliminate additional tax preferences made it clear that they would vote against the bill and petition the caucus to allow floor amendments if changes they desired were not presented to the full House for a vote. With the Democratic majority for the bill thus threatened and the prospect of caucus intervention again raised, Chairman Ullman and committee Democrats agreed in a closed-door caucus to request a rule allowing floor votes on the strengthening amendments. As on the oil depletion issue earlier the same year, the Ways and Means dissidents proved to be in step with House sentiment; three of the five amendments restricting tax preferences were adopted before the House passed the Ways and Means bill on December 4 by a 257-168 vote.[16] A confrontation with President Ford over the spending ceiling issue resulted in a veto of the tax reduction component of the bill, but a revised version was repassed in late 1975. After a very long debate in the Senate, the tax revision component of the bill was enacted the following year as the Tax Reform Act of 1976.[17]

Divided party control of Congress and the White House during the initial postreform years reinforced the partisan tendencies introduced into Ways and Means Committee politics by structural changes in the mid-1970s that encouraged greater responsiveness to the majority party organization and more partisan deliberations inside the committee. Ironically, given the view of many party government scholars that unified partisan control of government increases the effectiveness of party organization in Congress, not long after Democrat Jimmy Carter won the White House in 1976 Ways and Means Democrats found themselves unable to remain sufficiently unified to maintain control of committee deliberations.

Throughout the 1976 presidential campaign candidate Jimmy Carter called attention to tax reform as one of the changes he would immediately undertake to make government more fair and efficient. But once in office, events demanded that Carter act first on two other tax-related problems—a sluggish economy and the persistent problems the country was facing with fuel shortages and rising energy costs. Shortly after being sworn in Carter promised a comprehensive energy plan within ninety days. The resulting plan, submitted to Congress in April 1977, relied heavily on new tax provisions to deal with the energy situation. With an economic stimulus proposal and the energy plan dominating the time and attention of the House and Senate tax panels, tax reform was postponed until the second year of the Carter presidency.

The economic stimulus proposal was submitted to Congress first, in January of 1977. The tax component of the proposal involved $22 billion in tax cuts over fiscal years 1977 and 1978. The proposal included: 1) a fifty-dollar, onetime rebate of 1976 taxes to individuals and a payment of the same size to Social Security and Railroad Retirement beneficiaries ($11.4 billion); 2) an increase in the standard deduction for individuals and couples ($7 billion); and 3) tax relief for businesses in the form of an option to take a new tax credit for payroll taxes or an expanded investment tax credit ($3.6 billion).

Although few were enthusiastic about the idea, most committee Democrats supported Carter's request for tax rebates; Republicans opposed it, preferring permanent rate reductions to the "one-shot" rebate. Bipartisan cooperation emerged in support of revising the administration's business tax proposal to add a tax credit for hiring new employees, but in the 26-8 final vote on February 17 to report the package (H.R. 3477) to the House, the committee again broke along partisan lines with only three Republicans supporting the bill and only two Democrats in opposition.[18] Operating under a rule that prohibited noncommittee amendments, the House approved the Ways and Means package by a partisan 282 to 131 vote on March 8. After dropping the controversial rebates at the administration's request, the Senate passed the bill in April and a final version was approved in May.

While the Senate was still debating the economic stimulus proposal in April 1977, Carter unveiled his comprehensive energy plan. A major part of the 283-page proposal was a package of tax provisions to provide incentives for conservation of oil and natural gas and to encourage use of alternative energy sources. Although price controls on domestically produced oil were to remain in effect, a tax (called the crude oil equalization tax, or COET) was proposed to raise the cost of domestic oil to the world market price over the course of three years. To reduce industrial use of oil and natural gas, industries utilizing those energy sources would be subject to new taxes. To encourage greater use of coal, tax credits were to be provided to offset part of the costs of converting to the more plentiful fuel. To reduce gasoline consumption the president proposed a standby gasoline tax and a "gas guzzler" tax for inefficient automobiles, with rebates for purchasers of efficient models. Finally, the plan included additional tax provisions to spur conservation and development of new technologies: businesses and homeowners were to be given tax credits for conservation improvements and installation of new technologies such as solar or wind devices, and tax breaks were provided for development of geothermal and other new energy sources. To cushion the effects of increased energy taxes, the proceeds of the crude oil and gasoline taxes were to be rebated to consumers and taxpayers.

In Ways and Means Committee deliberations on Carter's energy proposals, each of the major tax provisions in the plan that passed committee scrutiny—a "gas guzzler" tax on inefficient new cars, a tax on crude oil, and tax credits for residential and business conservation expenditures—was approved by partisan votes in which Democrats defeated committee Republicans and a shifting group of majority members who were primarily seeking to defend regional interests against costs imposed by the plan. Although the Democratic majority made a number of major modifications in the Carter proposal, most Democrats supported the president's approach to energy policy while Republicans continued to criticize increased government regulation of energy markets and the lack of incentives for new oil and gas production. On the final 24-13 vote to report the bill (H.R. 6831), only two Democrats broke ranks to oppose the package, and only a single Republican supported it.[19]

These tax measures and the various other components of the Carter energy plan were then sent to a special Ad Hoc Committee on Energy.[20] The Ad Hoc Energy Committee reassembled the energy package in late July for submission to the House. With the exception of an amendment to restore part of the administration's proposed gasoline tax, only minor changes were made by the Ad Hoc Committee in the parts of the plan that had been reviewed by Ways and Means. The full House rejected the Ad Hoc Committee's gasoline tax amendment but otherwise approved the energy package—including the tax provisions developed by Ways and Means —by a partisan 244-177 vote. A much different sequence of events occurred in the Senate, where the administration's extensive program was reduced to a stripped-down version that included only a limited tax on industrial use of oil and gas and some new tax incentives for energy conservation and production. In the final version of the energy package that was signed by the president in November of 1978, of the original plan only the "gas guzzler" tax and tax incentives for conservation and development of new energy sources had survived.[21]

In contrast to the moderate partisanship characteristic of the committee during most of the Mills era, both committee deliberations *and* final votes on tax issues tended to be highly partisan in the initial postreform years (1975–77). The prereform pattern of restrained partisanship at the deliberative stage had given way to a thoroughgoing polarization along partisan lines in committee work on tax issues. This pattern is consistent with what one would expect from Fenno's theoretical framework. The addition of more policy-oriented committee members during the reform era and the institutional changes that increased the importance of partisan leaders and organization in the committee's environment suggested just such a change. Divided partisan control of Congress and the White House during 1975 and 1976 strongly reinforced the partisan tendencies in the new institutional environment.

Even though some Democrats and reformers were disappointed that sweeping new policy initiatives in areas such as tax reform did not occur after the committee was restructured, in most cases Ways and Means Democrats were sufficiently united on a liberal approach to the tax issues on the committee's agenda (i.e., dealing with a flagging economy by enacting mildly redistributive tax cuts and attempting to stimulate consumer demand, eliminating some special tax preferences to achieve greater equity in tax burdens, expanding government intervention in energy markets to encourage conservation and manage fuel shortages) to maintain control of committee decisionmaking. The result was limited participation in deliberations by committee Republicans and, despite reforms that "opened up" committee decisionmaking, limited influence for clientele groups whose goals were inconsistent with the liberal policy objectives of the Democratic majority in the House.[22]

The overall pattern of clientele influence in committee decisionmaking on the five tax bills reported between 1975 and 1977 is mixed, but these bills do not provide evidence of any dramatic increase in the distribution of tax benefits to clientele or constituency interests in the aftermath of the reforms. The 1975 tax reduction bill reported by the Ways and Means Committee increased the size of the tax cut proposed by President Ford from $16 billion to almost $20 billion, but it also shifted the balance of the cut toward low income taxpayers. By way of comparison, the Senate Finance Committee bill increased the annual tax reduction for 1975 to almost $30 billion by adding additional revenue-losing provisions that included tax credits designed to benefit specific industries (housing, automobile manufacturing, and others).[23] In the energy area, the committee approved conservation-oriented bills in 1975 and 1977 that were opposed by a large number of well-organized industry groups. Although some clientele groups won modifications in the president's proposals during Ways and Means deliberations on energy taxes in 1977, the House panel again demonstrated greater independence from clientele interests than did the Finance Committee, which gutted House-passed tax provisions that were opposed by the oil industry, the automobile industry and industrial users of oil and gas. Finally, though the Ways and Means Committee backed away from a more ambitious tax reform package sought by some Democratic members, it did vote to restrict a number of tax shelters and special preferences in the 1975 tax revision bill (which became the Tax Reform Act of 1976).[24]

The Exhaustion of Liberalism and the New Politics of Economic Growth, 1978–1981

One might have anticipated that unrestrained partisanship and a liberal cast to policy outcomes would continue to characterize committee decisionmaking during the late 1970s. Not only were reforms encouraging increased control of committee decisionmaking by the majority party still in place, but voters continued to reelect large Democratic majorities to the House [66.9 percent in the Ninety-fifth Congress (1977–78) and 63.7 percent in the Ninety-sixth Congress (1979–80)]. Instead, 1978 marked the beginning of a major shift in tax politics on the Ways and Means Committee. As a new economic policy agenda began to appear in the late 1970s, the politics of committee decisionmaking and the direction of policy outcomes witnessed important changes from the patterns that had been present in the initial postreform years.

A sluggish economy, persistent inflation, and a growing middle-class "tax revolt" all contributed to the rise of the new economic policy agenda. Traditional liberal concerns with distributional equity began to be eclipsed by a new emphasis on reducing tax burdens on middle-income taxpayers and encouraging savings and investment. By the late 1970s, economic policy debates began to be dominated by proposals for reducing marginal tax rates across the board for individuals, creating (or restoring) incentives for capital investment, and reducing economic inefficiencies resulting from federal regulation. In the context of this new agenda, Ways and Means Committee politics began to exhibit a great deal of volatility. This new pattern in committee politics first appeared in 1978 in deliberations on a tax reform and reduction proposal developed by the Carter administration.

In his 1978 State of the Union message President Carter announced that he would seek passage of a combination of tax reductions and revenue increases. In late January Carter requested a net annual tax reduction in 1979 of $24.5 billion, to come from $33.9 billion in tax cuts, and "reforms" eliminating $9.4 billion in tax deductions and preferences. Of the reductions, $23.5 billion involved cuts in personal taxes. The personal cuts were targeted primarily at taxpayers at the lower end of the income scale, with the largest proportional reductions going to families with incomes of $15,000 or less. Given the changes occurring in the economic policy agenda at the time, the proposal represented yet another example of the Carter administration's insensitivity to political realities in Congress. As John F. Witte notes, "Never in the history of the income tax were proposals so out of step with congressional intentions, and never were they so completely defeated."[25]

Ways and Means deliberations on the proposal found committee Democrats sharply divided on the president's recommendations. When the committee reached a standstill because of opposition to the Carter plan, an informal, bipartisan group of committee members including Ullman, Rostenkowski, James R. Jones (D-Okla.), Conable, and William Steiger (R-Wis.) began working on an alternative bill. According to a committee staffer who attended the meetings of the group, members of the majority and minority "sat down . . . and negotiated out every single provision in that bill as equals." After the informal group completed its work, the committee approved the alternative plan by a 25-12 vote in July. Rather than targeting cuts at low income families and curtailing tax preferences, the alternative bill provided for individual cuts distributed across all income levels and created new incentives for capital investment by cutting capital gains rates.[26]

In contrast to the highly partisan tax politics of the preceding years, the 1978 bill passed the House in an atmosphere of bipartisan cooperation. Conservative Republican Bill Archer of Texas, who had complained on the House floor the previous year that energy tax measures had been "railroaded" through by the majority party, praised Chairman Ullman's approach in formulating the 1978 measure. "This has not been an easy bill to craft," Archer stated on the House floor, adding: "The gentleman [Ullman] has been eminently fair to all members of the committee of all persuasions."[27] Unlike the previous tax bills that had been reported since the 1974 reforms, in this case it was the liberal Democrats who exercised little influence in committee deliberations. As one, Charles Vanik of Ohio, explained in the floor debate: "The final product was approved by thirteen Democrats and all twelve Republicans. The other twelve Democrats were left talking to one another."[28] On August 10, by a 362-49 vote, the House approved the Ways and Means bill unchanged from the form in which it had been reported by the committee. The size of the tax cut was almost doubled in the Senate version passed in October, but was reduced to within $3 billion of the original $16 billion House figure in conference.

The final major tax measure reported during the Carter years found the Ways and Means Committee back in the center of the divisive debate over energy policy. Only months after the final passage of the remnants of the first Carter energy plan, conditions in world oil markets brought on by an interruption in Iranian exports began to produce shortages and a new round of major price increases. In response, the Carter administration proposed a new round of energy initiatives in 1979. On April 5 Carter announced his intention to begin removal of price controls on domestic oil in order to increase incentives for conservation and new production. Because decontrol would bring substantial increases in already high oil company profits, the president also requested that Congress enact a "windfall profits tax" on increased revenues that would accrue to oil producers. The proceeds of the tax would go to an Energy Security Fund, to be used for assisting low-income families with fuel bills, funding mass transit programs, and development of petroleum reserves and new energy sources.

As the Ways and Means hearings progressed, it became clear that the real issue was not whether or not a windfall tax should be imposed on profits from oil production but whether the tax should in fact be heavier than the one the administration had proposed. Also controversial were questions of how the revenues would be used—whether they would go to a trust fund as the president had proposed, go to general revenues, or be "plowed back" to the energy industry to encourage new production.[29]

Deliberations on the bill were neither strictly partisan nor consensual, but instead involved a kaleidoscopic pattern of shifting committee coalitions. In a series of votes pitting Republicans and oil state Democrats (J. J. Pickle of Texas and James Jones of Oklahoma) against other Democrats, the committee decided to raise the tax rate on revenues from decontrol of existing oil production above the administration proposal. But on the taxation of future oil discoveries, Chairman Ullman and ten other Democrats joined the Republicans in supporting an amendment to reduce the tax. Democrats reunited to vote down (14-22) an amendment to add further production incentives through a "plow back" tax credit for oil exploration and to reject (16-20) a substitute package developed by Democrat James Jones and Republican W. Henson Moore of Louisiana that would have reduced rates on existing oil production and set a 1990 termination date for taxes on new production. The decision to report the bill came on a 20-16 vote with all of the Republicans and four Democrats voting no.[30]

The Ways and Means bill came to the floor on June 28 under a modified closed rule. The rule allowed votes on the Ways and Means bill, on amendments proposed by liberal Ways and Means Democrats who sought higher levies than those in the committee bill, and on the Jones-Moore substitute. The rate structure in the Ways and Means Committee bill was rejected when an overwhelming majority of Republicans joined ninety Democrats to approve the Jones-Moore substitute by a 236-183 margin. After the changes incorporated in the Jones-Moore substitute were approved, final passage came on a voice vote.[31] The final bill would have raised an estimated $277 billion in new revenues over a ten-year period. The version of the windfall profits tax approved by the Senate in December 1979 would have raised an estimated $178 billion over the same period. In final action on the bill in 1980, a package halfway between the House and Senate figures was agreed to. After the windfall profits tax became law in 1980, energy tax issues receded from the committee's agenda. But conditions the following year proved to be ripe for major income tax policy changes in the direction of those enacted in 1978.

Support for further growth-oriented tax reductions had been building even before Ronald Reagan and Republican congressional candidates scored impressive electoral successes in the fall of 1980. Prior to his nomination as Republican presidential candidate, Reagan joined with tax cut proponents Congressman Jack F. Kemp of New York and Senator William V. Roth of Delaware, senior Republicans Barber Conable of the House Ways and Means Committee and Robert Dole of the Senate Finance Committee, and a number of other fellow party members in advocating a 10 percent cut in personal rates for 1981 and the so-called 10-5-3 depreciation plan, which would cut business taxes by reducing the time required to write off capital expenditures. The House in 1980 went along with a Carter administration request to postpone action on taxes until after the election, but a bipartisan majority of the Senate Finance Committee approved a package of personal and business cuts in August that would have reduced taxes by $39.4 billion in 1981. Although the full Senate voted to table the Finance Committee bill when it reached the floor in September, leaders in both chambers agreed that tax reduction would be enacted in the next Congress.[32] Speaker Thomas P. O'Neill commented after meeting with President Carter and Democratic congressional leaders in July, "There's no question in all of our minds that there will be a tax cut in 1981."[33]

During the campaign Reagan embraced a three-year, across-the-board cut in individual marginal tax rates that had been proposed by Congressman Kemp and Senator Roth. Both the Kemp-Roth plan and the accelerated depreciation proposal had also been incorporated as planks in the

1980 Republican platform. The outcome of the election—a Reagan land-slide, Republican control of the Senate for the first time since 1954, and an increase of thirty-three Republican seats in the House—provided a very favorable climate for enactment of the tax policies sought by the new administration.

After the election Reagan moved quickly on a tax proposal.[34] In tele-vised addresses on February 5 and February 18, 1981, the newly elected president outlined his economic program of tax and budget cuts and ap-pealed for public support. The president's tax proposal called for a 10 percent cut in marginal rates on personal income each year for three years, and a modified version of the 10-5-3 accelerated depreciation plan (also known as the Accelerated Cost Recovery System, or ACRS) that he had endorsed before the election. According to Treasury Department estimates, the proposal would reduce tax revenues $718 billion over fiscal years 1981 through 1986 by providing $554 billion in personal tax reductions and $164 billion in cuts for businesses.[35] In the February 18 message, Reagan also announced his intention to deal with other tax issues in a second tax bill to be submitted after the basic economic program was in place. Addi-tional tax objectives mentioned by the president included indexing personal tax brackets for inflation, ending the "marriage penalty" (rate structures that make taxes on working couples higher than those on single wage earners), providing tuition tax credits, and restructuring inheritance taxes.

Despite the otherwise favorable political conditions for winning pas-sage of a major tax cut, the Reagan proposal encountered a number of obstacles on Capitol Hill. Still reeling from Republican gains in the 1980 election, Democrats criticized the proposal as overly generous to upper-income taxpayers, and argued that the overall size of the cuts would be inflationary. Some Republicans were also uncomfortable with the size of the cuts given the existing budget constraints. Members of both parties and clientele groups that sought tax changes other than those in the initial administration proposal were skeptical that a second bill would be feasible if the large reductions in the initial plan were approved. As a result of these factors, Republican leaders representing the new majority in the Senate as well as the chairmen of both tax committees indicated that some modifica-tions would have to be made in the president's proposal to secure passage.

In the hearings that began on February 24, the new chairman of the Ways and Means Committee, Dan Rostenkowski, announced his preference for a compromise bill. "It is my desire," he stated to Treasury secretary Donald T. Regan, "that a consensus bill emerge from this committee . . . and be signed into law; even if it does not fully resemble the plan President Reagan has laid before us."[36] After Ways and Means hearings were con-cluded in April, Rostenkowski announced a tentative plan that included personal cuts that were smaller overall, but more favorable to taxpayers in the middle-income range ($20,000 to $50,000) than the administration proposal. Informal discussions among congressional leaders including Rostenkowski and Finance Committee chairman Robert Dole began in May on a compromise plan, but negotiations broke off in early June when Ways and Means Democrats and the House majority leadership refused to agree to a three-year package of personal rate cuts and the administration decided (in part because it had already defeated the House Democratic leadership in May on the first budget resolution for fiscal year 1982) that sufficient support existed among Republicans and conservative Democrats to pass a bill closer to the original Reagan proposal. After the negotiations between the administration and Democratic leaders in the House collapsed, formulation of tax legislation proceeded on three fronts.

On June 4 the White House announced a revised proposal to be introduced in the House by Ways and Means ranking Republican Barber Conable and Democrat Kent Hance of Texas. The Conable-Hance proposal scaled back the first year of the personal rate cut from 10 to 5 percent and revised the depreciation provisions, making them less generous than those initially proposed. In a number of other areas, however, the revised plan upped the ante by adding new provisions intended to win support from a crucial bloc of mostly southern Democrats. Now included in the bill were increased tax credits for rehabilitation of older buildings, an immediate reduction in the top rate on unearned income from 70 to 50 percent, a deduction to offset the marriage penalty, increased allowances for contributions to IRA and Keogh plans, permanent status for an expiring provision that allowed increased deductions for dividend and interest income, new exemptions from estate and gift taxes, tax reductions for Americans working abroad, and an extension and increase in exemptions for small oil royalty holders who were subject to the windfall profits tax. When business interests protested the less favorable treatment in the revised depreciation proposal, the administration quickly restored most of the business cuts that had been included in the original plan and added a new provision allowing companies with limited tax liabilities to transfer tax breaks to more profitable companies (by selling and then leasing back assets—a practice known as safe-harbor leasing). These changes made the revenue losses in the Conable-Hance bill comparable to those in the original Reagan proposal, despite the reduced size of the personal rate cuts.

As Conable-Hance was introduced in the House, both the Finance Committee and Ways and Means began marking up tax bills in mid-June. By a 19-1 vote the Finance Committee approved a bill on June 25 that included not only most of the provisions contained in the administration's most recent proposal, but also new tax cuts in other areas as well. Probably most important in the long term, the Finance Committee voted to offer as a committee amendment a provision to require indexation of the personal income tax system for inflation.[37] Floor debate in the Senate on the Finance Committee bill had already begun when Ways and Means reported its version of the tax bill on July 23.

Deliberations on Ways and Means had become highly partisan. Formulation of the committee bill occurred primarily in partisan caucuses and through task forces of Democratic members assigned different substantive areas. The central feature of the resulting committee bill was a two-year, 15 percent cut in personal rates aimed primarily at middle- and lower-income groups, with a third-year cut of an additional 10 percent to take effect only if favorable economic conditions existed. Speaker O'Neill took an active role in persuading Rostenkowski to develop a Democratic alternative of this type.[38] Although the overall business tax reductions in the Ways and Means bill were comparable in size to the administration proposal, Ways and Means Democrats took a somewhat different approach by proposing cuts in corporate tax rates and a depreciation plan that included "expensing" (one-year write-off) for some capital expenditures.

But offsetting much of the smaller cut the committee had made in individual rates, the Ways and Means bill also incorporated new provisions in the bidding for floor support. To name a few, in the area of personal taxes, child care credits were expanded, capital gains provisions for home sales liberalized, deductions for IRAs increased, and reductions in estate and gift taxes approved. Specific clientele interests were also targeted for more favorable tax treatment. On the condition that the money would go for new investment, refunds of unused investment tax credits of over $3 billion were approved for certain industries (airlines, automobile manufacturers, mining, paper, steel, and railroads). Research and development credits beneficial to high technology companies were expanded. Finally, in the early morning hours of the final day of the markup, the committee voted to exempt all oil producers from windfall profits taxes on 500 barrels of oil per day.

Not to be outdone, the administration again revised the Conable-Hance proposal, incorporating some provisions (such as more liberal treatment of estate and gift taxes) from the Ways and Means bill, and adding others, including an allowance for charitable deductions by nonitemizers, indexation of personal tax rates, and a reduction in windfall profits tax rates, that had been incorporated in the Senate bill by the Finance Committee. The Republican cosponsor of the administration bill, Barber Conable, publicly expressed dismay over the bidding contest that had developed, but stated that it had become unavoidable under the circumstances in order to ensure adoption of the president's basic economic program.[39]

The total impact of the final administration package was estimated at $754 billion in reduced revenues over fiscal years 1981 through 1986, $36 billion more than the original Reagan proposal. By comparison, the Ways and Means bill would have reduced revenues by almost as much, an estimated $620 billion over the same period.[40] Although the committee reported its tax package (H.R. 4242) by a voice vote, the deep partisan split on the panel was indicated by a unanimous minority report advocating passage of the administration bill.[41]

The tax bill came to the House floor on July 29 under a modified closed rule that allowed votes only on the Ways and Means bill, the Conable-Hance substitute, and a last-minute substitute introduced by Democrat Morris Udall of Arizona, which included a much smaller tax cut than either of the other proposals. As the vote approached, the White House launched an all-out lobbying effort. Despite a last-minute plea by Speaker O'Neill for Democratic support for the Ways and Means bill, forty-eight Democrats supported the Conable-Hance substitute, giving the Reagan administration a 238-195 victory on the House floor. The final Senate vote on the tax bill also came on July 29, when a much amended version of the administration's proposal passed by a bipartisan 89-11 margin. Because both bills were based on the administration's three-year personal rate reduction and accelerated depreciation proposals, and because the Conable-Hance substitute had embraced many provisions initially approved in the Senate as the bidding escalated, relatively few major issues remained to be resolved in conference. The passage of the 1981 tax bill (formally known as the Economic Recovery Tax Act of 1981) marked the ascendancy of the new economic policy agenda that had emerged in the late 1970s; after 1981 a much different type of agenda began to shape Ways and Means Committee politics.

In terms of both partisanship and responsiveness to clientele interests, Ways and Means Committee decisionmaking exhibited a great deal of volatility over the period between 1978 and 1981. A bipartisan pattern in both deliberations and the final vote on taxes in 1978 was followed by a mixed pattern on the oil windfall profits tax and then a highly partisan deliberative process on the 1981 tax bill.

Some clientele interests clearly benefited from the committee's rejection of President Carter's 1978 reform proposal in favor of a bill that created new tax incentives for capital investment. Still, at least some aspects of the traditional patterns of limited responsiveness to clientele groups and concern with fiscal responsibility remained visible in Ways and Means members' actions. The overall size of the annual tax reduction voted by Ways and Means in 1978 ($16 billion) was considerably smaller than that approved by the Senate ($29 billion), and in time-honored fashion Ways and Means members pushed in conference to scale back the size of the Senate cuts (to $18.7 billion).[42] Moreover, it would be hard to construe the committee action on windfall profits as evidence of increased clientele influence in Ways and Means decisionmaking. The committee voted to raise tax rates on existing oil production above the Carter administration proposal, and the committee bill would have collected an estimated $29 billion in revenues from the oil industry over the period from 1980 to 1984. Although the House ultimately approved a less stringent tax than the one reported by Ways and Means, the Finance Committee approved a bill that would have further reduced the taxes on the oil industry by almost one-half over a ten-year period, compared to the House version.[43]

The deliberations on the 1981 tax cuts, however, offered a striking case of permeability to demands for tax benefits from particularistic interests and clientele groups. In this case, the postreform pattern in committee decisionmaking suggested by the electoral connection model seems unmistakable. As Catherine E. Rudder has written: "Absent were careful deliberation, a sense of limits, an ability to say no to claimants, and an overriding concern for the quality of the bill and for the integrity of the tax code."[44] A number of Ways and Means members publicly conceded that the process had gotten out of hand. Speaking on the House floor, Democrat Robert Matsui of California commented: "The Senate Finance Committee, our committee, and the administration got involved in a game in which we now have bills that all of us are supporting but none of us is really happy about."[45] As the vote on the bill approached, ranking Republican Barber Conable of New York commented: "If I were writing this bill, I would write it differently and so would every member of this Congress."[46]

The new economic policy agenda that emerged in the late 1970s had a divisive effect on an already factionalized Democratic majority in the House. This divisive effect of the new agenda on House Democrats rendered ineffective the new institutional arrangements that allowed greater majority party control over committee decisionmaking. The result in the tax area was a sharp swing toward more conservative policy outcomes in Ways and Means Committee bills and a period of volatility in committee decisionmaking—including wide variations in the level of partisanship and the hyperresponsiveness to clientele and constituency interests that occurred in 1981 as Ways and Means Democrats tried to hold together a majority coalition on the House floor. The revenue effects of the 1981 bill, however, and the onset of a major recession combined to usher in a new type of agenda that would influence committee politics throughout the 1980s.

Deficit Politics, 1982–1984

In 1981 the Reagan administration had projected that the president's new economic program would result in deficits for fiscal year (FY) 1982 of $45 billion. Instead, the recession that developed later in the year quickly drove deficit projections much higher, creating a crisis atmosphere in financial markets and among policymakers in Washington. In February 1982 the Congressional Budget Office estimated that deficits would reach $109 billion in FY 1982 and $157 billion in FY 1983 under existing policies. Even with the $43 billion in reductions in domestic programs and $87.6 billion in revenue increases over three years requested in the Reagan administration's budget for FY 1983, the president's budget plan submitted in early 1982 still projected deficits for FY 1983 of $91.5 billion.[47] Most members of Congress of both parties viewed budget deficits of this magnitude—and the even larger ones that actually developed—as both politically and economically dangerous.

Despite pressures to reduce the unprecedented peacetime deficits that occurred after 1981 (see Table 6-1), the Reagan administration between 1982 and 1984 refused to accept changes in the basic tax program enacted in 1981 and continued to request substantial real increases in defense spending in the budgets it submitted to Congress. As each budget cycle began, deficit reduction measures proposed by the White House focused primarily on cuts in domestic programs and small-scale tax increases (usually characterized as "user fees," "loophole closers," or "revenue enhancements"). Thus 1982 began a period in which tax policy became one dimension of a deficit politics in which the White House refused to initiate any major policy changes in response to growing deficits other than cuts in domestic spending, House Democratic leaders sought to protect domestic programs by pushing for increased revenues and a slowdown in the pace of defense spending, and Senate Republicans—though generally sympathetic to the president's goals of strengthening defense, restraining domestic spending, and keeping taxes low—were often cast in the difficult role of seeking out compromises needed to head off even higher deficits. The ability of Senate Republicans to agree among themselves and with the White House on a compromise budget package in 1982 shifted the initiative in tax policy deliberations to the upper chamber.[48]

In the weeks following the introduction of the Reagan budget for FY 1983, the negative reaction in Congress to the president's budget priorities resulted in a series of informal negotiations between the two branches. House and Senate party leaders and members of the budget and tax committees from both chambers met with White House chief of staff James A. Baker III and Office of Management and Budget director David A. Stockman (this group became known as the "Gang of 17") to try to work out an alternative budget plan. Recognizing that any budget that reduced the deficit substantially would have to include politically ticklish tax increases and reductions in proposed levels of defense spending, House Democrats refused to initiate action on a budget resolution or tax increase legislation without White House endorsement of a compromise plan. A general consensus emerged on the need for increased revenues, smaller defense increases, and reductions in some domestic entitlement programs, but the talks eventually broke down in late April when the White House and the

Table 6-1
Federal Budget Deficits, Fiscal Years 1975–1987

Year	Billions of Dollars	Percent of GNP
1975	53.2	3.5
1976	73.7	4.3
1977	53.6	2.8
1978	59.2	2.7
1979	40.2	1.6
1980	73.8	2.8
1981	78.9	2.6
1982	127.9	4.1
1983	207.8	6.3
1984	185.3	5.0
1985	212.3	5.4
1986	221.2	5.3
1987	149.7	3.4

Source: Office of Management and Budget, *Budget of the United States Government, Fiscal Year 1990*, pp. 10-38, 10-39.

House Democratic leadership could not reach agreement on a specific plan. With the failure of bipartisan negotiations, House Budget Committee chairman James R. Jones and Ways and Means chairman Dan Rostenkowski announced their intentions to let their Republican counterparts in the Senate take the first step in revising the Reagan budget proposals.[49]

Early in May, Senate Budget Committee chairman Pete V. Domenici of New Mexico reached agreement with the administration on a budget that would reduce defense expenditures requested by the president by $22 billion, cut $40 billion in spending from the Social Security program, and increase revenues by $95 billion over the next three fiscal years. After Senate leaders dropped the controversial Social Security provisions, a budget resolution was adopted by the Senate on May 21. Democrats on the House Budget Committee reported a resolution calling for $147 billion in new revenues for fiscal years 1983 through 1985, but the committee resolution and seven alternative versions were defeated by a divided House. On June 10 forty-seven Democrats joined House Republicans in approving a resolution similar to the one that had been adopted earlier by the Republican Senate. The final version of the FY 1983 budget approved by both houses in late June called for $20 billion in new revenues in FY 1983, $35 billion in FY 1984, and $40 billion in FY 1985. Reconciliation instructions included in the resolution required the Senate Finance Committee to report spending cuts and revenue increases by July 12. Standing committees in the House were to report spending and revenue measures by August 1.

Although the Ways and Means Committee held a series of hearings from February through May 1982 on revenue and spending measures for the upcoming fiscal year, the committee waited for its Senate counterpart to act on the legislation required by the budget resolution. Chairman Robert Dole of the Finance Committee, who had been an advocate during the spring budget negotiations of increased taxes to reduce the deficit, moved quickly to develop a bill that would produce $95 billion in new revenues and $17 billion in spending cuts over three years. Dole conducted two days of closed-door meetings among Finance Committee Republicans and Treasury officials to decide the basic content of the bill. After two days of markups, on July 2 the committee approved a $98 billion tax increase in the form of an amendment to a minor tax bill that had previously passed the House. With Democrats complaining they had little opportunity to influence the measure, the tax increase was reported by the Finance Committee on a straight party-line vote.[50]

The Finance Committee bill did not delay or defer the third year of individual rate cuts from the 1981 act as some Democrats had advocated, adopting instead a wide range of smaller tax increase provisions acceptable to President Reagan. The president had endorsed "closing loopholes," but rejected any major changes in the administration's basic tax program. The largest single component of the Finance Committee bill ($29.1 billion) was a package of compliance measures that would require withholding of part of interest and dividend income and establish more stringent reporting and enforcement measures.[51] The bill also included provisions to tighten up exclusions in business and personal taxes, in some cases restricting preferences enacted in the previous year's bill. Finally, the bill raised $19 billion from an array of miscellaneous measures that included restrictions on tax-exempt industrial development bonds used by state and local governments, increased excise taxes on telephone service and cigarettes, increased federal unemployment taxes, and increased taxes on air travel and aviation fuel.[52]

The Ways and Means Committee not only deferred to the Senate in initiating tax legislation in 1982, but voted on July 28 to go directly to conference rather than reporting its own bill for consideration by the House. The partisan 26-7 vote in favor of this move found only four Republicans voting yes and only one Democrat opposed. After the Senate bill was reported by the Finance Committee, the majority and minority staffs on Ways and Means had developed a tentative proposal that was accepted by Rostenkowski and Conable as a starting point for the Ways and Means markup. But when Rostenkowski called a caucus of committee Democrats on July 21 to discuss the proposal, a majority of Democrats rejected it, preferring instead to allow the Senate bill to set the terms of the tax increase.[53]

The constitutional provision requiring initiation of revenue-raising bills in the House of Representatives (Article 1, section 7) does not appear to have weighed very heavily in the decision for most committee members. "The constitutional question never really entered our minds. We were going to leave that to the constitutional lawyers to decide," one majority staffer recalled. Chairman Rostenkowski argued in favor of writing a bill in order to protect the prerogatives of the committee. As he later described the argument he made to committee Democrats: "The Constitution provides that *we* write the tax bills and send them over to the Senate. I was afraid that if we go to conference we set a precedent here where the majority in the Senate starts writing tax legislation."[54] But most other members were less concerned about constitutional issues or the committee's prerogatives than they were about the partisan conflicts surrounding economic and budget policy at the time.[55]

Many Democrats on Ways and Means simply did not want to be associated with a major tax increase they saw as necessitated by the failure of the economic program of the Reagan administration. One member put it bluntly in explaining the outcome in the Ways and Means caucus:

> The president was running around saying he wasn't going to raise taxes. The president said he represents the party of lower taxes. He said Democrats are always trying to raise people's taxes. So we said "to hell with him."

Some Democrats also cited concerns over whether their party could maintain control over the formulation process as a reason to defer to the Senate on the bill. With deficits growing at an alarming rate, some contended that severe repercussions in financial markets might have occurred if the tax package had begun to unravel through partisan competition to control the outcome. "I was concerned," one Democrat explained, "that given the level of partisanship on our committee and on the floor in general, it would have been impossible to do a serious tax bill." By accepting the increased revenues in the Senate bill, he concluded, "we abrogated our authority to good effect."

On July 28 the House voted 208-197 to go directly to conference on the tax bill. On the House floor Rostenkowski prefaced his appeal for support of the motion by expressing "deep personal misgivings" over the unusual procedure. But the political situation in the House and the need for new revenues, he argued, made this a necessary action.[56] A number of Republicans, including W. Henson Moore (La.) and Phillip Crane (Ill.) of the Ways and Means Committee, strongly criticized the procedure as a violation of the constitutional provision requiring origination of revenue bills in the House. But House minority leader Robert Michel and ranking Ways and Means Republican Barber Conable both supported going to conference with the Senate as the only practical way to achieve the deficit reductions that both houses and the president agreed were needed. "The long and short of it," Conable stated on the floor, "is that if we want to bring down the budget deficit now, we are led inexorably toward a conference with the other body. Neither time nor the majority will allow us to follow the other course."[57] The conferees reported back a slightly modified version of the Senate bill that would raise $98.3 billion in new revenues over the fiscal years from 1983 through 1985 and, with an aggressive White House lobbying effort behind the bill, both houses approved the tax increase on August 19.

After the passage of the Senate-initiated tax increase in the summer of 1982, it was 1984 before major tax legislation was taken up again by both houses of Congress. The intervening year witnessed a number of tax initiatives, but none attracted sufficient political support to produce any major change in federal tax policy. The president's February 1983 budget proposal requested a "standby tax" to be triggered if deficits were still high (over 2.5 percent of GNP) in FY 1986. Neither chamber took any action on the proposal. House Democrats passed a cap on the third year of the Reagan personal tax cut to limit benefits for upper-income taxpayers but, as predicted, the bill went nowhere in the Republican Senate. The FY 1984 budget that was finally adopted in the summer of 1983 called for $73 billion in new revenues, a figure neither tax committee seriously tried to meet. A smaller tax bill was developed by the Ways and Means Committee in 1983, however, and although it failed to win passage, it laid the groundwork for a bipartisan effort on taxes in 1984 that was curiously reminiscent of the tax politics of the Mills era.

With little support existing in either house for the FY 1984 Reagan administration budget submitted in February of 1983, a budget resolution was approved in June that included smaller reductions in domestic spending, less for defense, and more new revenues than the president had requested. The reconciliation instructions incorporated in the budget resolution gave the tax committees one month to report legislation to raise an additional $73 billion in revenues over the next three fiscal years. Senate Finance Committee chairman Robert Dole described the reconciliation provisions as politically unrealistic, arguing that mandating such a large revenue increase would simply be "giving this dead cat to the Finance Committee."[58] Although Dole tried later in the year to develop a tax package in the $50 billion range, divided opinion in the Senate prevented anything but a minor bill from being reported by the Finance Committee in 1983.

In July of 1983 the Ways and Means Committee began work on a series of tax bills to correct abuses and rewrite expiring sections in the tax code, and in doing so returned to the old practice of holding tax bill markups behind closed doors. In October of 1983 the committee reported a bill to reduce costs in the Medicare program (mandated by the FY 1984 budget resolution) and enact changes in tax law that would produce approximately $8 billion in new revenues over the FY 1984–86 period. Sections of the bill dealing with fringe benefits and life insurance were written by the Select Revenue Measures Subcommittee, marking the first time since the reforms in 1974 that major tax provisions had been developed outside the full committee.[59]

In sharp contrast to committee deliberations on tax issues during the two previous years, the 1983 bill was a bipartisan effort. As members described the formulation process in interviews, Select Revenue Measures Subcommittee chairman Fortney H. (Pete) Stark of California and ranking Republican W. Henson Moore of Louisiana worked together closely to draft the insurance provisions at the subcommittee level, and Rostenkowski and Conable shared responsibility in the full committee in assembling some of the other components of the bill. Further evidence of the reemergence of bipartisanship was the decision to approve the package by a voice vote, and the absence of minority views in the committee's report.[60]

Even with a unified committee, the bill met with controversy when Chairman Rostenkowski requested a closed rule for debate of the bill on the House floor. Opponents of industrial development bond restrictions included in the bill demanded a separate vote on that issue. A group of freshman Democrats strongly protested to the leadership that the bill would not allow a vote on a revenue package large enough to meet the $73 billion figure required by the budget resolution. In response to demands for additional revenues, Rostenkowski announced his intention to offer an amendment to "freeze" pending income and excise tax reductions amounting to $11.5 billion. Additional amendments to increase revenues were also developed outside the committee by the Democratic Study Group and the group of Democratic freshmen.

Despite a compromise on the development bond restrictions agreed to by Rostenkowski and accommodation by the Rules Committee of those groups of Democrats who were seeking votes on amendments to raise more revenue, the rule to debate the Ways and Means bill was defeated on the House floor November 17. Heavy lobbying by state and local governments against the bond restrictions that remained in the bill, and controversial changes in the Medicare program also included in the package were cited by Ways and Means members as the major reasons for the 214-204 defeat on the rule.[61]

Early in 1984, as bipartisan deficit-reduction talks again were initiated in response to the administration's FY 1985 budget proposals, the Ways and Means Committee and the Finance Committee began working on legislation independently of the budget negotiations. The president's budget requested $33.7 billion in new revenues over three years, but sentiment existed in both houses for a larger figure if it were part of a package to achieve larger deficit reductions than the president had proposed. As the budget talks dragged on, both tax committees began working on bills to increase revenues.

After two days of closed markups, on March 1 the Ways and Means Committee reported a tax bill based on the one that had failed to reach the House floor the year before. Changes were again made in the tax-exempt bond restrictions to defuse opposition to the bill, but other major provisions were left unchanged. Added to the package were the chairman's "freeze" proposal of the previous year and new provisions (some of which had been requested by the administration's FY 1985 budget) to restrict or close tax shelters and increase compliance. Overall, the 1984 bill increased revenues by $49.3 billion over the FY 1984–87 period.[62]

Maintaining the bipartisan cooperation that had emerged the year before, the Ways and Means Committee again reported the tax bill by a voice vote.[63] At Rostenkowski's request, the Rules Committee agreed to a closed rule on the revenue package, with a separate vote to be taken on the Medicare and other spending provisions that were also contained in the bill. Rostenkowski emphasized the bipartisan consensus behind the tax package in appealing for support when the bill reached the floor on April 11. "This is not a Democratic tax bill. It is not a Republican tax bill," he explained. "Its passage was virtually unanimous on both sides of the Committee— a rare event in this period of political posturing and mistrust."[64] With amendments prohibited by the rule, the bill (H.R. 4170) passed by an overwhelming 319-97 majority. After Senate passage of a tax increase bill on April 13, a final version of the bill, raising revenues by $50.7 billion over the FY 1984–87 period, emerged from a lengthy conference. Both houses approved the final version of the Deficit Reduction Act of 1984 on June 23.

With the focus on the fiscal objective of enacting revenue increases to reduce budget deficits and the reemergence of bipartisan committee deliberations, the action by the Ways and Means Committee on the 1984 tax bill could hardly have provided a sharper contrast with the intense partisan conflict and runaway clientelism that characterized committee decisionmaking on tax legislation in 1981. Under Rostenkowski's leadership and the fiscal and political pressures created by massive budget deficits, by 1984 politics on the committee appeared in some respects to have come almost full circle since the reforms—back to the moderate partisanship, attention to fiscal responsibility, and consensual decisionmaking style of the Mills years.

Conclusion: Reform, Agenda Change, and Committee Politics, 1975–1984

For most of the Mills era, moderate partisanship was the norm in Ways and Means Committee decisionmaking. Partisanship tended to be restrained at the deliberative stage, where members of both parties usually participated, although partisan splits were not unusual in the final stages of committee decisionmaking. Responsiveness to clientele interests was also fairly selective. The expectations derived from viewing reform-era institutional changes from the perspective of Fenno's theoretical framework—that the pursuit of partisan and policy goals would be of greater importance in committee politics—proved accurate for tax decisionmaking in the initial postreform years. On most tax bills between 1975 and 1977, both committee deliberations *and* final votes were highly partisan. Also consistent with increased concern with advancing policy goals, committee majorities throughout this period showed a willingness to report out controversial bills, risking (and experiencing in a number of cases) defeats on the House floor. After 1978, however, partisanship in committee decisionmaking on tax issues became more variable, and by the mid-1980s partisanship began to resemble the more restrained pattern of the prereform years.

The almost indiscriminate distribution of tax benefits in the committee bill produced in 1981, on the other hand, seemed to confirm the basic proposition about effects of reform-era institutional changes suggested by Mayhew's electoral connection model, that is, that a reduction in internal prestige associated with Ways and Means Committee membership would produce increased clientelism and particularism in committee decisionmaking at the expense of broader fiscal objectives. But other cases over the postreform period showed more selective responsiveness to group demands, especially after 1981.

In discussing factors influencing tax politics, a number of members emphasized the importance of the massive budget deficits that have been present since 1982. As one committee member stated:

> Tax bills used to be used to reduce taxes. And those bills could be used by members to achieve social objectives . . . as well as for special interest provisions. The big change of the last couple of years is that because of the deficit and the need to raise revenue it is very difficult to imagine the tax code being used anymore to be the engine for social and economic changes. For example, with the tax bill in 1984, I *know* that there were members who had amendments they wanted to offer to help this or that constituent. But they just didn't get offered because we couldn't afford to lose any money.

Said a second member early in 1985: "In 1981 we gave away the store. Since that time the realities of the budget situation mean that the Ways and

Means Committee is at best striving to maintain the revenue or increase it."

Although many in Congress sought to keep deficit reduction the priority issue on the tax policy agenda, the Reagan administration took a strong stand against any major revenue increases during the 1984 election campaign, and temporarily reordered the congressional agenda by submitting a proposal for comprehensive tax reform in the spring of 1985. The approval of a comprehensive tax reform package by the Ways and Means Committee marked an even more striking contrast to the extreme responsiveness to clientele interests that occurred in the development of tax legislation in 1981. Chapter 7 examines in detail the role of the Ways and Means Committee in the enactment of comprehensive tax reform during 1985–86, and considers the implications of the overall patterns in postreform committee behavior on tax issues for the theoretical perspectives that have informed the analysis of the effects of institutional change.

The Politics of Tax Reform, 1985–1986

Tax reform was the major domestic initiative of President Ronald Reagan's second term, and the resulting legislation represents one of the most dramatic changes in economic policy in recent decades. What makes the passage of tax reform also of particular interest to students of Congress is that, on balance, the legislation advanced a number of broad, diffuse, or poorly organized interests in American society at the expense of many very well-organized, well-funded clientele groups. That the postreform Ways and Means Committee would act on a comprehensive tax reform package of this type flies directly in the face of the expectations derived from the electoral connection model; only a more complex view of congressional politics can account for the politics and outcome in this final case of tax policymaking on the postreform Ways and Means Committee.

The first objective of this chapter is to examine in detail the role of the Ways and Means Committee in the development of the comprehensive tax reform package that won passage by the House of Representatives in December 1985 and by the Senate the following year. In addition to interview data and materials from the documentary record, the chapter also draws on *Showdown at Gucci Gulch*, a detailed account of the enactment of tax reform by journalists Jeffrey H. Birnbaum and Alan S. Murray. A second objective of this chapter is to examine the tax reform case in the context of the overall patterns in committee tax decisionmaking during the postreform years. Finally, the chapter will offer some summary conclusions on the usefulness of the electoral connection model on the one hand, and Fenno's multiple goal framework on the other, for understanding Ways and Means Committee politics in the postreform House.

The Ways and Means Committee and the Puzzle of Tax Reform

After revising an initial Treasury Department proposal that had been unveiled in late 1984, the Reagan administration formally submitted a major tax reform proposal to Congress in May 1985. The main features of the president's proposal were reductions in both individual and corporate rates, combined with the curtailment of a number of major individual and corporate tax preferences and deductions. The elimination of preferences weighed heaviest on corporations, which faced an overall tax increase estimated at $120 billion over five years. Individual taxpayers, under the president's plan, would receive a tax cut over the same period estimated at $147 billion.[1] The president insisted that any reform plan enacted in Congress be "revenue neutral"—that is, neither raise tax revenues nor increase the size of the federal deficit. Much to the surprise of many seasoned observers of congressional politics, in December 1985 the House approved a major reform plan of the same general type that the president had proposed, and Senate approval of an even more radical reform package followed in June 1986. Differences in the two plans were worked out during the summer, and Ronald Reagan signed the Tax Reform Act of 1986 into law in October.

Tax policy analyst James M. Verdier noted shortly after the enactment of tax reform that this sequence of events during 1985 and 1986 presents a "puzzle" to students of policymaking in the U.S.[2] The puzzle, in Verdier's view, was the enactment of non-incremental tax reform in a system usually understood to be oriented toward incremental policy changes. A review of the basic features of the Tax Reform Act lends additional support to the characterization of the outcome in this case as a puzzle.

By the mid-1980s, the federal tax code had become burdened with an extremely complex system of special provisions and preferences that provided tax benefits and incentives to various groups in American society. The goal of tax reform, as the issue became defined in the mid-1980s, was to eliminate many of these special provisions and preferences in order to create a broader tax base and allow lower tax rates. Elimination of tax preferences was considered both a matter of equity—"Make the bastards who aren't paying, pay," as one Ways and Means member put it—and a way to increase economic efficiency by reducing tax-induced distortions in the economy. For those who held to "supply-side" theory, the lower marginal rates made possible by fewer preferences were also seen as a way to stimulate new economic growth.

As shown in Table 7-1, the tax reform legislation enacted in 1986 brought substantial rate reductions. However, while rates were reduced on both individual and corporate income, the net effect of the reform act (reflecting the structure of the president's proposal) was a tax cut for individual taxpayers and a substantial corporate tax increase. The lower individual rates were financed in part through the elimination or reduction of corporate tax preferences (see Table 7-2). This occurred in spite of the fact that many corporate tax preferences were defended by active lobbying efforts. Moreover, each of the versions of the tax reform plan gave the largest personal tax cuts to taxpayers earning $20,000 or less (see Table 7-3). According to Brookings Institution economist Henry J. Aaron, when the effects on individuals of corporate tax increases are taken into account, the

Table 7-1
Individual and Corporate Rates in Existing Law, House Bill, Senate Bill, and Final Tax Reform Legislation

	Individual	Corporate
Existing law	14 rates, 11–50%	15, 18, 39, 40, 46%
House bill	15, 25, 35, 38%	15, 25, 36%
Senate bill[1]	15, 27%	15, 25, 33%
Final act[1]	15, 28%	15, 25, 34%

Source: Joint Committee on Taxation, *Summary of H.R. 3838, Tax Reform Act of 1985, as Reported by the Committee on Ways and Means on December 7, 1985*; Joint Committee on Taxation, *Summary of H.R. 3838, Tax Reform Act of 1986, as Reported by the Senate Committee on Finance*; Joint Committee on Taxation, *General Explanation of the Tax Reform Act of 1986*.

1. The individual and corporate rate structures in the Senate bill and the final act included provisions to "phase out" the effects of certain deductions and/or lower rates for those whose incomes exceed a specified level within the highest bracket. Therefore, under the new law, the *marginal* tax rates for some individuals and corporations will be 33 and 39 percent, respectively.

Table 7-2
Revenues Gained from Elimination of Tax Benefits and Preferences and Net Change in Income Tax for Individuals and Corporations in House Bill, Senate Bill, and Final Tax Reform Act, over Five Years (in billions of dollars)

	Preferences Eliminated[1]		Net Change in Tax	
	Individuals	Corporations	Individuals	Corporations
House bill[2]	185.6	236.8	− 139.8	+ 138.9
Senate bill[3]	243.1	236.0	− 99.1	+ 95.0
Final act	257.3	257.5	− 122.0	+ 120.3

Source: See Table 7-1.

1. Figures for preferences eliminated were calculated from estimates of revenue effects of all individual and corporate provisions shown to increase revenues. Compliance measures are not included in these totals.

2. House figures are for fiscal years 1986–90. Figures for Senate and final act are for fiscal years 1987–91.

3. Figures for the Senate bill are based on the bill reported by the Finance Committee and do not reflect the effects of amendments adopted on the Senate floor.

Table 7-3

Estimated Change in Income Tax Liability in 1988 by Income Class in House Bill, Senate Bill, and Final Tax Reform Act

Income Class	Percent of Estimated Change		
	House Bill	Senate Bill	Final Version
Under $10,000	− 74.7	− 63.0	− 65.1
$10,000–20,000	− 22.8	− 20.1	− 22.3
$20,000–30,000	− 9.7	− 8.1	− 9.8
$30,000–40,000	− 9.3	− 5.0	− 7.7
$40,000–50,000	− 7.9	− 6.6	− 9.1
$50,000–75,000	− 7.8	− 3.9	− 1.8
$75,000–100,000	− 6.0	− 3.3	− 1.2
$100,000–200,000	− 7.5	− 3.8	− 2.2
$200,000 and above	− 6.0	− 4.7	− 2.4

Source: Joint Committee on Taxation, *General Explanation of the Tax Reform Act of 1986*; Eileen Shanahan, "Tax Bill Wins Senate Approval, Post Recess Conference Next," *Congressional Quarterly Weekly Report* 44 (June 28, 1986): 1456.

reform act actually increased the overall progressivity of the income tax by reducing the tax burden on individuals in the low- and middle-income brackets while increasing it on individuals with incomes of $50,000 or higher.[3] A final feature of each of the tax reform plans was that revenues generated by the elimination of preferences were also used to eliminate tax liability for approximately six million low-income taxpayers.

As will be discussed below, some corporate interests directly benefited from reform, and some organized and lobbied actively for its enactment. Other groups and particular interests were successful in protecting tax preferences. Still, it would be accurate to describe the overall outcome on tax reform as a case where a number of broad, diffuse interests (greater equity and economic efficiency) and some poorly organized interests (low- and middle-income taxpayers) were advanced at the expense of and in the face of opposition from many well-organized corporate beneficiaries of existing tax preferences.

Tax reform on this scale seemed highly unlikely when viewed in the context of long-term trends in tax politics. John F. Witte, the political scientist who had undertaken the most comprehensive study of federal tax politics to date, expressed skepticism that anything resembling the Reagan administration proposals would become law.[4] The most powerful dynamic in federal tax politics, Witte argued, had been a "tax reduction bias" produced by the responsiveness of congressional decisionmaking to ever-present demands for tax relief from both particular interests and broader constituencies.[5] He observed that in the past a pattern of incremental addition of new tax reduction provisions had been only marginally affected by tax reform efforts and had been effectively constrained only by revenue crises on the order of war or depression.[6]

When tax reform is viewed from the perspective of Mayhew's electoral connection model, the Ways and Means Committee, if it were still functioning as a "control committee," might be expected to restrain the flow of tax benefits to local constituencies and organized groups, but the large-scale elimination or reduction of existing tax preferences to achieve general rate reductions is a puzzling outcome indeed—especially after the 1970s reforms had substantially weakened incentives for committee members to be attentive to institutional concerns or policy goals other than targeting benefits to local constituencies or organized clientele groups. Thus the puzzle presented by tax reform consists not only in an outcome in which broader societal interests prevailed over many well-organized clientele interests, but also in the fact that the critical first step in enacting reform was successfully undertaken by the Ways and Means Committee, whose power, autonomy, and centralized leadership had been major targets of the congressional reform movement of the 1970s.

Why, then, did a committee that was "opened up" in the 1970s to greater participation from the broad array of interests that benefited from existing preferences and special provisions in the tax code vote to enact a tax reform bill in the 1980s that was actively opposed by many of those interests? Three factors are most important in providing the answer to this part of the tax reform puzzle: 1) institutional changes since the reform era that have reestablished some committee autonomy from clientele groups and reimposed a more restrictive decisionmaking process in the House; 2) the reemergence of stronger committee leadership under Chairman Dan Rostenkowski; and 3) some distinctive characteristics of the tax reform issue and the policy context within which it emerged in the mid-1980s.[7]

The Reestablishment of Committee Autonomy

As we have seen in Chapters 5 and 6, by the time tax reform was taken up by the Ways and Means Committee in 1985, the committee had moved some distance from the more open politics of the reform era in the direction of closing off some of the new participation and reestablishing procedural autonomy in the House. These postreform adjustments include changes in both formal procedures and informal practices affecting the committee's operation. The most significant of these changes include: 1) a return to closed committee bill-drafting sessions; 2) the development of a revised closed rule procedure for debating tax legislation on the House floor; and 3) a return to recruitment practices that restrict committee appointments to experienced members from "safe" districts.

The return to closed door sessions for deliberations on tax issues first began in July 1982, when the Ways and Means Committee voted on two consecutive days to debate procedural issues relating to a Senate-initiated tax increase (H.R. 4961) in executive session. The following year it became clear that the committee was breaking with a decade-long practice of open markups when sessions in July and October to draft additional revenue-raising provisions (H.R. 4170) were closed to the public. Since 1983, all major tax legislation has been drafted in closed session. It is difficult, if not impossible, to isolate the effects of closing markup sessions. However, interviews with committee members suggest that the return to closed sessions may have reduced the influence of particular interests and clientele groups in committee decisionmaking and may have also encouraged members to take a broader view of the issues at stake in recent tax legislation.[8]

First, committee members stated that the presence at markups of representatives of clientele groups and constituency interests would make it difficult for them to support measures that might impose costs on their own constituencies or groups that had provided support in past elections. These comments confirm that the pull of the electoral connection is an important influence on members' behavior. Said one committee member, on the difficulty of writing tax legislation in public sessions: "You're not going to solve problems in front of an audience. We're politicians and part of that is a public posture that's required of us." A second member was more explicit:

> Say you've got a special problem in your district and those people that support you are sitting out there in front. When you're marking up a bill, all you're going to talk about is *your* interest at home. You're not going to talk about your interest in the context of a bill as weighed against other competing interests and seek a reasonable solution. You're going to take a hard line for what your people want.

In a scenario that was repeated a number of times in other interviews, another member explained the different environment that exists when deliberations are shielded from direct public observation:

> A member can enter a mild protest about the defeat of an amendment he might otherwise feel compelled to support. . . . Then, when the markup is over, the member can go out into the hall and say to the lobbyist, "I worked to get your amendment adopted but I just got outvoted."

Although many issues are resolved by recorded votes in closed markups (forty-eight recorded votes on substantive issues were taken during the Ways and Means markup of tax reform legislation in 1985), the committee has often made decisions in closed sessions through informal agreement, a show of hands, or voice votes. As one member pointed out, even with closed sessions: "Sometimes we don't want to take a recorded vote when there are a lot of lobbyists out there."

An example from the Ways and Means Committee tax reform markup illustrates the importance to members of avoiding recorded votes on—and hence individual responsibility for—certain types of provisions. Ways and Means Committee Democrats had agreed in the final stages of the markup to eliminate part of a tax preference strongly supported by organized labor (exemption of employee fringe benefits) on the condition that no recorded vote would be taken on the issue. When Republicans, frustrated by their limited influence on the bill's development, refused to cooperate and demanded a recorded vote on the issue, Democrats balked at eliminating the labor-supported preference, deciding instead to set the top corporate rate a percentage point higher to pick up the revenue needed to maintain revenue neutrality.[9]

The ability to resolve issues in closed sessions allows members to avoid some of the direct responsibility for imposing costs on constituency interests or group allies, as was almost inevitable with tax reform.[10] To use the formulation developed by R. Kent Weaver, closed meetings are in part a mechanism for blame avoidance on issues that may have negative consequences for committee members' constituencies.[11]

According to some members, a closed deliberative process, by weakening the pull of particularistic interests, encourages members to consider broader issues that may be at stake in committee bills. One member observed that he and his colleagues tend to be much more "outspoken" about "what is right for the country" in closed sessions. Said another on the effects of closing markups: "We don't think so much about the posturing, about satisfying someone sitting there watching you, as the needs of other members and what *we* perceive to be important." Finally, one senior Republican stated directly: "I think without the closed markups [Rostenkowski] . . . couldn't have passed the tax reform act."

The return to closed committee deliberations is one factor that helps explain the outcome on tax reform. Closed markups allowed members to avoid individual responsibility (and thus individual blame) for eliminating some of the tax preferences important to clientele groups, and thus helped shift the focus of the committee's deliberations from protecting parochial interests to achieving broader objectives through tax reform.

A second factor that has increased the autonomy of the Ways and Means Committee during the 1980s has been the acceptance in the House of more restrictive procedures for considering tax legislation on the House floor. After decades of debating tax legislation under closed rules prohibiting amendments not approved by the Ways and Means Committee, the House acted between 1973 and 1975 to alter this practice in order to allow broader participation in tax decisionmaking.[12] However, after a single case of successful intervention in a tax bill (H.R. 2166) by the Democratic caucus and experimentation with an essentially open rule on energy tax legislation in 1975 (H.R. 6860), demands for broader participation have been accommodated through the use of modified closed rules negotiated through discussions between and among the leadership of the Ways and Means Committee, the majority leadership, the Rules Committee, and various blocs of members seeking changes in Ways and Means bills.[13]

On most of the tax measures reported since 1975, a limited number of specific amendments have been made in order, but floor amendments have otherwise been prohibited. Amendments allowed by the Rules Committee have included substitute measures for committee bills (often drafted by the Republican minority on the committee) as well as specific amendments sought by dissident committee members or others in the House. In any case, by late 1985 when the House was presented the tax reform package drafted by the Ways and Means Committee, the legitimacy of the modified closed rule procedure was well established. House members were offered the opportunity to vote on a Republican-backed substitute and two minor amendments, but otherwise the committee bill was protected from changes that might have restored tax benefits enjoyed by particular interests and undermined the tax reform effort.[14]

The third contributing factor in the reestablishment of committee autonomy has been a reversal of the trend toward more open committee recruitment that appeared during the reform era. Traditionally, seats on Ways and Means had been restricted to senior members from "safe" seats. As Rudder has emphasized, one effect of the House reform movement was to open committee selection to freshmen members and members from highly competitive districts. As was shown in Chapter 4, however, Ways and Means appointments during the 1980s have been more selective.

Since 1981 neither party has appointed a member who won less than 60 percent of the vote in the previous election. As a result, only four of the thirty-six committee members serving at the time of the tax reform markup in 1985 had won reelection in 1984 by less than a 60 percent margin.[15] In addition, the routine appointment of freshmen members (a practice limited to the Democratic side during the reform era) had also stopped (see above, Table 4-1). Therefore, to the extent that new members and members from marginal districts are especially responsive to constituent interests and clientele groups with resources to influence electoral outcomes, informal recruitment practices, along with closed markups and restrictive floor procedures, have contributed to the reestablishment of some "insulation" for the Ways and Means Committee from demands for tax benefits and have allowed the committee somewhat greater procedural autonomy in the House.

Committee Leadership

In interviews, Ways and Means members of both parties emphasized that Chairman Dan Rostenkowski's active coalition-building efforts were critical to committee approval of the tax reform package. Said a Democratic member: "He really brought the Democrats along on this. There was no real interest—well maybe from [Donald J.] Pease [D-Ohio] and [Byron L.] Dorgan [D-N.D.] and one or two others—but most of us did not want to do tax reform." A committee Republican offered a similar view: "I don't know of anybody else who could have gotten a consensus—or *created* a consensus—on a bill given the obstacles in its way at the beginning. There was no political consensus out among the rank-and-file for a bill." Chapter 5 described Rostenkowski's leadership style as the *machine Democrat as chairman*. Techniques involved in this approach include encouraging group solidarity, early consultation and negotiation to win firm commitments, threatening dissidents and freezing out defectors, and centralized control over organizational resources. All of these techniques—together with appeals directed at committee members' prestige, policy, and constituency or electoral concerns—came into play in Rostenkowski's successful coalition-building efforts on tax reform.

Before the Reagan administration proposal was formally submitted to Congress in May 1985, Rostenkowski began meeting with small groups of committee Democrats. According to members who attended these early meetings, Rostenkowski sought to build support on the committee for tax reform by characterizing the forthcoming Reagan administration proposal as a major opportunity to advance good public policy. Said one participant in these meetings:

> Most of us had made speeches in favor of tax reform at every civic club. Rostenkowski seized on this and said: "Now you people have been talking about reforming the tax code and making it fairer for the lower income people, the average working person. You will never get a better opportunity to get this than now because I've got the president on board and he's going to be the lead person out there, which gives everyone cover. If you want to get reform you've got to do it under these circumstances. You can't get it when a Democratic president is out there because you will get slaughtered by the Republicans. But we can get it this year."

In describing how Rostenkowski framed the issue, the same member noted: "He has told me time and again that he thinks it's awful that young people pay so much in taxes as compared to corporations." Rostenkowski himself commented on how he tried to persuade committee Democrats to support reform:

I said we're going to take 6 or 7 million people that are poor off the rolls. We're going to do more for the lower end of the tax structure and corporate America is going to wind up paying more in taxes. Those are the arguments I kind of shamed my colleagues into accepting.[16]

Committee hearings on the president's proposal ran from May through late July. As the hearings progressed Rostenkowski and/or Ways and Means Committee staff consulted individually with each committee member to gauge support for specific aspects of a reform plan.[17]

Over the weekend of September 7–8, Rostenkowski also convened a committee retreat outside Washington at Airlie House in rural Virginia. Along with committee members, staff, and a number of high level Treasury Department officials, the chairman invited a group of economists to discuss the policy effects of tax reform. "We were there for two days of straight B.S. with many of the leading economists in the country," one committee member recalled. "There was nothing else to do—no televisions in the place, no telephones. A lot of the discussion was about what was good for the economy, good for growth, and this and that."

"Finally, at the end," the same member continued, "[Rostenkowski] threw everybody out but the members." In the closed meeting that concluded the retreat, Rostenkowski attempted to galvanize committee support for a reform package by characterizing the issue both as an opportunity to advance good public policy and as one on which the committee members' reputations would be riding. As one Ways and Means member recounted Rostenkowski's appeal:

He said, "Look, we have an opportunity here to do something historic." . . . He also said, "The tax code is not fair." . . . He told a story about when his daughter was living at home and he picked up her pay stub and saw how much money was being taken out of her salary, and said, "This just isn't fair." Tears started coming into his eyes. He said, "This is not fair and we're going to do something about it."

Recalled another member:

Airlie House was important in terms of bringing the committee together and really did help to develop a sense of history. He said this was an historic moment, a great opportunity for the committee to recapture some of the glory it had lost because we had lost fights on the floor of the House in years before.[18]

Although many members remained less than enthusiastic about comprehensive tax reform, Rostenkowski was able to secure an informal agreement at the Airlie House retreat to move ahead to a committee markup that would start from a draft proposal prepared by the majority and minority staffs. Perhaps overstating the group solidarity that existed at this point, Rostenkowski remarked to the *Washington Post* as the tax reform markups began in September: "There is a genuine feeling of pride in the Ways and Means Committee. I don't remember when we have visibly been so cohesive and bipartisan. I'll take a small bow for instilling that camaraderie."[19]

Once the committee markup was under way, a senior majority staffer commented, "it was a whole new ballgame." To maintain support for a reform package, Rostenkowski was forced to shift from a coalition-building strategy stressing opportunities for enhancing prestige and enacting good public policy to a strategy that included negotiating changes to accommodate local or group interests of importance to individual committee members. As one committee member described the markup process, "There was an awful lot of protection going on—in terms of protecting what's good for your state, your region, your district." By the count of a staffer who worked closely with the chairman, five of the twenty-eight members of the coalition that ultimately approved the committee bill (four Democrats and one Republican) supported the chairman consistently from the outset; the remainder exacted as a condition for support at least some concessions for interests of local or regional concern.

To achieve lower tax rates without increasing budget deficits, a number of major tax preferences had to be eliminated or substantially reduced. One of the preferences slated for reduction in the Ways and Means bill, the deductibility of state and local taxes, proved to be a major obstacle in maintaining a committee coalition in support of tax reform. Ways and Means members from high-tax states in the northeast were strongly opposed to any plan that curtailed deductions for state and local taxes, and they began actively to seek allies among oil state members and others who were concerned about regional interests affected by the plan.[20] According to a committee aide, New York Republican Raymond McGrath made it clear that his position on the issue reflected electoral concerns. As the staffer recalled it, McGrath told the chairman: "Look, I can't exist out on Long Island unless you give me this." Another committee member explained that he had told Rostenkowski: "Unless you allow for the deductibility of state and local taxes, I don't care what you do, I'm not for this."

Seeking to contain defections from the tax reform effort, Rostenkowski negotiated an agreement with a group of committee members from the northeast; he would preserve the full deductibility of state and local taxes, and they would support the committee bill. Rostenkowski, a senior committee aide explained, "began meeting with [Thomas] Downey [D-N.Y.], [Charles] Rangel [D-N.Y.], [Barbara] Kennelly [D-Conn.], and McGrath. . . . He made it clear that state and local would not hold up the bill."[21] As one committee member recalled it, "He said 'OK, I'm gonna give in to this but now you have to support it [the committee bill].'"

Rostenkowski also firmed up allegiance to the committee bill by allowing members to make some revisions in the plan through informal task forces and by threatening members when support wavered. As one member noted: "The [preservation of] the second home mortgage deduction came in from a task force. That was one I went after hard because it impacts my state." Another member stated: "In some of the major areas we have been left to write the legislation [in task forces] but we have almost signed on in blood." Rostenkowski made it clear in the later stages of the markup that those who voted against him would stand to lose out in the drafting of transition rules for the bill—special exceptions to revenue-raising provisions that may be used to confer tax benefits on particular individuals, localities, or industries. As one member described the chairman's response to an unwanted amendment that lost revenue:

> He just looked at all of us sitting there and said "I just want to tell you that if this thing passes any accommodations I have made to any member of the committee for this are null and void." He just said that. Two or three people changed their votes."[22]

Other aspects of Rostenkowski's coalition-building strategy that were at least partly oriented toward members' electoral concerns were: 1) attempting to use the favorable disposition of the press toward tax reform to encourage support for the committee bill; and 2) emphasizing to committee Democrats that they and their party would likely be blamed for killing tax reform if the committee failed to act on the Reagan proposal.[23] When the survival of tax reform appeared threatened in mid-October by a committee vote that substantially expanded tax deductions for banks, the committee was portrayed very unfavorably in a number of editorials and in accounts of the vote that appeared in major newspapers.[24] "There was a furor in the press," one member recalled. Apparently anticipating this negative reaction, Rostenkowski told staffers he would let committee members "stew in it for a while," rather than attempting to have the committee reconsider the vote immediately.[25] Whether out of concern for reputation in the Washington community or fear of being branded a protector of "special interests" in future elections, some members' support for tax reform appeared to have been reinvigorated by the negative press. As a committee staffer described the press response and its effects on Ways and Means Democrats: "There were some scorching editorials. . . . These guys were being held up to ridicule for caving in, for dropping the ball. That softened the boys up."

In discussing how Rostenkowski kept committee Democrats behind the reform plan, another senior committee aide noted:

> When we had trouble, when we lost on the bank vote, . . . [the chairman's] argument tended to be: "We can't do this. The Democrats are

going to get blamed for killing tax reform. I can hear Ronald Reagan out there right now saying your rates are now 50 [percent] and I could have lowered them to 35 [percent]."

Rostenkowski, he explained, "clearly made the political pitch," to committee Democrats, but the chairman's approach was described as "always a combination of policy and politics."

A final aspect of the chairman's successful push to report a tax reform bill was active use of the committee's majority staff. In the tax area, the pattern of centralized control by the chairman over organizational resources is especially pronounced. During his tenure as chairman, Rostenkowski has built up the majority tax staff and placed it under his direct control. As a senior member of the tax staff explained:

> Prior to 1981 you had several different staffs—a full committee tax staff, a subcommittee tax staff, and separate from that, the former chairman [Ullman] had a series of individuals without title who were his principal advisers on issues. Mr. Rostenkowski swept all that away and said we are going to have one group to do all those things. Also there is no separate group of advisers you have to deal with as a staff person. You deal directly with the chairman.

Throughout the tax reform markup, the expertise and loyalty of the majority tax staff allowed Rostenkowski to work independently of Treasury analysts in developing a plan that could win support of a committee majority. The use of staff also provided the chairman with a means of staying abreast of members' concerns and a capability for monitoring decisions made by task forces during the markup. On a number of occasions Rostenkowski intervened in task force deliberations after having been notified by staff that targets he had set for eliminating preferences were in jeopardy.[26]

The tax reform package was reported favorably by the Ways and Means Committee in November 1985. All twenty-three Democrats supported the committee bill, joined by five of the panel's thirteen Republicans. In contrast to the assumptions underlying the electoral connection model, goals other than reelection clearly played a major role in the coalition-building strategy used by Rostenkowski to assemble a committee majority in support of tax reform. However, the politics of the tax reform issue were also distinctive in some important respects. Both to understand why a majority of committee members supported a policy change that advanced broad, diffuse interests over interests of organized clienteles, and to judge the significance of this case for evaluating the two purposive theories that provide the focus for this part of the study, it is necessary first to look at some characteristics of the tax reform issue itself and the context in which it arose during the mid-1980s.

The Politics of Tax Reform

Both postreform institutional changes and active committee leadership contributed to the approval by the Ways and Means Committee of a tax reform package that cut tax rates by reducing or eliminating tax preferences defended by well-organized interests. The final set of factors that help to explain the "puzzle" of tax reform are some aspects of the issue itself that facilitated coalition building in the Ways and Means Committee, on the House floor, and later in the Senate as well.

In a book that appeared the year tax reform deliberations began in Congress, Martha Derthick and Paul J. Quirk attempted to identify the conditions under which "particularistic, well organized interests can successfully be subordinated to diffuse, far more encompassing, but ill-organized interests."[27] Concluding that such an outcome occurred in Congress in a number of cases of procompetitive deregulation in the late 1970s and early 1980s, they observe that this was partly due to issue-related factors: "The evidence . . . does not suggest that Congress's preference for broad 'public' interests is firm and reliable. . . . Procompetitive reform was in some respects an unusual issue. Presenting . . . a rare liberal-conservative coalition, an academic consensus, and intuitively persuasive arguments connected to problems of high public concern, reform policies were especially suited to elicit a congressional response oriented to general interests and shaped by ideas."[28] After procompetitive regulatory reform was pushed to the forefront of the agenda by actors outside of Congress (primarily independent regulatory commissions), Derthick and Quirk found that congressional leaders and majorities in both houses supported policy change despite public complacency and active opposition by well-organized economic interests. The issue of tax reform, as it became defined in 1985, exhibited some of the same characteristics. Hence Derthick and Quirk's analysis helps a great deal in solving the puzzle of tax reform.

Elite Consensus. Policy prescriptions advocated by regulatory reformers in the 1970s, Derthick and Quirk found, were based on a broad consensus among policy experts and were "politically adaptive," that is, they related to areas of public concern and "could be rendered in simple, symbolic, intuitively appealing terms."[29] Although economists and tax specialists differed on the merits of the specific proposals developed by the Reagan administration, the Ways and Means Committee, and the Finance Committee, by 1985 there was near unanimity among tax policy experts on the desirability of reforms that would broaden the tax base by curtailing tax preferences.

Much like the issue of regulatory reform, elite support for tax reform arose in part from studies by policy experts (in this case indicating that the existing tax code was creating economic inefficiencies and compliance problems),[30] as well as from the convergence of objectives traditionally sought by liberals and conservatives.[31] For liberals, tax preferences had been seen primarily as a device by which corporations and wealthy individuals avoided paying their "fair share" of the tax burden. Liberal intellectuals and politicians, therefore, had long sought elimination of tax preferences as a means of broadening the revenue base needed to fund social programs, and as a matter of distributional equity. Conservatives, on the other hand, had begun during the 1970s to emphasize the importance of low marginal tax rates as incentives for work, savings, and investment. The major tax reform proposals on the agenda after 1982, following an approach pioneered by Senator Bill Bradley (D-N.J.), began to generate broader support by forging "a link between the base-broadening thrust of traditional liberal reformers and the rate-reduction thrust of supply-side conservatives."[32]

Political Adaptability. The tax reform issue satisfied the basic criterion for political adaptability by lending itself to simplification in symbolic terms relating to problems of public concern. In a nationally televised speech broadcast the evening before his proposal was submitted to Congress, Ronald Reagan characterized the issue as one pitting fairness, simplicity, and lower taxes against "the special interest raids of the few."[33] Opinion polls confirmed that Americans thought the federal tax system was too complicated and unfair, but public support for comprehensive tax reform never became overwhelming or even very intense.[34]

The picture of limited public support for tax reform was reinforced by comments of Ways and Means members about constituency reactions. When asked about the level of constituent interest in tax reform, one member remarked:

> You just didn't find any. There was no burning desire in this country for us to do this. It became an issue that took on a life of its own because of internal politics in Washington. . . . You got outside of Washington and nobody gave a tinker's damn about it.

Birnbaum and Murray report that other Ways and Means members found a similar lack of constituent interest in the weeks preceding the Ways and Means markup.[35] How, then, did the politics of the issue encourage members to respond to the broader interests served by the elimination of tax preferences and the shift to lower tax rates?

First, from the outset the politics of the tax reform issue were somewhat more favorable to nonincremental change than was the case with regulatory reform. In the cases studied by Derthick and Quirk, "the dominant industry interests were overwhelmingly opposed" when the policy change was initially proposed.[36] Although more organized interests opposed than supported tax reform, business interests were divided on the issue in 1985. Some businesses had benefited relatively little from the major tax preferences that were being cut back (the investment tax credit and

accelerated depreciation), and actively supported reform to gain lower overall corporate rates or in anticipation of general economic benefits. Among
the early supporters of tax reform were a number of corporate giants including IBM, General Motors, Procter and Gamble, General Foods, and
J. C. Penney.[37] However, if the division among business interests helps
explain why reform was possible, it does not explain why the issue "took on
a life of its own."

Elite consensus and press coverage. The convergence of elite consensus
with the apparent *possibility*, if not the actuality, of intense public concern
helps explain why the tax reform issue took on a life of its own in Congress.
On an issue of this type, policy and political goals are likely to converge for
many members in support of policy change. Again, note the similarity of
the tax reform case to the pattern found by Derthick and Quirk in the area
of regulatory reform: "The leading sources of pertinent guidance concerning the public interest . . . were in substantial (and unusual) agreement, all
favoring procompetitive reform. For members disposed to make policy
judgments independently [of political incentives], this was directly important. *It also meant that political elites and the media would tend to approve of
actions taken to promote reform*, as would probably the general public, to the
extent of its awareness [emphasis mine]."[38]

By 1985 sufficient elite consensus existed on the view that tax reform
was in the public interest for that view to be widely reflected in press
coverage of congressional action. As Derthick and Quirk point out, the
attention of the media and political elites is focused on those in leadership
positions in Congress, creating incentives for committee leaders concerned
about their prestige in the Washington community and beyond to pursue
broadly oriented policy goals.[39] The behavior of Rostenkowski on the tax
reform issue and the favorable treatment of his role in the press lend support to this view.[40] The prospect of negative coverage in the press for
opposing reform may create political incentives for rank-and-file members
to support policy change as well.

Elite consensus and partisan politics. With the elite consensus on tax
reform reflected in the coverage of the issue by the mass media, a second set
of political incentives for supporting tax reform also developed with the
prospect that the *party* seen as responsible for reform stood to gain support
in the electorate, and that, once the issue was on the congressional agenda,
blame would be focused on either party if its members were seen as responsible for blocking or killing reform. Some congressional Democrats—including Rostenkowski—initially interpreted the Reagan administration tax
reform proposal as an attempt to make permanent inroads on the Democratic electoral coalition by portraying the Republicans as allied with average taxpayers against "special interests."[41] Also, in 1985 congressional
Democrats still held tremendous respect for Ronald Reagan's ability to

mobilize public opinion and his willingness to focus public attention on resistance to his policy objectives from Democrats. As Rostenkowski noted in his first major speech embracing tax reform: "Those who are gathering to derail tax reform should recall [Reagan's] knack for dividing complex issues into two simple parts—good and bad, fair and unfair, givers and takers—and asking, 'Which side are you on?' It's not beyond the president to ask television viewers across the nation why the most powerful special interests should stand between the least powerful and the tax cuts they deserve. It's a devastating question that could unleash a potent backlash."[42]

But what made partisanship a more important factor than it otherwise might have been was the peculiar configuration of divided party government that existed in 1985–86: Republican control of the White House, Democratic control of the House, and Republican control of the Senate. Contrary to the conventional view that divided party government fragments power and thus makes major policy change unlikely, on an issue marked by a high degree of elite consensus and the potential for simplification in attractive symbolic terms, divided party control may actually help drive policy change in Congress as leaders (and to a lesser extent, rank-and-file members) of the two parties compete for credit—or, perhaps just as important in this case, seek to avoid responsibility for failure.[43]

Due to the constitutional responsibility of the House for initiating revenue legislation, after a Republican president put tax reform on the congressional agenda House Democrats had the opportunity to "win back" the tax reform issue. As Rostenkowski put it, one of his objectives was "to put a Democratic twist on the bill."[44] But the prospect of being blamed by the president for the failure of tax reform provided an added incentive for House Democrats to support reform. According to an account in the *Washington Post*, Speaker O'Neill had made it clear by October 1985 that he was "determined to get the tax bill out of the House so that if the measure does not pass this year the Republicans in the Senate will be blamed."[45] As was noted above, Rostenkowski made sure Democratic Ways and Means members realized that *they* would be blamed if the committee failed to report a credible reform package. Thus the partisan dynamic generated by the tax reform issue may have created additional incentives for Ways and Means Democrats to support reform, as well as the incentives that clearly were present for committee and party leaders.

Once reform was placed on the agenda by the Reagan administration, the issue "took on a life of its own" because of elite consensus in support of tax reform and the potential for simplification in attractive symbolic terms by the press and/or a popular president. In addition to those members who supported reform primarily because virtually all the experts agreed that it was good public policy, the politics of the tax reform issue (including the way it was framed by congressional leaders) created incentives to support reform for those concerned about prestige in the Washington community, partisan goals, and reelection as well. Chairman Dan Rostenkowski's strategy for building a majority coalition in support of tax reform on the Ways and Means Committee incorporated appeals to committee members involving *all* of these motivations.

Tax Reform and Deficit Politics

As seen in the previous chapter, Ways and Means Committee decisionmaking on tax issues has shown very limited responsiveness to clientele interests since the appearance of large deficits in 1982. Although the tax reform issue generated its own political dynamic, independent in many respects of the immediate fiscal pressures of the deficit, the constraints imposed by the fiscal context are visible in committee deliberations on the tax reform issue as well. Responsiveness to clientele groups seeking to maintain tax preferences was strictly constrained by the political imperative to get tax rates down, coupled with the fiscal imperative to at least maintain the existing revenue base. As one Ways and Means member described the operation of the committee task forces that worked on tax reform, "We only had so much revenue; if you gave up revenue in there you had to get it somewhere else." Said a second member: "If I wanted to bring an amendment to help some special industry or group of people, I had to pay for it. I had to include in my amendment the additional revenue. That slows things down in a hurry." Although some clientele interests were successful in protecting tax preferences in the Ways and Means bill, committee decisionmaking on the tax reform issue clearly demonstrated independence from the numerous organized economic interests that ended up shouldering much of the burden of the rate reductions that were achieved.

The moderate partisanship that characterized much of the committee's work on the tax reform issue also fit with the patterns that had been present in tax deliberations in 1983 and 1984. Although the committee ultimately broke along party lines on the final vote to report the tax reform package, members of the minority actively participated in informal task forces set up by Rostenkowski to revise parts of the committee bill. Said one Ways and Means Republican on the role of minority members in the task forces: "Many of the things we were opposed to in the beginning we were able to modify some. That's where the give and take began to take place." Commented another Republican on the task forces in which he participated: "We never took formal votes; we didn't gang up on each other or have caucuses of Republicans and Democrats. Here was the goddam problem, you have forty-eight hours to deal with it, what were you going to do?" The locus of decisionmaking later shifted to the committee's Democratic caucus as Republicans grew frustrated with their inability to achieve more extensive changes in the committee bill, but five Republicans still voted with a unanimous Democratic majority to report the tax reform package (H.R. 3838) in December 1985.[46]

Tax Reform and Purposive Theories of Congressional Politics

The politics and the outcome in the tax reform case directly contradict the basic assumptions and hypotheses about committee behavior derived from the electoral connection model. Both the prominence of appeals to members' concerns with good public policy in Chairman Dan Rostenkowski's coalition-building strategy, and an outcome in which broad, diffuse, and poorly organized interests were advanced over those of well-organized clientele groups show that congressional politics, in at least some cases, are more complex than Mayhew's model assumes. To put it simply, a theoretical framework that incorporates goals other than reelection is needed to explain the politics and outcome in this case.

What, then, are the implications of the tax reform case for judging the relative usefulness of Mayhew's and Fenno's theories of congressional politics? One possibility is that the tax reform case—though important as a major economic policy decision—was the result of the convergence of factors so unusual or unique as to offer little of importance to students of Congress who seek generalizations about how the institution works. However, when set in the context of the longer term patterns in tax politics and policy outcomes on the postreform Ways and Means Committee (discussed in more detail below) and the accumulating empirical evidence on the importance of goals other than reelection in congressional behavior, a more plausible conclusion is that the tax reform issue evoked policy and prestige concerns that are almost always important to some degree in congressional politics and thus merit consideration—along with more narrow electoral motivations—in purposive theorizing.[47]

The tax reform case does suggest that goals other than reelection are more likely to assume greater importance in congressional policymaking in certain institutional settings and on certain types of issues than others.[48] Ways and Means members stated in interviews that they felt greater freedom to attend to concerns other than immediate demands of constituency and clientele groups when deliberations were closed to the public and press. Procedures that allow some insulation of committee deliberations from direct constituency and group pressures thus appear to allow greater freedom for members to act to advance policy or prestige goals in cases where these may be in tension with electoral incentives. Aggressive leadership of the type undertaken by Rostenkowski also may provide some insulation from particularistic demands. As Rostenkowski described how committee members view his role as chairman, "I've heard some [committee members] say—not all—that I give them cover so they don't have to compromise with the pressure groups on the outside—blaming the chairman."[49]

In addition, the tax reform case suggests that policy and prestige motivations are likely to play a more important role in congressional policy-making on issues on which a high degree of elite consensus exists in support of a particular policy change. When experts and issue activists cannot agree on an issue, members have greater freedom to respond to narrower electoral incentives. It is only natural, when "the experts" disagree, for representatives to embrace policy arguments that coincide with their electoral/constituency interests whenever possible. However, when experts, policy activists, and others who populate the networks surrounding various policy issues do agree on what advances the public interest, the course of action for achieving good public policy goals is marked out more clearly for most members, and is therefore likely to be more of an independent factor in decisionmaking. If, as was the case with procompetitive deregulation and tax reform, elite consensus develops on an issue that may be defined in appealing symbolic terms, the conditions are set for a convergence of prestige, policy, *and* electoral concerns—and thus a major policy breakthrough—if the issue reaches the congressional agenda. Here again, leadership in Congress may play an important role in framing deliberations so that members recognize the prestige and policy dimensions of issues as well as the possible electoral consequences.

The Ways and Means Committee and the Politics of Taxation, 1975–1986

Both of the purposive theories that have provided the framework for the analysis of consequences of reform-era institutional changes find some support in the behavior of the Ways and Means Committee on tax issues over the postreform period. The basic patterns in committee decisionmaking on tax issues during the 1975–86 period are summarized in Table 7-4.

Viewed from the perspective of Fenno's multiple goals framework, changes in members' goals and environmental constraints that occurred during the 1970s suggested that Ways and Means members would become less oriented toward limiting conflict to maintain prestige and a record of floor success, and more oriented toward pursuit of policy goals—especially partisan policy goals. Between 1975 and 1977 both committee deliberations and final committee votes tended to break down along partisan lines. To the extent that a dominant decision rule existed on the committee during this unsettled period after the committee was restructured, it was pursuit of the policy goals of majority members. But with a major shift in the committee's agenda in 1978, this pattern began to change.

The new economic policy agenda in the late 1970s involved a shift

Table 7-4

Ways and Means Committee Decisionmaking on Major Tax Bills, 1975–1986

Bill	Partisanship Deliberations	Final Vote(IP)[1]	Clientele Influence	Floor Action
Tax Reduction Act, 1975 (H.R. 2166)	mixed	bipartisan (41)	low	amend (major)
Energy Tax Bill, 1975 (H.R. 6860)	partisan	partisan (83)	low	amend (major)
Tax Reduction/Reform Act, 1975 (H.R. 10612)	partisan	partisan (72)	low/ moderate	amend (major)
Tax Reduction Act, 1977 (H.R. 3477)	partisan	partisan (68)	low	W&M bill
Energy Tax Act, 1977 (H.R. 6831)	partisan	partisan (84)	low/ moderate	amend (minor)
Revenue Act, 1978 (H.R. 13511)	consensual	bipartisan (48)	moderate	W&M bill
Windfall Profit Tax, 1979 (H.R. 3919)	mixed	partisan (83)	low	amend (major)
Economic Recovery Tax Act, 1981 (H.R. 4242)	partisan	partisan (95)[2]	high	admin. bill
Tax Equity/Fiscal Responsibility Act, 1982 (H.R. 4961)	partisan	partisan (63)[3]	low	Senate bill
Deficit Reduction Act, 1984 (H.R. 4170)	consensual	bipartisan (17)[2]	low	W&M bill
Tax Reform Act, 1985 (H.R. 3838)	mixed	partisan (62)	low	amend (minor)

1. Partisan votes are those in which a majority of one party opposes a majority of the opposing party. The number in parentheses for each bill is the index of partisanship (IP) for the final Ways and Means Committee vote on the bill. The index is calculated by subtracting the percentage of members of one party voting for a bill from the percentage of members of the other party voting for the bill. See Fenno, *Congressmen in Committees*, pp. 207–8.

2. No recorded final committee vote taken. IP for the 1981 bill calculated from the vote on the House floor on the Conable-Hance substitute to the Ways and Means Committee bill. IP for the 1984 bill calculated from floor vote on passage.

3. Because the committee decided not to report a bill, the IP was calculated from the committee vote to go directly to conference.

from traditional liberal concerns with achieving greater distributive equity through an activist government to a new emphasis on stimulating economic growth. The Democratic majority on the committee fragmented in response to these new economic policy issues. As may be seen in Table 7-5, both Democratic cohesion and partisanship in committee tax votes were at their lowest point in the twelve-year postreform period during 1978 when this shift occurred. Partisanship varied widely on tax bills as the committee responded to the new agenda in the period from 1978 through 1981. In the context of the deficit politics that emerged after 1981, Democratic members of the Ways and Means Committee (and the House) became more unified and committee voting has been more partisan.

However, by the mid-1980s something like the restrained partisanship of the prereform years, where members of both parties usually participated in committee deliberations, reemerged on tax issues. This reflected in part Dan Rostenkowski's style as leader, which is oriented toward building bipartisan coalitions where possible to enhance the prospects for winning passage of committee bills on the House floor. But it also reflected the deficit-driven agenda within which the committee has operated since 1981. Bipartisan cooperation on tax legislation has been in part what Weaver has termed a "circle the wagons" strategy employed by committee members for diffusing individual and partisan responsibility for politically unpopular tax increases and entitlement program cuts needed to achieve the policy goal of controlling the size of budget deficits.[50]

Viewed from the perspective of Mayhew's electoral connection model, the 1970s reforms reduced the institutional prestige of the Ways and Means Committee, and hence weakened incentives for members to resist opportunities for delivering particularistic benefits to constituencies and servicing clientele groups in making tax policy decisions. The evidence for increased particularism and clientelism in Ways and Means Committee deliberations on major tax legislation over the 1975–81 period is mixed, primarily because of the bidding war that developed in the enactment of tax cut legislation in 1981. With the fiscal constraints that have existed since the emergence of massive deficits and the policy breakthrough on tax reform, responsiveness to clientele interests in committee decisionmaking has been very limited since 1981.[51]

Only in the case of the multibillion-dollar bidding war in 1981 did committee members' behavior definitely appear to fit the pattern of policymaking suggested by Mayhew's electoral connection model. Rather than serving its traditional "control committee" function of restraining distribution of tax benefits, Ways and Means Committee Democrats engaged in a coalition-building contest with House Republicans and the Reagan administration in which participants on both sides acknowledged that short-term political advantage took precedence over responsible policymaking.

Table 7-5
Ways and Means Committee Partisanship on All Recorded Committee Tax
Votes, 1975–1986

Year	Index of Partisanship[1]	Index of Cohesion[2] Democrats	Republicans	Percent of Votes Partisan	Total Votes
1975	47	40	63	68	187
1976	49	44	73	70	33
1977	45	39	71	65	57
1978	39	28	60	62	73
1979	49	41	59	64	56
1980	46	63	66	65	20
1981	70	71	84	82	33
1982	52	62	61	80	10
1983	65	59	76	86	14
1984	57	68	48	67	9
1985	52	56	55	83	57
1986	20	60	100	0	1

Source: Compiled by author from recorded votes in Ways and Means Committee files.

1. Index of partisanship is the mean for all recorded votes each year. On the calculation of the index, see Table 7-4, n. 1.

2. Index of cohesion is calculated by dividing the total number of party members voting with their party majority on all roll calls by the total number of votes cast. See Rice, *Quantitative Methods*, pp. 208–9, and Turner and Schneier, *Party and Constituency*, pp. 20–21.

But in explaining why the committee helped "give away the store" in 1981 by adding more and more particularistic tax benefits, there is much more to the story than the scenario of a weakened control committee whose members were no longer willing to refrain from distributing tax benefits to constituents and clientele groups. It is important to recognize that what set off the bidding war in the House was *partisan* competition based on different views of economic policy. A very popular Republican president with a plausible claim to represent a shift in majority opinion in the country defined the scope of deliberations on tax policy in 1981 with a very large tax reduction proposal.[52] The Democratic leadership in the House sought to protect the revenue base for social welfare programs and limit some of the tax relief for upper-income groups in the Reagan plan. When the majority leadership and Ways and Means Democrats agreed that a *smaller* overall cut less generous to upper-income taxpayers should be developed as an alternative to the president's program—but then could not assemble a majority coalition in the House to support the alternative—a very unstable situation developed.

Consistent with the more partisan institutional environment in the postreform House, when push came to shove between the Republican president and the Democratic House leadership, Ways and Means Democrats under Rostenkowski's leadership joined the bidding war rather than acquiescing to an administration bill that might have kept a lid on some of the particularistic demands in the House. The result was a deliberative process in which restraint and fiscal responsibility became secondary to partisan competition to control the outcome by distributing tax benefits.

Mayhew's electoral connection model helps in explaining why members seek particularistic benefits when opportunities such as the bidding war over tax policy in 1981 are present, but proves to be of limited use for understanding the overall patterns in tax decisionmaking on the postreform Ways and Means Committee, especially in the case of tax reform. Fenno's theory of committee politics, by taking into account the importance of members' conflicting views of good public policy as a factor influencing congressional behavior, as well as the importance of different environmental factors, provides a more useful approach for understanding the increased importance of policy partisanship in decisionmaking on the reformed committee and the shifts that have occurred in committee politics due to agenda changes. Together with a discussion of the effects of the 1970s reforms for the problem of deliberation in the House, some of the broader theoretical issues raised by the Ways and Means case will be considered in more detail in the concluding chapter.

Chapter 8

Conclusion

Over the period since the congressional reforms of the 1970s, the politics of the House Ways and Means Committee have differed in significant ways from those of the prereform years. In this concluding chapter answers to questions about why change occurred in this key congressional committee will be reviewed, as will those on the effects of reform-era institutional changes on policymaking in the area of taxation. This review will provide a basis for addressing two broader issues raised by the Ways and Means case. First, tax policymaking on the postreform Ways and Means Committee provides an important case for evaluating the two competing theories of congressional politics that have been used to examine the effects of institutional change: David R. Mayhew's electoral connection model, which views members as if they were "single-minded reelection seekers," and the theoretical framework developed by Richard F. Fenno, Jr., which views the behavior of members of Congress as the product of more complex motivations and environmental constraints. Second, while there is little doubt that structural changes of historic proportions were achieved by House reformers during the 1970s, the important question of how these changes have affected capabilities for dealing with the problem of deliberation in the House of Representatives remains to be addressed.

Explaining Change

The Ways and Means Committee of the 1950s and 1960s was an integral part of the decentralized institutional order of the postwar House. At one level, explaining change in the Ways and Means Committee during the 1970s and 1980s requires a focus on the parent institution and the political and social environment within which it functions. After a period of relative political stability following World War II, during the late 1960s and early 1970s important changes began to occur in public opinion on institutional legitimacy, in electoral politics, in the governmental agenda, and in executive-congressional relations. As a result, the prerogatives of the Ways and Means Committee, its leadership, and established mode of operation were challenged by the emergence of an active procedural majority in the revitalized Democratic caucus in the early 1970s. The committee's prereform role was further challenged by a breakdown in the effectiveness of an informal process of fiscal control in Congress.

Major structural reforms in the House of Representatives resulted in the 1970s, enacted primarily by the Democratic caucus. Among the most important reforms for this case were requirements for election of committee chairmen by the caucus rather than automatic appointment by seniority, expansion of the size of the Ways and Means Committee, enactment of a rule to require creation of Ways and Means subcommittees, establishment of more open procedures designed to allow broader participation in committee decisionmaking, and transfer of the committee assignment power for House Democrats from Ways and Means Democrats to a party body. The reforms targeted at Ways and Means were motivated partly by demands for a more open, participatory decisionmaking process in the House, but also by a desire among liberal Democrats to transform the cautious decisionmaking style the committee had adopted under the leadership of Chairman Wilbur D. Mills into a more active, more partisan policymaking role. In the other major area of reform that became important for the Ways and Means Committee in later years, conflicts with the president over spending authority and frustrations in Congress with the ineffectiveness of the existing informal, decentralized process of budgetary control led to the creation in 1974 of a new budget process and new organizational units with authority for coordinating revenue and spending decisions. The budget committees and the Congressional Budget Office possessed authority and expertise to become involved in policy issues within the jurisdiction of the Ways and Means Committee, and together with the budget resolution/reconciliation procedure, further challenged the autonomy of the committee. After 1975, then, the Ways and Means Committee was larger and less centralized in its internal organization, and a new institutional context existed in the House in which the distinctive procedural autonomy of the prereform committee had been reduced through reforms that increased the authority of the majority caucus and its leadership and established a new budget process.

The Consequences of Reform

For evaluating the effects of reform-era institutional changes on the Ways and Means Committee over the 1975–86 period, a second perspective is useful, one that focuses on purposive behavior of individual House members. The theoretical frameworks of this type proposed by David R. Mayhew and Richard F. Fenno, Jr., both offer insights into institutional factors that were important influences on the behavior of members of the prereform committee, but suggest different consequences from the institutional reforms of the 1970s.

The fundamental premise of Mayhew's approach is that a great deal about congressional politics may be understood by viewing members as single-minded reelection seekers. With few electoral reasons to attend to their responsibilities as national legislators or contribute to the collective performance of their political party, House members, in this view, engage instead in advertising, position taking, and credit claiming in order to attract and maintain electoral support. Only the selective incentive of institutional prestige associated with positions of leadership or membership on a few top committees (control committees) keeps the policy effects of the electoral connection within tolerable limits, those effects being delay and symbolism, and distribution of benefits to local constituencies and organized groups who provide electoral support in return.

The House Ways and Means Committee was one of the panels identified by Mayhew's analysis as a "control committee." When the institutional changes of the reform era are viewed from the perspective of the electoral connection model, the key factor in the Ways and Means case is committee prestige. Reform-era changes that expanded the size of the Ways and Means Committee, removed the committee assignment power for House Democrats, and created expanded opportunities for subcommittee leadership positions on other panels reduced the internal prestige associated with membership on Ways and Means. When viewed from the perspective of the electoral connection model, then, reform-era changes weakened incentives for Ways and Means members to attend to fiscal effects and institutional prerogatives, and therefore should result in greater particularism and clientelism in committee decisionmaking—especially in policymaking on tax issues where opportunities for distributing benefits through special tax provisions abound.

Fenno's theoretical perspective, on the other hand, suggests somewhat different consequences of reform-era institutional changes for the behavior of this committee. Committee decisionmaking processes and policy outcomes, Fenno argues, result from the interplay of members' goals with the different environmental constraints within which members of committees work. In addition to the reelection goal singled out by Mayhew, Fenno also assumes that concerns with enacting good public policy and enjoying influence or prestige are important motives for members of Congress.[1] When postreform changes in Ways and Means members' goals and the committee's environmental constraints are considered, a different pattern in committee politics is suggested.

Fenno's theory differs from the electoral connection model in suggesting the proposition that the changes of the reform era should result in a more ideological and partisan committee politics. With increased recruitment of policy-oriented members, and changes in the committee's structure and institutional environment that encouraged increased attention to partisan goals, Fenno's framework suggests a shift away from the prereform pattern of restrained partisanship and orientation toward writing bills assured of House passage toward a decisionmaking process in which pursuit of partisan and/or policy goals becomes more important. Although some reform-era changes reduced the procedural autonomy of the committee and as a result made clientele groups more important in the committee's environment than was the case before the mid-1970s, the limited number of members on the postreform committee citing electoral or constituency concerns as a reason for joining the panel suggests that increased clientelism in committee decisionmaking would be relatively limited.

Patterns in committee decisionmaking on tax issues over the 1975–86 period do not fit neatly the expectations of either increased policy activism and partisanship or increased particularism and clientelism, but show considerable variation over both dimensions. In comparison to the Mills-era committee, increased partisan conflict was present in committee deliberations during the initial postreform years, but this gave way to a more volatile pattern from 1978 to 1982, after which a more moderate partisanship reminiscent of the prereform committee began to appear. No dramatic increase in clientelism or in the distribution of particularistic tax benefits was evident in the initial postreform years. Yet, in competing with the Reagan administration to enact tax reduction legislation in 1981, the committee incorporated a plethora of special tax provisions which helped bid up federal revenue losses by tens of billions of dollars. After 1982 the committee has demonstrated much greater attention to broader economic policy objectives (primarily deficit reduction) and independence from clientele interests in developing a tax increase package in 1984 and a comprehensive tax reform bill in 1985.

By incorporating a more realistic conceptualization of members' goals and incorporating both policy and institutional aspects of committee environments, Fenno's theory provides the more useful framework for understanding the politics of taxation on the postreform Ways and Means Committee. The electoral connection model does find support in the distribution of tax benefits that was attempted by Ways and Means Democrats in order to win passage of the committee's tax reduction package in 1981. But even in that case, the bidding war for control of tax policy was set off by partisan competition between the Democratic leadership in the House and the Reagan administration.

The Ways and Means Committee, of course, is not just a tax committee. Major health care issues (Medicare), Social Security, other social welfare programs (Supplemental Security Income, Aid to Families with Dependent Children, Unemployment Compensation), and trade policy also fall within the committee's jurisdiction. A more comprehensive analysis of committee politics, looking at each of these policy areas as well as taxation, would yield a more complete picture of the consequences of reform-era institutional changes.[2] However, if the focus on a single policy area necessarily results in only a partial account of postreform committee politics, both interview and voting data suggest that taxation offers an appropriate case for examining the questions posed by the competing purposive theories of Fenno and Mayhew.

Issues within the committee's jurisdiction may be categorized according to two dimensions: the intensity of clientele or interest group activity and the importance of partisan or ideological considerations.[3] Figure 8-1 depicts the issue areas in the committee's jurisdiction based on interviews with committee members and staff. Members and staff characterized health and taxation as the issue areas with the heaviest lobbying or clientele activity, with trade and Social Security in a middle range, and welfare issues lowest. Health and welfare issues were described as the most ideological or partisan, with Social Security and taxation in a middle range, and trade least. No attempt has been made independently to confirm the categorization of issues in terms of clientele activity, but recorded committee votes over the 1975–86 period were broken out by issue area and examined for the incidence of partisan votes, and a mean index of partisanship was calculated for votes in each issue area.[4] Table 8-1 shows that patterns in committee voting during the 1975–86 period are consistent with the rankings derived from interviews regarding the partisan/ideological dimension of the issues.

The characterization of issues in Figure 8-1, which is simply a composite "snapshot" of impressions of members and staff at a single point in time (the mid to late 1980s), provides a rough but useful means for placing tax legislation within the broader range of issues for which the Ways and Means Committee is responsible. Taxation was described by members and staff as distinctive in the number and sophistication of clientele groups involved in lobbying the committee, but was described as falling in a middle range in terms of the importance of ideology or partisanship. As an issue area for evaluating the usefulness of the electoral connection model, taxation would appear to be close to ideal; what members describe as distinctive about this area of the committee's jurisdiction—intense clientele activity—should make it a relatively "easy" case if the electoral connection model accurately captures the essential features of congressional politics. Taxation is an issue area in which committee members have abundant opportunities to distribute electorally targeted benefits through special tax provisions, and it is also an area in which large numbers of requests for these types of benefits from organized clientele groups are present.[5]

If the electoral connection model helps explain why members will support particularistic tax provisions and why an irresponsible bidding contest could develop during enactment of tax reduction legislation in 1981, it is otherwise of limited usefulness for explaining the patterns in tax politics

Figure 8-1
Issues in the Jurisdiction of the Ways and Means Committee

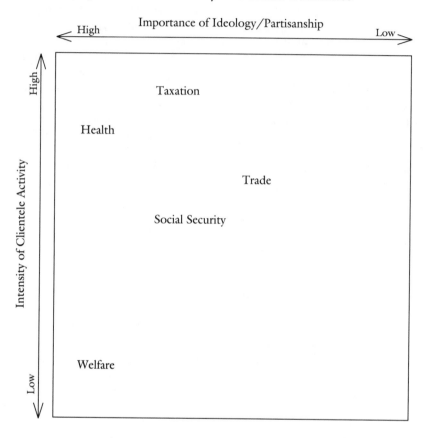

over the postreform period, especially in the case of the major policy break-through that occurred on tax reform in 1985–86. R. Douglas Arnold has noted that "whenever one attempts to generalize about a complex political process there is an ever present danger that one may strip away its barest essentials along with less important features."[6] The electoral connection model has the virtue of parsimony and is useful in highlighting political incentives created by institutional arrangements and the electoral process, but it fails to capture some essential features of the politics and outcomes of Ways and Means Committee tax decisions over the postreform period.[7]

Fenno's theoretical framework, by incorporating goals other than re-election and emphasizing the interplay between members' goals and environmental constraints, offers a much more useful perspective for under-standing the politics of the postreform committee—even if it does not fully

Table 8-1
Index of Partisanship and Percent Partisan Votes by Issue Area, 1975–1986

Issue Area	Index of Partisanship[1]	Percent Partisan Votes
Health	64	89
Welfare	61	74
Social Security	53	72
Taxation	49	69
Trade	43	60

Source: Compiled by the author from recorded votes in Ways and Means Committee files.

1. Calculation of these scores is described in n. 4 of this chapter.

account for some of the agenda-driven changes that have occurred in committee politics over the period *since* the reforms. In Fenno's framework, a committee's environmental constraints are defined by those individuals outside the committee who take an ongoing interest in committee decisions and can affect the achievement of its members' goals. This conceptualization of the committee's political environment assumes a more stable environment than was present in this case. The configuration of outsiders (in the parent chamber, the executive branch, clientele groups, and the leadership of the two parties) interested in Ways and Means Committee tax decisions did not change appreciably from 1981 to 1984, for example, but because of the rise of massive budget deficits after 1981, the environmental constraints faced by committee members changed markedly. Fenno did point out the more volatile politics that may occur on committees for which partisan coalitions are a major environmental influence, noting that shifting partisan objectives and coalitions in the environment of the House Education and Labor Committee meant that it had "the most unstable environment of the six committees [analyzed]."[8] Partisan leaders had always been a significant factor in the Ways and Means Committee's policy environment, and became even more so after the 1970s reforms, introducing greater instability as demonstrated by the volatility in committee politics in the context of a highly fragmented Democratic party in the House in the late 1970s and early 1980s.

Patterns in partisanship and responsiveness to clientele interests in Ways and Means Committee tax policymaking over the 1975–86 period have been strongly influenced by changes in the economic policy agenda. After the reforms of the 1970s recast the committee's institutional environment, a series of major agenda changes each created new environmental constraints for committee members and resulted in new patterns in committee politics. These shifts in committee politics occurred in part because of the increased importance of party leaders and organizational units in the postreform committee environment, but also because of changes in the nation's fiscal situation. As Roger H. Davidson has noted, the contractive fiscal agenda of the 1980s has had effects on committee politics for other panels as well as for Ways and Means.[9]

The analysis of the consequences of the 1970s reforms for Ways and Means Committee politics in the tax area leads, then, to three basic conclusions. First, in this case, Mayhew's electoral connection model oversimplifies congressional politics by failing to take into account the importance of members' concerns with good public policy and the complexities of the institutional and policy environments within which members act. Second, Fenno's theoretical framework, though more helpful for understanding the politics of the postreform Ways and Means Committee, does not account fully for the dynamism of the committee environment that occurred with a major change in the fiscal situation (the onset of large deficits). Therefore attempts by scholars such as David Price and Steven S. Smith and Christopher J. Deering to develop more dynamic conceptualizations of committee policy environments are on the right track, even if the specific categories they have suggested (primarily salience, conflict, and fragmentation) do not appear to have been the critical ones in the Ways and Means case.[10] The Ways and Means case suggests the need to add an additional dimension to conceptualizations of committee environments, the *fiscal* environment.

After 1981, opportunities and constraints for pursuing prestige, policy, or constituency goals were defined in part by deficit politics. Prestige and policy considerations both encouraged a focus on deficit reduction: the latter to demonstrate that the committee and the Congress retained the power to govern and the former because of the elite consensus (supplysiders excepted) that extremely large deficits are economically unwise, if not dangerous. For those committee members who sought to channel tax or other benefits to local constituencies or group allies, opportunities to do so were severely constrained in a deficit-dominated agenda. Deficit politics also have had important effects on committee decisionmaking processes. A period where committee politics have been primarily about increasing taxes and cutting existing spending programs has at times encouraged bipartisanship as a way to diffuse individual and partisan responsibility for policy changes needed to reduce deficits.

All other things being equal, an expansive fiscal environment tends to foster decentralization as priority-setting among alternative programs or policy areas is less of an ongoing problem for the committee system; a contractive fiscal environment where existing commitments consume available resources, or far exceed revenues as during the deficit politics of the 1980s, tends to foster attempts to strengthen priority-setting mechanisms in the committee system, either through more centralized patterns of authority internal to committees, or across committees by realigning jurisdictions, or—more recently—through the creation and manipulation of the budget process.[11] Dan Rostenkowski was able to reestablish an assertive and more centralized leadership style on the Ways and Means Committee in part because of committee members' recognition of the need for greater control over committee deliberations in order to make headway (or avoid losing ground) on the deficit.

A third and final conclusion is that leadership proved to be a more important factor in postreform committee politics than one might have anticipated from the emphasis that has been placed in recent years on contextual factors as the primary determinants of leaders' styles and their effectiveness. Although contextual factors continued to define certain broad limits for the exercise of leadership on the Ways and Means Committee after the mid-1970s reforms, personal factors proved important in defining an effective leadership style for the postreform committee. As a participatory democrat, Al Ullman maintained a permissive style of leadership that did little to address the sense of "wandering in the desert" that was felt by some members during the volatile committee politics of the late 1970s. Ullman's successor after 1980, Dan Rostenkowski, brought a more active and prestige-oriented style of leadership to Ways and Means. Although his effectiveness as leader has been determined in part by the larger policy and partisan dynamics of issues within the committee's jurisdiction, when conditions have allowed (as on tax bills in 1984 and 1985–86), Rostenkowski's personal political skills and concern with protecting committee power and prestige have been important factors in moving the Ways and Means Committee back somewhat in the direction of the autonomy and more moderate partisanship of the Mills years.

The 1970s Reforms and the Problem of Deliberation

As a legislative body that exercises real authority in the American constitutional system, the House of Representatives faces an ongoing problem of deliberation. Its members must faithfully represent the diversity of opinions and interests in American society, yet somehow reach agreement to make authoritative decisions for the society as a whole. As was argued in Chapter 1, legislative deliberation—the activity of reaching agreement among representatives on rules to govern the political community—requires three basic conditions in order to be effective: information about issues on the legislative agenda and on alternative courses of action; time to engage in discussion and discover grounds for agreement; and an appropriate institutional setting, where members representing the range of views in the body may be heard, but where the number of participants is small enough to allow serious discussion, and conditions allow members to speak frankly and remain open to compromise or persuasion. How then have the reforms of the 1970s, including those targeted at the Ways and Means Committee, affected the deliberative capabilities of the House? Although this study has focused on a single policy area and a single House committee, its findings do suggest some observations regarding the consequences of the reform era for the problem of deliberation in the House.

One area in which there appears to have been an improvement in deliberative capabilities is in the provision of more information to more members. Increased staffing on the Ways and Means Committee and the creation of the Congressional Budget Office and budget committee staffs have made more information available to more members on the tax and other issues in the jurisdiction of Ways and Means.[12] Some observers, though, including some senior Ways and Means members interviewed for this study, see increased staffing as a mixed blessing for the quality of committee deliberations. Along with providing access to more information, these members observed, the availability of staff may encourage legislators to become overly dependent on staffers rather than personally mastering and discussing the issues that must be decided.[13]

In terms of allowing time for conducting deliberations, the structural reforms in the Ways and Means Committee have brought some positive changes as well. The creation of legislative subcommittees in 1975 allowed for a more efficient division of labor on the committee, reducing to some degree the time pressures that were present when all of the issues in the committee's broad jurisdiction had to be handled one by one by the full committee.[14] However, the reconciliation procedure that evolved from the budget reforms, together with the political and fiscal conditions present in the 1980s, have often created time constraints under which members and staff report feeling that they have had insufficient time to look thoroughly at some major policy decisions.

Regarding the third condition for deliberation, an appropriate institutional setting, one clear effect of the reforms was to reduce the autonomy of the Ways and Means Committee as the principal deliberative body in the House on the economic and social welfare issues within its jurisdiction. One indication of the reduced autonomy of the postreform committee is the fact that five of the ten major tax bills reported by the panel between 1975 and 1986 were rejected or substantially amended on the House floor (see Table 7-4). Some view this as a more "democratic" arrangement, and hence a positive change. The new authority placed in the majority party organization and the budget process have created the potential for a more integrative approach to the problems on the congressional agenda than was the case when standing committees were more able to conduct autonomous deliberations. Whether the quality of deliberation in the more open and complex institutional setting in the postreform House has actually improved is open to question. A brief discussion of the effects of opening up committee procedures and of the role of the majority party in House deliberations on economic policy issues during the 1975–86 period will serve to illustrate the point.

For the members of the Ways and Means Committee who were interviewed for this study, perhaps the clearest lesson of the 1970s reform era is that opening bill-writing sessions to the public detracts from the quality of deliberation. Contrary to the hopes of reformers, according to most committee members the change to open committee markups in the mid-1970s tended to strengthen the pull of the electoral connection as members often felt pressured to stake out uncompromising positions when working under the watchful eye of representatives of local interests or groups who were electoral allies (or potential enemies). Problems Smith and Deering have noted with open bill markups on Senate committees are present for House committees as well: "Such an open environment is not conducive to give-and-take between members, discourages junior members from admitting ignorance by asking questions of knowledgeable colleagues, and puts a premium on grandstanding in front of the audience."[15] As discussed in Chapter 7, Ways and Means members attribute the success of the committee in developing deficit reduction measures and reporting out a tax reform bill in part to the more conducive setting for committee deliberation that has been present since the panel returned to the practice of closed markups in 1983.

In addition to creating a more open legislative process, another goal of some of the reformers during the 1970s was to create more party-centered deliberation on major policy issues. Reforms consistent with this goal included the increased party ratio on Ways and Means, election of committee chairmen by the caucus, and appointment of standing committees through a party body chaired by the Speaker.

In the context of the economic policy agenda of the mid-1970s and the large Democratic majorities in the House at that time, these reforms were successful in imparting a more partisan orientation to deliberations on the Ways and Means Committee. Something like a party-centered pattern of deliberation, for example, occurred in the House in response to President Carter's energy package submitted in 1977. Carter secured the active support of Democratic leaders in the House, and the administration's energy plan was revised and approved by partisan majorities with Republican members having very limited influence in committee deliberations or on the final outcome on the floor.

Although the reforms facilitated this shift toward a greater role for the majority party in the performance of deliberative functions in the House, by the late 1970s a paradoxical situation existed. Reforms had created a more party-centered institutional structure in the House, but the majority party's public philosophy no longer defined the national agenda and its members were deeply split on the economic policy issues that did dominate the agenda (e.g., across-the-board cuts in personal taxes and new incentives for business investment).[16]

The problem of disarray on economic policy issues in the House Democratic party was compounded by the election of Ronald Reagan and a Republican Senate in 1980. Attempts by Ways and Means Chairman Dan Rostenkowski and the House Democratic leadership to use the new organizational clout of the House majority party to moderate the scope of the Reagan tax and budget proposals in 1981 were not supported by party majorities on the House floor, and in effect forced deliberations on the issues on the new agenda outside the normal institutional channels in the House (i.e., the tax and budget committees). This situation helped create the chaotic tax policy process in 1981. In 1982 new patterns of deliberative activity again developed as the Senate Budget and Finance committees took control of the initiation of tax legislation when Democratic House leaders were reluctant to come to the aid of a Republican administration that found itself with a staggering revenue shortfall.

The 1970s House reforms—including those in the Ways and Means Committee—created greater *potential* for a party-centered deliberative process in the House, but the House Democratic party, by the late 1970s, was simply too fragmented to realize that potential.[17] As Richard P. Conlon, the executive director of the Democratic Study Group and an active figure in the House reform movement, summed up the situation in 1981: "Today, thanks to the reforms, House Democrats have the tools to deal with a chairman or any other member who obstructs the party program. Unfortunately we no longer have much of a program to obstruct."[18] Faced with the necessity of responding to the budgetary priorities of the Reagan administration and the pressures of deficits, House Democrats had achieved greater unity by the mid-1980s, but still showed limited success in realizing the potential for an ongoing party-centered deliberative process.[19]

In terms of conducting deliberations on economic policy issues, House reformers were successful in "opening up" a committee-centered deliberative process, but achieved only limited success in establishing an alternative in the majority party organization. In the postreform House, standing committees, the budget process, the majority party organization, and the House floor all exist as possible settings for performing deliberative functions formerly dominated by committees.[20] In contrast to the highly institutionalized patterns that structured deliberations in the postwar House, deliberative activity today is much more likely to occur on an ad hoc basis in a variety of institutional settings and be shaped by individual actors and shifting situational factors.[21]

Under the influence of Dan Rostenkowski's active but pragmatic leadership and the pressures of massive budget deficits, the Ways and Means Committee achieved some success in reasserting control over House deliberations on tax issues during the mid-1980s. Some senior members even suggested in interviews that the committee seemed to be moving back to a role similar to the one it had performed in the Mills era. However, with the persistence of large deficits, the potential for increased partisanship in the configuration of divided party control of the White House and Congress that has now become the norm, and the new avenues for deliberation that exist with the budget process and the majority party organization, it is highly unlikely that anything resembling the stable, committee-centered deliberative pattern of the Mills era can be reestablished in the postreform House. Because of its broad jurisdiction and the representative character of its membership, Ways and Means will continue to be an important deliberative body, but the most likely prospect is for more ad hoc policymaking in which this committee will be only one of a number of institutional units and informal groups that will be involved in framing policy choices for the House.

Notes

Preface

1. Sundquist, *Decline and Resurgence*, p. 482. For another general overview of the 1970s reform era in Congress, see Rieselbach, *Congressional Reform*.

2. Davidson and Oleszek, *Congress Against Itself*, p. 270.

3. For a bibliography on congressional reform in the 1970s, see Rieselbach, *Congressional Reform*, pp. 159–66.

4. See Patterson, "Legislative Reform," "The Semi-Sovereign Congress," and "Understanding Congress in the Long Run."

5. Dodd, "Universal Principle of Change," p. 39.

6. For the most comprehensive statement of this view, see Sheppard, *Rethinking Congressional Reform*.

7. Patterson, "The Semi-Sovereign Congress," pp. 176–77. For an analysis of the 1970s reforms that also emphasizes increased capabilities for involvement in more aspects of policymaking activity, see Jones, *United States Congress*, chap. 15.

8. Alexander, *History and Procedure of the House*, p. 234, quoted in Manley, *Politics of Finance*, p. 3.

9. See Furlong, "Origins of the Committee on Ways and Means," and Wander, "Patterns of Change." The most extensive historical account of the committee is the recently published, Committee on Ways and Means, *The Committee on Ways and Means: A Bicentennial History, 1789–1989*.

10. Alexander, *History and Procedure of the House*, pp. 107–36; Galloway, *History of the House*, p. 107.

11. Alexander, *History and Procedure of the House*, pp. 81–83; Hasbrouck, *Party Government*, pp. 42–43.

12. See Fleming, "Re-establishing Leadership"; Galloway, *History of the House*, pp. 136–41; Ripley, *Majority Party Leadership*, pp. 95–98.

13. Brown, *Leadership of Congress*, p. 185.

14. See Manley, *Politics of Finance*, pp. 53–57.

15. On the problems associated with identifying and evaluating change in Congress, see Jones, "How Reform Changes Congress," and Patterson, "Legislative Reform."

16. For an overview of the factors associated with change in congressional committee politics, see Smith and Deering, *Committees in Congress*, pp. 3–5.

17. Manley, *Politics of Finance*; Fenno, *Congressmen in Committees*; Rudder, "Committee Reform," "Policy Impact," "Tax Policy," "Fiscal Responsibility"; Smith and Deering, *Committees in Congress*.

18. See, for example, March and Olsen, "The New Institutionalism" and "Popular Sovereignty and the Search for Appropriate Institutions."

19. On institutional factors in congressional politics, see, for example, the wide range of essays collected in McCubbins and Sullivan, *Congress: Structure and Policy.*

20. A total of forty-three individuals were interviewed for this study between 1985 and 1989. Included in this total were thirty-one current and former Ways and Means Committee members (six of whom were interviewed at least twice), seven committee staff, one member of the Congressional Budget Office tax staff, and four lobbyists. The partisan breakdown of the committee members interviewed was twenty Democrats and eleven Republicans. Committee staff included five members of the majority staff and two from the minority. Interviews were open-ended, semistructured, and lasted from fifteen minutes to one hour and fifteen minutes. In all but one case, interviews were first recorded on tape, then transcribed. With the single exception of Chairman Dan Rostenkowski (D-Ill.), all of those interviewed were promised anonymity.

Chapter 1

1. See Rudder, "Committee Reform," "Policy Impact," "Tax Policy"; Surrey, "Our Troubled Tax Policy." Richard E. Cohen, "Requiem for a Heavyweight," *National Journal* 11 (November 3, 1979): 1857; I. M. Destler, "'Reforming' Trade Politics: The Weakness of Ways and Means," *Washington Post*, November 28, 1978, p. A15.

2. See Rudder, "Fiscal Responsibility."

3. Manley, *Politics of Finance*, p. 211; see also Fenno, *Congressmen in Committees*, p. 205.

4. Mikva and Saris, *The American Congress*, p. 292. For a similar view, see the volume from the Ralph Nader Congress Project, Spohn and McCollum, *The Revenue Committees.*

5. Cooper, "Organization and Innovation," p. 326, emphasis mine. For other statements of Cooper's theoretical framework, see "Strengthening the Congress," "Congress in Organizational Perspective," and Cooper and Brady, "Toward a Diachronic Analysis." On some of the problems involved in applying organization theory to legislatures in general and the U.S. Congress in particular, see Patterson, "Understanding Congress in the Long Run," and Polsby, "Studying Congress."

6. Among the works that might be cited as examples of this approach to legislative politics are studies drawing on group and role theory (Truman, *The Governmental Process, The Congressional Party*; Huitt and Peabody, *Congress: Two Decades of Analysis*), on systems theory (Wahlke et al., *The Legislative System*; Fenno, *Power of the Purse*; Rieselbach, *Congressional Politics*; Jewell and Patterson, *Legislative Process*), and on the concept of institutionalization (Polsby, "Institutionalization of the U.S. House"). Other studies drawing directly on organization theory include Froman, "Organization Theory," and Davidson and Oleszek, "Adaptation and Consolidation."

7. On the rise and development of this school of legislative scholarship, see Ferejohn and Fiorina, "Purposive Models," Sinclair, "Purposive Behavior," and Shepsle, "Prospects for Formal Models."

8. Fenno, *Congressmen in Committees* and *Home Style*; Mayhew, *Congress: The Electoral Connection.*

9. Polsby, "Legislatures," p. 260.

10. Lowenberg, "Role of Parliaments," p. 3.

11. Hamilton, Madison, and Jay, *The Federalist*, p. 79.

12. Bessette, "Deliberative Democracy," p. 107.

13. These formulations are from, respectively: Vogler, *Politics of Congress*; Cooper, "Congress in Organizational Perspective"; Rieselbach, *Congressional Reform*; and Jones, "House Leadership."

14. Jones, *United States Congress*, p. 26.

15. Malbin, "Factions and Incentives," p. 94.

16. For a treatment of legislative deliberation that emphasizes discussion of the public interest but views bargaining among competing interests (partisan mutual adjustment) as a flawed form of deliberation, see Maass, *Congress and the Common Good*, chap. 1. Following the work of Jane J. Mansbridge, David J. Vogler and Sidney R. Waldman have termed these two types of deliberation adversary and unitary. See Vogler and Waldman, *Congress and Democracy*.

17. This statement of the requisites for effective legislative deliberation draws on discussions of this question by Bessette, "Deliberative Democracy" and "Is Congress a Deliberative Body?"; Malbin, "Factions and Incentives"; Rudder, "Tax Policy"; Jones, "Limits of Leadership" and "House Leadership"; Maass, *Congress and the Common Good*; Cooper, "Strengthening the Congress"; and Vogler and Waldman, *Congress and Democracy*.

18. Whether disciplined parties encourage greater deliberation on broad interests in a society or simply encourage a different type of particularism is an open question. In any case, the presence of disciplined parties tends to move the focus of deliberative activity outside the legislature to a cabinet and/or party organizations.

19. Brady, *Congressional Voting*, p. 23.

20. On the role of party leadership in the House in the early twentieth century, see also Brown, *Leadership of Congress*; Hasbrouck, *Party Government*; Fleming, "Reestablishing Leadership"; and Galloway, *History of the House*, chap. 9.

21. Cooper and Brady, "Institutional Context," p. 416.

22. On the role of party leadership in the House prior to the reforms of the 1970s, see Jones, *Minority Party*, and Ripley, *Party Leaders* and *Majority Party Leadership*. For the period since the 1970s, see Sinclair, *Majority Leadership*, and Smith, "O'Neill's Legacy."

23. Cooper and Brady, "Institutional Context," p. 417.

24. See Davidson, "Representation and Committees," and "Breaking Up Those Cozy Triangles"; Shepsle, *Giant Jigsaw Puzzle*, chap. 10.

25. Ripley, *Party Leaders*, p. 86.

26. Sundquist, *Decline and Resurgence*, p. 418.

Chapter 2

1. Manley, *Politics of Finance*; Fenno, *Congressmen in Committees*.

2. Fenno, *Congressmen in Committees*, p. 84.

3. Manley, *Politics of Finance*, pp. 268–91. See also Fenno, *Congressmen in Committees*, pp. 153–54.

4. Derthick, *Policymaking for Social Security*, p. 49. Derthick points out that this norm in fact allowed incremental expansion of the program, but that Ways and Means members still acted as a "brake" on program expansion by insisting on tax increases to fund new benefits. Other studies that describe a similar policymaking role for the prereform Ways and Means Committee include Schick, *Congress and*

Money, chap. 12; Pastor, *Congress and the Politics of Foreign Economic Policy*; and Moynihan, *Politics of a Guaranteed Annual Income*.

5. Manley, *Politics of Finance*, pp. 63–90. See also Fenno, *Congressmen in Committees*, pp. 83–86.

6. Manley, *Politics of Finance*, pp. 21–22.

7. Fenno, *Congressmen in Committees*, pp. 2–5. Manley, *Politics of Finance*, pp. 55–58.

8. Fenno, *Congressmen in Committees*, pp. 15–21.

9. Ibid., p. 18.

10. Manley, *Politics of Finance*, p. 111.

11. Ibid., pp. 144–49.

12. Ibid., pp. 89–90.

13. Ibid., p. 110.

14. Fenno, *Congressmen in Committees*, p. 117.

15. Ibid.

16. Manley, *Politics of Finance*, p. 212.

17. The following section draws primarily on Cooper, "Organization and Innovation." For further elaboration of Cooper's theoretical framework, see the additional sources cited above, Chapter 1, n. 5.

18. Cooper, "Organization and Innovation," p. 331.

19. Nie, Verba, and Petrocik, *Changing American Voter*, chap. 3; Mann and Wolfinger, "Candidates and Parties," p. 620.

20. Clapp, *The Congressman*, p. 397.

21. Ibid.

22. Cooper and Brady, "Institutional Context," p. 417.

23. Sinclair, *Congressional Realignment*, chaps. 3–5.

24. Ornstein, Mann, and Malbin, *Vital Statistics*, p. 56.

25. Ibid., p. 17.

26. Ibid., chap. 6.

27. Sinclair, *Congressional Realignment*, pp. 46–47. See also pp. 101–11, 116–24.

28. See Sundquist, *Politics and Policy*.

29. Schultze et al., *Setting National Priorities*, p. 394.

30. Schick, "The Distributive Congress," p. 264. The classic study of budgetary politics during this era is Wildavsky's *Politics of the Budgetary Process*.

31. Greenstein, "Change and Continuity," p. 57.

32. Ibid., p. 58.

33. Hess, *Organizing the Presidency*, pp. 78–110.

34. Davis, "Congressional Liaison."

35. See Huntington, *American Politics*; Ceaser, "Direct Participation in Politics."

36. Almond and Verba, *The Civic Culture*, p. 102.

37. Davidson, Kovenock, and O'Leary, *Congress in Crisis*, p. 53.

38. Lipset and Schneider, *The Confidence Gap*, p. 15.

39. Cooper and Brady, "Institutional Context," p. 419.

40. See Asher, "The Norm of Specialization."

41. Fenno, "Internal Distribution of Influence," p. 73.

42. Sundquist, *Decline and Resurgence*, p. 72. On the origins and development of the norm of balanced budgets, see Savage, *Balanced Budgets and American Politics*.

43. Masters, "Committee Assignments," p. 357.

44. Ibid., p. 352.

45. Ibid., p. 353.

46. For the period between 1955 and 1967, for example, Fenno found that the East was heavily overrepresented on Education and Labor, and that western states controlled a full 50 percent of the seats on Interior. *Congressmen in Committees*, p. 62. Jones's study of the Agriculture Committee in the late 1950s found that only one member came from a district without significant agricultural production. "Representation in Congress." On the tendency of the committee selection process during this period to produce unrepresentative committee memberships, see also Shepsle, *Giant Jigsaw Puzzle*, chap. 10.

47. Fenno, *Congressmen in Committees*, p. 18.

48. Beer, "A New Public Philosophy," pp. 27–28.

49. Lipset and Schneider, *The Confidence Gap*, p. 17.

50. Ibid., pp. 48–49.

51. Davidson and Oleszek, *Congress and Its Members*, p. 152.

52. Lipset and Schneider, *The Confidence Gap*, pp. 41–66.

53. "Political Briefs," *Congressional Quarterly Weekly Report* 26 (June 14, 1968): 1487. "Polls on Electoral Reform," *Congressional Quarterly Weekly Report* 26 (September 27, 1968): 2567. "Campaign Financing: Growing Pressure to Go Public," *Congressional Quarterly Weekly Report* 32 (March 30, 1974): 797. "Congressional Term Limits Get More Public Support But Still Unpopular on Hill," *Congressional Quarterly Weekly Report* 36 (February 25, 1978): 533–34.

54. This argument was made repeatedly in House debates on committee reform in 1974. See remarks by Bill Frenzel (R-Minn.) and David T. Martin (R-Neb.), *Congressional Record*, September 30, 1974, pp. 32954–55, and by Patricia Schroeder (D-Col.), *Congressional Record*, October 8, 1974, p. 34469.

55. Davidson and Oleszek, *Congress Against Itself*, p. 71.

56. The phrase is Richard Bolling's (D-Mo.). Bolling, *House Out of Order*, p. 11.

57. Jacobson, *Politics of Congressional Elections*, p. 60.

58. Nie, Verba, and Petrocik, *Changing American Voter*, p. 57.

59. Shelley, *Permanent Majority*, pp. 140–41.

60. Congressman Moffett also stated in a 1977 interview:

> Every time I went to a [party] meeting, all the officials would say I was a Johnny-come-lately to the Democratic Party. Well that was the best thing that could happen in 1974—to be accused of being a Johnny-come-lately to politics. This is what happened to a lot of . . . [new Democrats]. . . . So they come here and don't feel any great allegiance to any party. . . . You have to be aware of how politically advantageous it is to be viewed as a maverick now. The public is almost insisting on it.

"Connecticut's Toby Moffett—'Liberating' the House Liberals," *National Journal* 9 (December 31, 1977): 1994–95.

61. Ornstein, Mann, and Malbin, *Vital Statistics*, pp. 165, 170.

62. For a more detailed account of why the informal postwar budgetary process broke down, see Wildavsky, *New Politics of the Budgetary Process*.

63. Office of Management and Budget, *Budget, Fiscal Year 1990, Historical Tables*, pp. 134–37; Schultze, *Setting National Priorities*, pp. 400–401.

64. Ibid., p. 409.

65. Reichley, *Conservatives in an Age of Change*, p. 246.
66. Jones, "Limits of Leadership," p. 617.
67. Stevens et al., "The Democratic Study Group," p. 667.
68. Ibid., pp. 667–71; Kofmehl, "Institutionalization of a Voting Block."
69. Davidson, Kovenock, and O'Leary, *Congress in Crisis*, chap. 5.
70. Ornstein and Rohde, "Political Parties and Congressional Reform," pp. 281–83.
71. Ibid., p. 282.
72. Schick, *Congress and Money*, chap. 3.
73. Ippolito, *Congressional Spending*, p. 60.

Chapter 3

1. Albert R. Hunt, "Waning Institution? Even if Mills Stays On, Ways and Means Panel Faces a Loss of Power," *Wall Street Journal*, July 10, 1973, p. 1.
2. Ibid.; "A Committee and Its Chairman Face Uncertain Futures," *Congressional Quarterly Weekly Report* 31 (July 14, 1973): 1892–93; Daniel J. Balz, "Ways and Means Seeks to Maintain Power and Prestige," *National Journal* 6 (June 22, 1974): 913–20.
3. Unekis and Rieselbach, *Congressional Committee Politics*, p. 39. On the importance of partisan/ideological alignments in committee voting during this period, see also Parker and Parker, *Factions in House Committees*. The increased number of committee roll call votes may also have reflected a heavier legislative agenda in the Ninety-third Congress. In the Ninety-second Congress (1971-72) the committee held 14 separate sets of hearings that extended over 72 days, and held executive sessions on 119 different days. During the Ninety-third Congress (1973-74) 17 sets of hearings were held extending over 102 days, with executive sessions occurring on 176 different days. Committee on Ways and Means, *Ninety-Second Congress Legislative Record of the Committee on Ways and Means* and *Ninety-Third Congress Legislative Record of the Committee on Ways and Means*.
4. See Balz, "Ways and Means"; "Committee and Its Chairman."
5. Balz, "Ways and Means," p. 915.
6. On Archer's role in committee deliberations on oil industry tax issues in 1974, see James G. Phillips, "Congress Moves toward Repeal of Oil Depletion Allowance," *National Journal* 6 (April 13, 1974): 544–53, and Morrison, "Energy Tax Legislation."
7. See above, Chapter 2, and Manley, *Politics of Finance*, pp. 88–90.
8. Hunt, "Waning Institution," p. 19. See also Balz, "Ways and Means," p. 914.
9. See Bowler et al., "Political Economy of National Health Insurance."
10. Ibid., p. 123; see also Richard D. Lyons, "House Panel Rift Appears to Doom Health Cost Bill," *New York Times*, August 22, 1974, pp. 1, 55.
11. *Congressional Quarterly Almanac, 1974*, p. 392.
12. Phillips, "Congress Moves toward Repeal," p. 549.
13. Ibid.
14. Unless otherwise noted, the following account is based on Morrison, "Energy Tax Legislation." On the politics of energy tax legislation during this period, see also Gilligan and Kreibel, "Complex Rules and Congressional Outcomes."
15. Mary Russell, "Mills Defiance on Oil Taxes Strains Democratic Ties," *Washington Post*, May 24, 1974, p. A2.

16. Ibid.

17. Both oil state members and liberal Democrats were opposed to the bill. See Daniel J. Balz, "Split Committee Is Unlikely to Produce Passable Bill," *National Journal* 6 (October 5, 1974): 1500–1502.

18. The first incident occurred in Washington on October 9, 1974, when the woman, Annabella Battistella, jumped from Mills's car into the Tidal Basin after the car was stopped by police for speeding and driving without headlights. The second incident occurred on November 30, 1974, when Mills appeared onstage with the dancer at a nightclub in Boston's "Combat Zone." See "New Congress Organizes; No Role For Mills," *Congressional Quarterly Weekly Report* 32 (December 7, 1974): 3247–48; Mary Russell, "Representative Mills Gives Up Hill Post," *Washington Post*, December 11, 1974, pp. A1, A8; "The Fall of Chairman Wilbur Mills," *Time*, December 16, 1974, pp. 22–26.

19. Balz, "Ways and Means," p. 915.

20. See Richard L. Lyons, "Battle on Spending May Determine Mills' Clout," *Washington Post*, October 9, 1972, p. A21.

21. Derthick, *Policymaking for Social Security*, p. 366.

22. Ibid., pp. 350, 367; "House Hinges Social Security Boosts to Living Costs," *Congressional Quarterly Weekly Report* 28 (May 29, 1970): 1430–32; Weaver, *Automatic Government*, pp. 72-75.

23. "Social Security Boost, Debt Ceiling Measures Cleared," *Congressional Quarterly Weekly Report* 31 (July 7, 1973): 1831–33.

24. "Committee and Its Chairman," p. 1892.

25. Balz, "Ways and Means," pp. 915, 918.

26. Davidson and Oleszek, *Congress Against Itself*, p. 44.

27. Myra MacPherson, "Looking Back: Wilbur Mills Recalls His Bout With Alcohol," *Washington Post*, November 4, 1978, pp. B1, B3.

28. Prior to the incidents in 1974, part of the Mills mystique had been that the chairman avoided Washington social life, preferring instead to spend his evenings at home studying issues related to upcoming committee business. See the 1963 *Time* cover story, "An Idea on the March," *Time*, January 11, 1963, pp. 20–21. For a critical assessment of the admiring treatments Mills had been given in this and other portrayals in the press prior to 1974, see Walter Shapiro, "The Ways and Means of Conning the Press, *Washington Monthly*, December 1974, pp. 4–13.

29. Hunt, "Waning Institution," p. 1.

30. Rudder, "Committee Reform and the Revenue Process," "Policy Impact of Reform," "Tax Policy," and "Fiscal Responsibility." On the impact of reform, see also Smith and Deering, *Committees in Congress*, pp. 95–98; Schick, *Congress and Money*, pp. 483–500; Unekis and Rieselbach, *Congressional Committee Politics*, pp. 126–33; and Bowler, "The New Committee on Ways and Means."

31. Rudder, "Tax Policy," p. 202. Rudder also included "routine assignment of new members and members from unsafe districts to the Ways and Means Committee" as an important change during the 1970s. This and other aspects of committee recruitment are examined in detail below in Chapter 4.

32. Rudder, "Tax Policy," pp. 213–16, "Fiscal Responsibility," pp. 215–21; Bowler, "Politics of Federal Health Insurance Programs," pp. 209–10.

33. The original measure requiring a committee to vote to close a meeting was part of the Legislative Reorganization Act of 1970, but the Democratic caucus voted in 1973 and again in 1975 to strengthen rules encouraging open meet-

ings. A threefold increase in the allowance for committee staff and the requirement that Ways and Means set up subcommittees were part of the Committee Reform Amendments adopted as a House resolution in October 1974. Both provisions contributed to the staff buildup on Ways and Means, but only the subcommittee reform had originated in the Democratic caucus. See the discussion of the Democratic caucus reforms below.

34. Fenno, *Congressmen in Committees*, pp. 17–18.

35. Davidson and Oleszek, *Congress Against Itself*, p. 45. See also Sheppard, *Rethinking Congressional Reform*, pp. 70–72.

36. Ornstein, "Subcommittee Reforms in the House," pp. 92–94.

37. For a detailed account of the enactment of committee and subcommittee reforms in the Democratic caucus in 1971 and 1973, see Sheppard, *Rethinking Congressional Reform*, pp. 59–147. See also Ornstein, "Subcommittee Reforms in the House"; Rohde, "Committee Reform in the House"; Ornstein and Rohde, "Political Parties and Congressional Reform," pp. 283–86; and Sundquist, *Decline and Resurgence*, pp. 378–79.

38. *Congressional Quarterly Weekly Report* stated at the time that the closed rule reform was "aimed at the Ways and Means Committee." "House Reform: Easy to Advocate, Hard to Define," *Congressional Quarterly Weekly Report* 31 (January 20, 1973): 72. According to Manley, the practice of debating major tax bills reported by the Ways and Means Committee under closed rules had been well established since the 1930s, and the extension of the practice to other major bills reported by the committee had become equally well established by the late 1960s. *Politics of Finance*, p. 226.

39. Rudder, "Committee Reform and the Revenue Process," pp. 118–19; Marjorie Hunter, "Democrats Curb Secrecy in the House," *New York Times*, February 22, 1973, pp. 1, 24.

40. Davidson and Oleszek, *Congress Against Itself*, p. 179. See also Sheppard, *Rethinking Congressional Reform*, p. 122.

41. Hunt, "Waning Institution," p. 19.

42. Other areas removed from the jurisdiction of the Ways and Means Committee in the final proposal reported by the Bolling Committee were general revenue sharing, work incentive programs, and renegotiation of currency agreements. The food stamp program and issues involving foundations and charitable trusts were the only proposed additions. Davidson and Oleszek, *Congress Against Itself*, pp. 105–7; Sheppard, *Rethinking Congressional Reform*, pp. 142–43.

43. Davidson and Oleszek, *Congress Against Itself*, pp. 180, 193–94; *Congressional Quarterly Almanac, 1974*, p. 636.

44. Sheppard, *Rethinking Congressional Reform*, pp. 156–59; Davidson and Oleszek, *Congress Against Itself*, pp. 193–97.

45. Davidson and Oleszek, *Congress Against Itself*, p. 202.

46. Michael J. Malbin, "New Democratic Procedures Affect Distribution of Power," *National Journal* 6 (December 14, 1974): 1884.

47. *Congressional Record*, September 30, 1974, p. 32966.

48. Ibid., p. 33008.

49. Ibid., p. 32996.

50. MacFarland, *Common Cause*, pp. 119–22; "House Survey Hints Move to Curb Mills," *New York Times*, November 21, 1974, p. 48.

51. Richard D. Lyons, "Albert Favors a Stronger Role for Newer Members and the Dilution of Ways and Means Panel," *New York Times*, November 22, 1974, p. 17.

52. Sheppard, *Rethinking Congressional Reform*, pp. 194–95.

53. Albert R. Hunt, "Ebbing Influence: Weakened Rep. Mills and His Committee Face Rough Going," *Wall Street Journal*, November 29, 1974, p. 1. See also Richard L. Lyons, "Ways and Means Target of House Reformers," *Washington Post*, November 13, 1974, p. A2.

54. The account of the December 1974 organizational caucus is based on: Rudder, "Committee Reform and the Revenue Process," p. 120; "House Democrats Seek to Rewrite the Rules," *Congressional Quarterly Weekly Report* 32 (November 30, 1974): 3199–3201; "New Congress Organizes: No Role For Mills," *Congressional Quarterly Weekly Report* 32 (December 7, 1974): 3247–53; David E. Rosenbaum, "House Dems End Mills's Rule Over Committees," *New York Times*, December 3, 1974, pp. 1, 31; Richard D. Lyons, "Mills Goes Into Hospital After Being Told of Plan to Oust Him as Chairman," *New York Times*, December 4, 1974, pp. 1, 52; Malbin, "New Democratic Procedures," pp. 1884–85; Sheppard, *Rethinking Congressional Reform*, pp. 195–98.

55. Davidson, Kovenock, and O'Leary, *Congress in Crisis*, p. 162.

56. Fenno, *Congressmen in Committees*, p. 209.

57. Juan D. Cameron, "And They Call It the Most Important Committee in Congress," *Fortune* 93 (March 1976): 144.

58. "New Congress Organizes," p. 3250.

59. Davidson and Oleszek, *Congress Against Itself*, p. 43.

60. Sheppard, *Rethinking Congressional Reform*, p. 198.

61. See Schick, *Congress and Money*, *Reconciliation and the Congressional Budget Process*; Havemann, *Congress and the Budget*; Ippolito, *Congressional Spending*; LeLoup, *Fiscal Congress*; Penner, *The Congressional Budget Process*; Ellwood, "The Great Exception"; Wander, Hebert, and Copeland, *Congressional Budgeting*; Penner and Abramson, *Broken Purse Strings*; and Wildavsky, *New Politics of the Budgetary Process*.

62. See Davidson, "Two Avenues of Change," pp. 230–31; Ellwood and Thurber, "The Congressional Budget Process Re-examined."

63. Title X of the act also created new procedures for controlling presidential impoundments. See Schick, *Congress and Money*, pp. 401–12.

64. See Ellwood and Thurber, "The Congressional Budget Process Re-examined," p. 251; Schick, *Congress and Money*, pp. 51–81, 568–73; and Jones, "How Reform Changes Congress," pp. 20–21.

65. See Schick, *Congress and Money*, pp. 500–504; Havemann, "Budget Process and Tax Legislation."

66. Schick, *Congress and Money*, p. 503.

67. See Schick, *Reconciliation and the Congressional Budget Process*; Ellwood, "Great Exception"; Penner and Abramson, *Broken Purse Strings*, pp. 41–83.

68. Ellwood, "Great Exception," p. 331.

69. On the enactment of Gramm-Rudman-Hollings, see Strahan, "Governing in the Post-Liberal Era"; Ellwood, "Politics of the Enactment and Implementation of Gramm-Rudman-Hollings"; and White and Wildavsky, *The Deficit and the Public Interest*.

70. For a concise description of budget procedures after the enactment of Gramm-Rudman-Hollings, see Senate Committee on the Budget, *The Congressional Budget Process: An Explanation*.

71. See Strahan, "Governing in the Post-Liberal Era"; Ellwood, "Politics of the Enactment and Implementation of Gramm-Rudman-Hollings"; and White and Wildavsky, *The Deficit and the Public Interest*.

72. Ellwood, "Budget Reforms and Interchamber Relations," p. 101.

73. Schick, *Reconciliation and the Congressional Budget Process*, pp. 40–41.

Chapter 4

1. Michael J. Malbin, "New Democratic Procedures Affect Distribution of Power," *National Journal* 6 (December 14, 1974): 1884.

2. Mayhew, *Congress: The Electoral Connection*, pp. 49–77.

3. Ibid., p. 125.

4. Ibid., p. 132.

5. Ibid., p. 146.

6. Ibid., p. 158.

7. For a more detailed review and critique of Fenno's theory of committee politics, see Smith, "Central Concepts."

8. Fenno, *Congressmen in Committees*, p. 1. Mayhew does not deny that members may actually pursue goals other than reelection, but argues simply that a reelection-driven framework is the most powerful theoretical approach for explaining congressional politics. See *Congress: The Electoral Connection*, pp. 5–6, 13–17.

9. Fenno, *Congressmen in Committees*, p. xv.

10. On the limitations of Fenno's theoretical framework as a causal model or deductive theory in the precise sense, see Smith, "Central Concepts," especially pp. 11–12.

11. Jewell and Chu, "Membership Movement and Committee Attractiveness," pp. 433–41.

12. Ray, "Committee Attractiveness in the U.S. House."

13. The index used in both studies has a possible range of 0–1. Attractiveness is measured "by giving a committee three points each time a member gave up four or more terms of seniority on a different committee in order to secure the new assignment, two points if two or three terms of seniority were relinquished, one point if a single term was forfeited, and no points each time a freshman was assigned to a committee." The resulting total was divided by the number of new members assigned to the committee during the period studied, then divided again by three to produce the standardized score of 0–1. Ray, "Committee Attractiveness in the U.S. House," pp. 609–10. The scores of the top three committees reported in the two studies were as follows (p. 610):

	1963–1971	1973–1981
Ways and Means	.756	.431
Rules	.500	.389
Appropriations	.442	.438

14. Seniority figures were computed by the author from the *Congressional Directory*. See the discussion below of the importance of seniority in committee recruitment.

15. Jewell and Chu, "Membership Movement and Committee Attractiveness," p. 439.

16. See Smith and Deering, *Committees in Congress*, pp. 96–97; Rudder, "Committee Reform," pp. 128–29.

17. Mayhew, *Congress: The Electoral Connection*, p. 140.

18. See Ornstein, "The Open Congress Meets the President," pp. 195–204; Malbin, "Factions and Incentives," p. 100–106.

19. Mayhew, *Congress: The Electoral Connection*, pp. 142–45.

20. The most comprehensive study of the prereform committee selection process for House Democrats is Shepsle, *Giant Jigsaw Puzzle*.

21. Smith and Ray, "House Democratic Committee Assignments," p. 238.

22. Ibid., p. 238. See also Shepsle, *Giant Jigsaw Puzzle*, pp. 262–81; Smith and Deering, *Committees in Congress*, pp. 237–46.

23. Smith and Ray, "House Democratic Committee Assignments," p. 227.

24. Fenno, *Congressmen in Committees*, pp. 19–20.

25. Manley found that 62 percent of the Democratic vacancies between 1947 and 1969 were filled with members from the same state. *Politics of Finance*, p. 32.

26. Unsuccessful attempts to win seats on Ways and Means without a Steering and Policy nomination were undertaken in the caucus by Robert J. Cornell of Wisconsin in 1977, and James L. Oberstar of Minnesota and Ronnie L. Flippo of Alabama in 1979. Flippo later won the nomination from the Steering and Policy Committee and a Ways and Means seat in 1983.

27. Manley, *Politics of Finance*, pp. 22–38. On the prereform selection process for Ways and Means, see also Shepsle, *Giant Jigsaw Puzzle*, pp. 138–48.

28. Fenno, *Congressmen in Committees*, pp. 18–19.

29. The mean is skewed somewhat by the case of Omar T. Burleson of Texas, who had accumulated twenty-two years of seniority before joining the committee in 1969. Without Burleson the mean seniority for Mills-era Democratic appointments was still a considerable 8.5 years.

30. Interestingly, a second reason for selecting members from safe seats that was noted by Manley and by some of the senior members who discussed earlier recruitment practices—that relative freedom from worries about electoral defeat would allow more time to master the committee's complex subject matter—did not come up in interviews with more recent appointees. See Manley, *Politics of Finance*, p. 51.

31. Rudder, "Policy Impact," p. 79, "Tax Policy," p. 202.

32. Note the similarities to the desirable and undesirable personal characteristics mentioned by those interviewed by Fenno: "When money-committee members and their selectors discuss the reasons for their appointments, they typically mention personal attributes such as 'cooperative,' 'popular,' 'reasonable,' 'sober,' 'easy to work with.' Conversely they were not . . . 'screwballs,' 'running around kicking everyone in the teeth,' 'shooting their mouths off,' 'going off half-cocked.'" *Congressmen in Committees*, pp. 20–21.

33. The authors of the respected *Almanac of American Politics* described Stark as "by nature a kind of insurgent." Barone and Ujifusa, *Almanac of American Politics*, p. 116. By the mid-1980s, however, Stark had become a subcommittee chairman and a major force on the Ways and Means Committee. In interviews, a number of members were complimentary of Stark's legislative work (see the discussion in Chapter 6 of Stark's role in developing the 1984 tax bill).

34. Manley, *Politics of Finance*, pp. 38–40, 52–53.

35. The single Republican freshman who won appointment during this period was George Bush of Texas.

36. Manley, *Politics of Finance*, p. 22. On the involvement of House party leaders in postreform committee assignments, see also Smith and Deering, *Committees in Congress*, pp. 242–246.

37. Smith and Deering, *Committees in Congress*, p. 83.

38. Ibid., p. 96.

39. Manley reported that "two thirds of those interviewed . . . were attracted to the Committee because of its importance, power, and prestige." *Politics of Finance*, p. 56. Describing interviews with members of the Ways and Means Committee and the Appropriations Committee, Fenno observed that goals of prestige or influence in the House "were expressed by 75 to 80 percent of the members of both Committees." *Congressmen in Committees*, p. 3.

40. Smith and Deering found a similar change when comparing reasons given by junior House members who were interested in serving on Ways and Means in the Ninety-second (1971–72) and Ninety-seventh (1981–82) Congresses. In the Ninety-second Congress (according to interviews conducted by Charles S. Bullock), five of six junior members who expressed interest in Ways and Means cited prestige or influence as the reason. By the Ninety-seventh Congress, only about half (seven of thirteen) mentioned prestige. The remainder were attracted to the policy activity of the committee. Smith and Deering, *Committees in Congress*, p. 90.

41. One member did note in response to a different question that membership on Ways and Means was attractive because it made campaign fund-raising relatively easy.

42. Fenno, *Congressmen in Committees*, pp. 153–54.

43. Rudder, "Policy Impact," p. 77.

44. Daniel J. Balz, "Slow Progress on Tax Reform Issues," *National Journal* 7 (August 30, 1975): 1237.

45. Juan D. Cameron, "And They Call It the Most Important Committee in Congress," *Fortune* 93 (March 1976): 148.

46. Manley, *Politics of Finance*, pp. 160–61; see also Fenno, *Congressmen in Committees*, pp. 235–36. The decline in committee floor success reflects broader changes in amending activity in the House as well as shifts in Ways and Means members' goals and committee decisionmaking processes. On the increase in floor amending activity in the House during this period, see Bach and Smith, *Managing Uncertainty in the House*, and Smith, *Call to Order*, especially pp. 176–83.

47. See Manley, *Politics of Finance*, pp. 22–44.

48. Shelley, *Permanent Majority*, pp. 18–19.

49. Ibid., pp. 51–53.

50. Rudder, "Tax Policy," p. 158.

51. See Conable, "Legislative Persuasion," and Surrey, "Tribute to Woodworth."

52. See Manley, *Politics of Finance*, pp. 307–19; Malbin, *Unelected Representatives*, pp. 170–87; Reese, *Politics of Taxation*, pp. 61–68; and Conable, *Congress and the Income Tax*, pp. 28–30.

53. Ornstein et al., *Vital Statistics*, pp. 147, 149.

Chapter 5

1. Manley, "Wilbur D. Mills," p. 464.

2. See, for example, Cooper and Brady, "Institutional Context and Leadership Style"; Jones, "House Leadership"; Sinclair, *Majority Leadership*; Smith, "O'Neill's Legacy"; Loomis, "Me Decade"; Rohde and Shepsle, "Leaders and Followers." One exception to the focus on contextual factors in recent studies of leadership is Owens, "Wright Patman," which emphasizes the importance of both personal and contextual factors in the development of Wright Patman's "extreme advocacy" leadership style as chairman of the House Banking and Currency Committee.

3. Fenno, *Congressmen in Committees*, p. 133. In the case of committee leadership, Smith and Deering have argued that increased formalization of structure and procedures in the House during the 1970s made contextual factors "more useful in explaining differences among committee chairs' approaches to committee politics." *Committees in Congress*, p. 168. In the specific case of the Ways and Means Committee, they conclude: "On the surface, the approaches of Ullman and Rostenkowski appear less successful than were Mills', but the changing opportunities and constraints they face have dictated both their leadership styles and success ratios." *Committees in Congress*, p. 186.

4. Fenno, *Congressmen in Committees*, p. 117. Fenno has also noted the increased importance of personal factors in explaining members' "home styles" in cases where constituency characteristics are ambiguous. See *Home Style*, pp. 79, 91, 124–35.

5. See Cooper and Brady, "Institutional Context and Leadership Style"; Rohde and Shepsle, "Leaders and Followers"; and Jones, "The Limits of Leadership."

6. Swenson, "Influence of Recruitment."

7. The conceptual framework proposed here admittedly involves a certain degree of simplification. Although institutional, partisan, and issue-related factors may be highly interrelated over time, in conceptualizing the opportunities and constraints that exist for a leader at any given point in time, it is useful to consider each as analytically distinct.

8. Cited in Smith and Deering, *Committees in Congress*, p. 177.

9. Ibid., p. 177.

10. Dale Tate, "Ways and Means: Behind Closed Doors," *Congressional Quarterly Weekly Report* 41 (October 8, 1983): 2067; Jacqueline Calmes, "Few Complaints are Voiced as Doors Close on Capitol Hill," *Congressional Quarterly Weekly Report* 45 (May 23, 1987): 1059–60.

11. *Congressional Quarterly Almanac, 1985*, p. 452.

12. This is not to argue that increases in party unity are entirely due to agenda changes. David Rohde has shown that increased Democratic unity may also be associated with changes that have been occurring in party and electoral politics in the South. See Rohde, "Variations in Partisanship in the House of Representatives."

13. Manley, *Politics of Finance*, pp. 151–247; Sinclair, "Agenda, Policy, and Alignment Change," pp. 308–9.

14. Sinclair, *Congressional Realignment*, p. 145.

15. Unekis and Rieselbach, *Congressional Committee Politics*; Parker and Parker, *Factions in House Committees*.

16. See Sinclair, "Agenda, Policy, and Alignment Change," "Agenda Control and Policy Success"; Ellwood, "The Great Exception."

17. Calculated from scores reported in Ornstein et al., *Vital Statistics*, pp. 208–9. Scores have been normalized to remove the effects of missed votes. For a more detailed analysis of the increased Democratic unity in the House during this period, see Rohde, "Variations in Partisanship in the House of Representatives."

18. The index of cohesion was calculated by dividing the total number of party members voting with their party majority on all roll call votes each year by the total number of votes cast. See Rice, *Quantitative Methods*, pp. 208–9, and Turner and Schneier, *Party and Constituency*, pp. 20–21.

19. Davidson, "Committees as Moving Targets," p. 32.

20. Richard E. Cohen, "Al Ullman—The Complex, Contradictory Chairman of Ways and Means," *National Journal* 10 (March 4, 1978): 347.

21. Ibid.

22. Ibid.

23. Rudder, "Committee Reform," p. 131.

24. Tom Arrandale, "Ways and Means in 1975: No Longer Pre-eminent," *Congressional Quarterly Weekly Report* 34 (January 10, 1976): 44.

25. Juan D. Cameron, "And They Call It the Most Important Committee on Capitol Hill," *Fortune* 93 (March 1976): 142.

26. See Crook and Hibbing, "Congressional Reform and Party Discipline."

27. "Republicans: On the Sidelines," *Congressional Quarterly Weekly Report* 32 (March 15, 1975): 516.

28. Cohen, "Al Ullman," p. 347.

29. Personal interview with the author, March 8, 1989.

30. See Arrandale, "Ways and Means in 1975." See also Reese, *Politics of Taxation*, p. 113.

31. In this respect, Ullman's situation resembles that of Thomas Morgan, chairman of the House Foreign Affairs Committee during the period covered by Fenno's study of committee politics. In explaining the criticism he encountered of Morgan's leadership, Fenno noted that Morgan "is severely hampered in giving his members what they want because they do not really know what they want—not sufficiently to standardize and operationalize their desires in a satisfying set of decision rules." *Congressmen in Committees*, p. 133.

32. Personal interview with the author, March 9, 1989.

33. On Rostenkowski's political career before entering Congress and his ongoing ties to local politics in Chicago, see Snowiss, "Congressional Recruitment"; Irwin B. Arieff, "New Role for Rostenkowski Gets Him in the Thick of House Power-Playing," *Congressional Quarterly Weekly Report* 39 (May 16, 1981): 863–66; Steven V. Roberts, "A Most Important Man on Capitol Hill," *New York Times Magazine*, September 22, 1985, pp. 44–55; Birnbaum and Murray, *Showdown at Gucci Gulch*, pp. 103–4; Smith, *The Power Game*, pp. 553–55.

34. Personal interview with the author, March 9, 1989.

35. On Rostenkowski's leadership style, see also Conable, *Congress and the Income Tax*, chaps. 2 and 3.

36. A total of twenty-four Democratic appointments were made between 1975 and 1980, during which time the mean percentage of freshman Democrats in each of these three Congresses was 18.7 percent. Only twelve new Democratic members were appointed between 1981 and 1986, and the mean percentage of freshman Democrats in these three Congresses dropped to 11.7 percent. (Figures on freshmen from 1975–80 from Hinckley, *Stability and Change*, p. 130; others calculated by the author.)

37. See Birnbaum and Murray, *Showdown at Gucci Gulch*, pp. 116–17, and Bowler, "Preparing Members on Complex Issues," pp. 39–42.

38. Elizabeth Wehr, "Rostenkowski: A Firm Grip on Ways and Means," *Congressional Quarterly Weekly Report* 43 (July 6, 1985): 1318.

39. Pamela Fessler, "Rostenkowski Seeks More Influential Role," *Congressional Quarterly Weekly Report* 41 (January 29, 1983): 195; Birnbaum and Murray, *Showdown at Gucci Gulch*, p. 105; Conable, *Congress and the Income Tax*, p. 67.

40. See Birnbaum and Murray, *Showdown at Gucci Gulch*, pp. 96–100.

41. Snowiss, "Congressional Recruitment," p. 630.

42. Greenstein, *Personality and Politics*, p. 42.

43. Greenstein, "Personality and Politics," p. 20.

44. An interesting parallel to Rostenkowski's role as a committee leader in the 1980s may be Thomas B. Reed's role in refashioning majority leadership in the 1880s.

Chapter 6

1. Because of the large number of major tax bills enacted during these years (eleven), a more complete account of congressional tax politics during this period would be a book unto itself. Fortunately, most of the period is already covered in the most comprehensive study of federal tax politics to date, John F. Witte's *Politics and Development of the Federal Income Tax*. For more detailed discussions of other aspects of federal tax policy and politics over this period, see also the series of essays by Catherine E. Rudder; Reese, *Politics of Taxation*; Verdier, "The President, Congress, and Tax Reform"; Martin, "Business Influence and State Power"; Steinmo, "Political Institutions and Tax Policy"; King, "Tax Expenditures and Systematic Public Policy"; West, *Congress and Economic Policymaking*; Hansen, *Politics of Taxation*; and Pechman, *Federal Tax Policy*.

2. In addition to the concept of environmental constraints in Fenno's work, other studies that have emphasized the importance of jurisdictional or agenda-related influences on committee politics include Jones, "Representation in Congress"; Hinckley, "Policy Content, Committee Membership, and Behavior"; Price, *Policymaking in Congressional Committees*; and Smith and Deering, *Committees in Congress*.

3. Manley, *Politics of Finance*, p. 22.

4. Ibid., p. 11.

5. Fenno, *Congressmen in Committees*, p. 84.

6. Ibid., p. 157.

7. See Reese, *Politics of Taxation*, pp. 124–26.

8. Manley, *Politics of Finance*, pp. 272–79.

9. In addition to the specific citations in the text, the analysis of tax legislation in this chapter draws generally on Rudder, "Committee Reform," "Policy Impact," "Tax Policy," "Fiscal Responsibility"; Witte, *Politics of the Federal Income Tax*; and Conable, *Congress and the Income Tax*, chap. 3.

10. The account of congressional action on H.R. 2166 draws primarily on "Tax Cut Bill Adopted," *Congressional Quarterly Weekly Report* 33 (February 22, 1975): 351–52, and "House Passes Tax Cut With Depletion Repeal," *Congressional Quarterly Weekly Report* 33 (March 1, 1975): 419–23.

11. "Energy Tax Hearings," *Congressional Quarterly Weekly Report* 33 (March 8, 1975): 472–75; "Republicans: On the Sidelines," *Congressional Quarterly Weekly*

Report 33 (March 15, 1975): 516; "Energy Tax Package," *Congressional Quarterly Weekly Report* 33 (March 22, 1975): 580–81.

12. "Republicans: On the Sidelines," p. 516.

13. Tom Arrandale, "House Passes Stripped Down Energy Tax Bill," *Congressional Quarterly Weekly Report* 33 (June 21, 1975): 1275–76.

14. Rudder, "Policy Impact," pp. 84–86.

15. Tom Arrandale, "Ways and Means Divided on Tax Legislation," *Congressional Quarterly Weekly Report* 33 (November 8, 1975): 2429–31.

16. Tom Arrandale, "House Passes Tax Bill; Spending Cuts Blocked," *Congressional Quarterly Weekly Report* 33 (December 6, 1975): 2626–27.

17. See Witte, *Politics of the Federal Income Tax*, pp. 190–98.

18. Richard Cohen, "But for the Time Being, A Tax Credit for Business," *National Journal* 9 (March 19, 1977): 419–21; Judy Gardner, "Ways and Means Revises Carter Tax Plan," *Congressional Quarterly Weekly Report* 35 (February 19, 1977): 299–301.

19. Bob Rankin and Harrison H. Donnelly, "Committees Move on Carter Energy Bill," *Congressional Quarterly Weekly Report* 35 (July 2, 1977): 1335–37; see also Oppenheimer, "The Oil Pricing Issue."

20. See Jones, "The Making of Energy Policy"; Oppenheimer, "Policy Effects of U.S. House Reform."

21. Bob Rankin, "House Gives Carter Major Energy Victory," *Congressional Quarterly Weekly Report* 35 (August 6, 1977): 1623–95; Bob Rankin, "Senate Votes Energy Tax Bill," *Congressional Quarterly Weekly Report* 35 (October 5, 1977): 2355–58.

22. On the perceptions of Ways and Means Committee members and others that the oil industry and other business interests had lost influence in committee decisionmaking in the immediate aftermath of the 1974 reforms, see Allen Ehrenhalt, "Energy Lobby: New Faces at Ways and Means," *Congressional Quarterly Weekly Report* 33 (May 3, 1975): 939–46, and Rudder, "Policy Impact," pp. 76–77.

23. Witte, *Politics of the Federal Income Tax*, pp. 185–86.

24. See Ibid., p. 188.

25. Ibid., p. 207.

26. See Surrey, "Reflections on the Revenue Act"; Kantowicz, "Limits of Incrementalism"; and Conable, *Congress and the Income Tax*, pp. 49–53.

27. *Congressional Record*, August 1, 1977, p. 25900; *Congressional Record*, August 10, 1978, p. 25430.

28. *Congressional Record*, August 10, 1978, p. 25426.

29. See Oppenheimer, "The Oil Pricing Issue," pp. 213–19; Yager, "Energy Battles of 1979."

30. Anne Pelham, "Ways and Means Votes Tougher Windfall Tax on Profits of Oil Companies," *Congressional Quarterly Weekly Report* 37 (June 16, 1979): 1139–42.

31. Anne Pelham, "House Ignores Proposal by Ways and Means Panel, Passes Weaker 'Windfall' Tax," *Congressional Quarterly Weekly Report* 37 (June 30, 1979): 1283–85.

32. Dale Tate, "Reagan Calls for Tax Cuts; Senate Democrats Respond," *Congressional Quarterly Weekly Report* 38 (June 28, 1980): 1779–80; Dale Tate, "Carter, Congress Begin Talks on Tax Cut," *Congressional Quarterly Weekly Report* 38 (July 5, 1980): 1905; Irwin B. Arieff, "GOP's Detroit Convention Marked the Coronation of Supply Side Economics," *Congressional Quarterly Weekly Report* 38 (July 19,

1980): 2002–3; Dale Tate, "Tax Cut Hearings Reveal Sharp Democratic Split," *Congressional Quarterly Weekly Report* 38 (July 26, 1980): 2077; Dale Tate, "Political Campaigns Draw Battle Lines Over Tax Cuts," *Congressional Quarterly Weekly Report* 38 (August 2, 1980): 2155–58; Dale Tate, "Senate Finance Pushes $39 Billion Tax Cut," *Congressional Quarterly Weekly Report* 38 (August 23, 1980): 2443–44; Dale Tate and Harrison Donnelly, "GOP Taunts Democrats Over Pre-election Votes on Budget, Tax Issues," *Congressional Quarterly Weekly Report* 38 (September 20, 1980): 2753–54; Dale Tate and Harrison Donnelly, "GOP Forces Budget, Tax Votes," *Congressional Quarterly Weekly Report* 38 (September 27, 1980): 2811–12.

33. Tate, "Carter, Congress Begin Talks on Tax Cut," p. 1905.

34. The account of congressional action on the 1981 tax reduction bill is based on interviews with Ways and Means members; Witte, *Politics of the Federal Income Tax*, chap. 11; Richard Cohen, "A Reagan Victory on His Tax Package Could be a Costly One Politically," *National Journal* 13 (June 13, 1981): 1058–62; Dale Tate, "Reagan Tax Cut Meets Skeptical Hill Reception," *Congressional Quarterly Weekly Report* 39 (February 21, 1981): 336–37; Dale Tate, "Tax Cut Compromise Barred as Committee Markups Near," *Congressional Quarterly Weekly Report* 39 (April 18, 1981): 670–71; Dale Tate, "Tax Cut Agreement Proves Elusive," *Congressional Quarterly Weekly Report* 39 (May 30, 1981): 937; Dale Tate, "Reagan and Rostenkowski Modify Tax Cut Proposals to Woo Conservative Votes," *Congressional Quarterly Weekly Report* 39 (June 6, 1981): 979–80; Pamela Fessler, "Positions Harden as Panels Kick Off Tax Cut Markups," *Congressional Quarterly Weekly Report* 39 (June 13, 1981): 1027–28; Pamela Fessler, "House Panel Backs Business Tax Alternative," *Congressional Quarterly Weekly Report* 39 (June 20, 1981): 1088–1089; Pamela Fessler, "Finance Committee Clears President's Tax Cut Plan; House Panel Sets Timetable," *Congressional Quarterly Weekly Report* 39 (June 27, 1981): 1130–31; Bill Keller, "Democrats and Republicans Try to Outbid Each Other in Cutting Taxes for Business," *Congressional Quarterly Weekly Report* 39 (June 27, 1981): 1132–37; Pamela Fessler, "Senate Backs Indexing; House Bill Gels," *Congressional Quarterly Weekly Report* 39 (July 18, 1981): 1306–7; Pamela Fessler, "House Floor Battle Looming on Tax Cut," *Congressional Quarterly Weekly Report* 39 (July 25, 1981): 1323–26; Pamela Fessler, "Tax Cut Passed by Solid Margins in House, Senate," *Congressional Quarterly Weekly Report* 39 (August 1, 1981): 1371, 1374–76.

35. Committee on Ways and Means, *Hearings on Tax Aspects of the President's Economic Program*, p. 17.

36. Ibid., p. 4.

37. On the history and politics of the issue of indexing the federal income tax system for inflation, see Weaver, *Automatic Government*, chap. 9.

38. Smith, "Budget Battles of 1981," pp. 68–69.

39. Fessler, "House Battle Looming," p. 1323.

40. Joint Committee on Taxation, *Comparative Summary of H.R. 4242*.

41. Committee on Ways and Means, *Report on H.R. 4242, The Tax Incentive Act of 1981*, pp. 608–10.

42. See Witte, *Politics of the Federal Income Tax*, pp. 209–27.

43. Pelham, "Ways and Means Votes Tougher Windfall Tax"; Anne Pelham, "Senate Committee Passes Weakened Version of Oil Windfall Profits Tax," *Congressional Quarterly Weekly Report* 37 (October 27, 1979): 2414–17.

44. Rudder, "Tax Policy," p. 206.

45. *Congressional Record*, July 29, 1981, p. 18085.

46. Fessler, "House Battle Looming," p. 1324. See also Conable, *Congress and the Income Tax*, pp. 53–62.

47. Pamela Fessler, "$86 Billion Reagan Tax Proposal Outlined," *Congressional Quarterly Weekly Report* 40 (January 30, 1982): 149.

48. On the effects of the budget process on House-Senate relations, see Ellwood, "Budget Reforms and Interchamber Relations."

49. Dale Tate, "Budget Battle Erupts on Hill as Compromise Talks Fizzle," *Congressional Quarterly Weekly Report* 40 (May 1, 1982): 967–69. On the "Gang of 17" and the politics of budget negotiations in 1982, see also Light, *Artful Work*, pp. 140–51.

50. Dale Tate, "Senate Republicans, Reagan Press a New Budget Package," *Congressional Quarterly Weekly Report* 40 (May 5, 1982): 1037–40; Dale Tate, "GOP version of 1983 Budget Narrowly Approved by House, *Congressional Quarterly Weekly Report* 40 (June 12, 1982): 1387–88.

51. The requirement of withholding of taxes on interest and dividends was later repealed.

52. Rudder, "Fiscal Responsibility," pp. 216–217; Pamela Fessler, "Divided Finance Committee Approves Tax-Increase Plan," *Congressional Quarterly Weekly Report* 40 (July 3, 1982): 1575–76.

53. Pamela Fessler, "House Sends Tax Bill Directly to Conference," *Congressional Quarterly Weekly Report* 40 (July 31, 1982): 1808.

54. Personal interview with the author, March 8, 1989.

55. For a lively but oversimplified account of the Ways and Means decision that characterizes the outcome as influenced by committee members' concerns about raising taxes on clientele groups who had contributed campaign funds to congressional Democrats, see Drew, *Politics and Money*, pp. 43–45.

56. *Congressional Record* (Daily ed.), July 28, 1982, p. H4777.

57. Ibid., p. H4780. For Conable's account of the politics of the 1982 bill, see *Congress and the Income Tax*, pp. 62–66.

58. Dale Tate, "Congress Rebuffs President, Clears '84 Budget Resolution," *Congressional Quarterly Weekly Report* 41 (June 25, 1983): 1269–74.

59. Dale Tate, "Attack on Deficit Flounders as Congress Confronts Taxes," *Congressional Quarterly Weekly Report* 41 (October 22, 1983): 2159–61.

60. Committee on Ways and Means, *Report on the Tax Reform Act of 1983*, p. 484.

61. Dale Tate, "Tax Chairmen Offer New Plans as Deficit Cut Efforts Languish," *Congressional Quarterly Weekly Report* 41 (October 29, 1983): 2271–72; Dale Tate, "Deficit Reduction Moves Fail as Torn Congress Shies Away From Tax, Spending Mandate," *Congressional Quarterly Weekly Report* 41 (November 19, 1983): 2406–9.

62. Pamela Fessler, "Ways and Means, Finance Panels Fashion Deficit Reduction Bills," *Congressional Quarterly Weekly Report* 42 (March 3, 1984): 484–86; Rudder, "Fiscal Responsibility," pp. 218–19; Conable, *Congress and the Income Tax*, pp. 66–76.

63. Committee on Ways and Means, *Report on the Tax Reform Act of 1984*, p. 1829.

64. *Congressional Record* (Daily ed.), April 11, 1984, p. H2593.

Chapter 7

1. Joint Committee on Taxation, *Estimated Revenue Effects of the President's Tax Reform Proposal*, p. 15.

2. Verdier, "Tax Reform Act of 1986." See also "The President, Congress, and Tax Reform."

3. Aaron, "The Impossible Dream," p. 6.

4. Witte, *Politics of the Federal Income Tax*, pp. 385–86. Witte was hardly alone in this view. See, for example, Davies, *United States Taxes and Tax Policy*, chap. 14; King, "Tax Expenditures and Systematic Public Policy," pp. 29–30; and Conable, *Congress and the Income Tax*, p. xii.

5. The most important of the broader constituencies, according to Witte, has been the middle class. Witte argues that a major factor contributing to the tax reduction bias since World War II has been the goal of maintaining a stable tax burden on the middle class during periods of inflation. *Politics of the Federal Income Tax*, chaps. 4–12.

6. Ibid.

7. For an analysis of the enactment of tax reform that identifies some similar causal factors and offers a broader focus than the analysis of Ways and Means Committee politics in this chapter, see Conlan, Beam, and Wrightson, *Taxing Choices*.

8. On members' views of the effects of open markups, see also Rudder, "Committee Reform," pp. 124–26.

9. Birnbaum and Murray, *Showdown at Gucci Gulch*, pp. 148–51.

10. Concerning the consequences of closed sessions for tax bills prior to 1985, one Ways and Means member noted: "I think closed meetings were especially effective in developing the '83 and '84 tax bills, in removing exemptions, and [in] refusing to accept amendments that would have lost money for the Treasury."

11. Weaver, *Automatic Government*, chap. 2.

12. See Manley, *Politics of Finance*, pp. 220–33; Rudder, "Committee Reform," pp. 126–28, and "Policy Impact," pp. 81–86.

13. On the increased use of restrictive rules in the House during the 1980s, see Bach and Smith, *Managing Uncertainty in the House*, and Smith, *Call to Order*.

14. The two minor amendments, both of which were adopted, allowed exceptions in the bill for American Samoa, Guam, the Mariana Islands, and the Virgin Islands, and established a $100-a-year individual tax credit for contributions to congressional campaigns in the taxpayer's home state.

15. The four, all Democrats, were Sam Gibbons, D-Fla. (59 percent); Andy Jacobs, Jr., D-Ind. (59 percent); James R. Jones, D-Okla. (52 percent); Thomas J. Downey, D-N.Y. (54 percent). See Chapter 4, Tables 4–3 and 4–5.

16. Personal interview with the author, March 8, 1989.

17. Birnbaum and Murray, *Showdown at Gucci Gulch*, p. 108.

18. For a very similar account of the Airlie House meeting, see Birnbaum and Murray, *Showdown at Gucci Gulch*, p. 117.

19. Anne Swardson, "House Tax Bill About to Go On the Table," *Washington Post*, September 24, 1985, p. A3.

20. Birnbaum and Murray, *Showdown at Gucci Gulch*, pp. 113–16, 128–31.

21. See ibid., p. 134.

22. See ibid., pp. 146–47.

23. For a general discussion of the conditions under which politicians may seek to avoid blame for governmental actions or try to focus it on others, see Weaver, *Automatic Government*, chap. 2.

24. Birnbaum and Murray, *Showdown at Gucci Gulch*, pp. 124–27.

25. Ibid., p. 126.

26. Ibid., pp. 148–49.

27. Derthick and Quirk, *Politics of Deregulation*, p. 13.

28. Ibid., p. 146. For an examination of the importance in the tax reform case of expert consensus and the politics of ideas, as opposed to group or partisan factors emphasized in most studies of American public policymaking, see Conlan, Beam, and Wrightson, *Taxing Choices*.

29. Derthick and Quirk, *Politics of Deregulation*, p. 247.

30. For a brief summary of economists' views of the tax code as it existed in 1985, see Aaron and Galper, *Assessing Tax Reform*, pp. 2–6. On compliance problems, see Roscoe L. Egger, Jr., "Without Real Reform Our Tax System Could Collapse," *Washington Post*, February 10, 1985, pp. D1, D4.

31. On the similarity of tax reform and deregulation as issues on which liberal and conservative views had converged, see the comments by economist Joseph Pechman in Conable and Pechman, "Tax Philosophy," p. 3.

32. Verdier, "Tax Reform Act of 1986," p. 8; see also Birnbaum and Murray, *Showdown at Gucci Gulch*, pp. xv, 23–31.

33. Reagan, "Tax Reform: Address to the Nation," p. 707.

34. It is the relative lack of intensity of public support for policy change that distinguishes the politics of tax reform from the otherwise similar pattern of "policy escalation" that Charles O. Jones has identified in environmental policymaking in the early 1970s. See his *Clean Air*, chap. 7. On public opinion on the issue of tax reform during this period, see Everett Ladd, "Tax Attitudes," *Public Opinion* 8 (February/March 1985): 8–10, "Tax Americana," *Public Opinion* 8 (February/March 1985): 19–29, and "Reaction to the Reagan Administration's Tax Plan," *Public Opinion* 8 (August/September 1985): 29–32.

35. Birnbaum and Murray, *Showdown at Gucci Gulch*, pp. 108–10.

36. Derthick and Quirk, *Politics of Deregulation*, p. 17.

37. On the divergence of business interests in tax reform and the divided lobbying efforts this produced, see Birnbaum and Murray, *Showdown at Gucci Gulch*, pp. 80–81, 161; Pamela Fessler and Steven Pressman, "Tax Overhaul: The Crucial Lobby Fight of 1985," *Congressional Quarterly Weekly Report* 43 (March 9, 1985): 192–95; "Companies Upset by Tax Bill," *New York Times*, November 20, 1985, pp. 29, 55. On the interests of different economic sectors in relation to tax reform, see also Martin, "Business Influence and State Power."

38. Derthick and Quirk, *Politics of Deregulation*, p. 104.

39. Ibid., pp. 102–5.

40. See, for example, the front-page *Washington Post* article that appeared shortly after tax reform passed the House in December. Dale Russakoff, "Tax Vote Overhauls Rostenkowski's Image," *Washington Post*, December 19, 1985, p. A1.

41. Birnbaum and Murray, *Showdown at Gucci Gulch*, p. 107.

42. Committee on Ways and Means, "Speech of Rep. Dan Rostenkowski to Economic Club of New York,"p. 3.

43. On the conditions under which blame avoidance is likely to take prece-

dence over credit claiming for elected officials, see Weaver, *Automatic Government*, chap. 2.

44. Personal interview with the author, March 8, 1989.

45. Margaret Shapiro and Edward Walsh, "Democrats Say Tax Revision Faces Difficulty," *Washington Post*, December 7, 1985, pp. A1, A6.

46. See Birnbaum and Murray, *Showdown at Gucci Gulch*, pp. 121–51.

47. Among the works that have presented empirical evidence on the importance of goals other than reelection for understanding congressional politics, see especially Fenno, *Congressmen in Committees* and *Home Style*; Arnold, *Congress and the Bureaucracy* and "Local Roots of Domestic Policy"; Smith and Deering, *Committees in Congress*; Derthick and Quirk, *Politics of Deregulation*; Hall, "Participation and Purpose in Committee Decision Making"; and Weaver, *Automatic Government*.

48. On the relation of issue contexts to the importance of different goals, see Arnold, "Local Roots of Domestic Policy," and Weaver, *Automatic Government*, pp. 29–34.

49. Personal interview with the author, March 9, 1989.

50. Weaver, *Automatic Government*, pp. 26–27, 218–20.

51. Some might argue that the expansion of the system of tax preferences during this period is clear evidence of increased clientelism in tax decisionmaking. The sum of revenue losses from special tax provisions or "tax expenditures" expanded from $91.8 billion in fiscal year 1976 to $430.5 billion in fiscal year 1987 (see Office of Management and Budget, *Special Analyses* for FY 1976 and FY 1987 budgets), but as Witte argued based on extensive analysis of the tax expenditure system, it is an oversimplification to equate tax expenditures with clientele benefits. In any case, Witte concluded that "the evidence for the proposition that tax expenditures have proliferated in recent years is mixed." *Politics of the Federal Income Tax*, p. 290. The rate at which changes have been made to enlarge tax expenditure provisions has accelerated since 1970, but only one of the "big ticket" provisions that accounted for 79 percent of the 1982 total was enacted after 1975. That provision (safe harbor leasing) was initiated by the Reagan administration in 1981 but sharply curtailed after 1982. Ibid., chap. 13. For a second analysis that concludes that narrow clientele pressures have been of limited importance for the expansion of the tax expenditure system, see King, "Tax Expenditures and Systematic Public Policy."

52. For evidence that presidential proposals have tended to define the scope of congressional deliberations on taxes and spending, see Peterson, "The New Politics of Deficits."

Chapter 8

1. Although Mayhew's initial assumption about congressional politics is that members should be viewed as single-minded reelection seekers, he later introduces the prestige goal into the model in order to explain the politics of the prereform House (see the discussion of selective incentives above in Chapter 4). Mayhew, *Congress: The Electoral Connection*, pp. 141–58. Therefore, to speak precisely, the Mayhew model assumes that members are motivated by reelection and (for some at least) prestige.

2. Existing works that would provide the starting point for a more comprehen-

sive account of Ways and Means Committee politics and policymaking over the postreform period include: Derthick, *Policymaking for Social Security*; Light, *Artful Work*; Weaver, "Controlling Entitlements" and *Automatic Government*; Pastor, *Politics of U.S. Foreign Economic Policy* and "Congress and Trade Policy"; Bowler, "Politics of Federal Health Insurance Programs."

3. These are the distinctions members and staff made when asked to compare tax policy to other areas in the committee's jurisdiction.

4. Partisan votes are those in which a majority of one party opposes a majority of the other party. The index of partisanship is the mean for all recorded votes in each issue area. On individual votes, the index of partisanship is calculated by subtracting the percentage of one party voting yes from the percentage of the other party voting yes. See Fenno, *Congressmen in Committees*, p. 207, n. 18.

5. Moreover, if anything, the level of clientele activity was increasing during the 1975–86 period. See Edsall, *New Politics of Inequality*, chap. 3, and Conable, *Congress and the Income Tax*, p. 121.

6. Arnold, *Congress and the Bureaucracy*, p. 15.

7. To argue that a more complex conceptualization of members' goals is needed to understand the politics and outcomes in the Ways and Means case is not to deny that the reelection goal is probably primary in an abstract sense for most members. Just as most individuals' concerns tend to narrow to self-preservation when faced with a life-threatening situation, most members of Congress probably do tend to place first priority on electoral survival when it is thought to be directly at risk. But even if few members appear to feel totally secure about their prospects for reelection, it seems only reasonable to assume also that few, with the possible exception of a relatively small group of new members from highly competitive districts, are likely to view their political survival as being at stake on *all* issues, *all* the time. Most members probably feel free much of the time to pursue interests other than reelection. For similar views of the hierarchy of members' goals, see Fenno, *Home Style*, chaps. 6 and 7; and Derthick and Quirk, *Politics of Deregulation*, chap. 4. See also Fiorina's discussion of "reelection maintainers" in *Representatives, Roll Calls, and Constituencies*.

8. Fenno, *Congressmen in Committees*, p. 33.

9. Davidson, "Committees as Moving Targets" and "New Centralization."

10. David E. Price has identified salience and conflict across issues as incentives and disincentives for policy activism by committee members. *Policymaking in Congressional Committees*. Smith and Deering have developed a more complex framework for analyzing committee environments. Proposing that each committee's environment may be conceptualized as consisting of three components—a public environment, an interbranch environment, and a congressional environment—they have shown that each component of a committee's environment may vary in terms of fragmentation, salience, and conflict. *Committees in Congress*, chap. 3. For a thorough treatment of the complexities involved in conceptualizing committee environments, see Smith, "Central Concepts."

11. On the long-term effects on congressional structure and politics of major shifts in the fiscal context, see Wander, "Patterns of Change in the Congressional Budget Process."

12. See Rudder, "Tax Policy," p. 203.

13. On this point see Malbin, *Unelected Representatives*.

14. See Rudder, "Tax Policy," pp. 202–3.

15. Smith and Deering, *Committees in Congress*, p. 152. See also Bessette, "Is Congress a Deliberative Body?" p. 11, and Conable, *Congress and the Income Tax*, pp. 30–32.

16. See Beer, "In Search of a New Public Philosophy."

17. On the potential for increased party control over House deliberations in the aftermath of the reforms, see Jones, "House Leadership," and Ornstein and Rohde, "Political Parties and Congressional Reform."

18. Conlon, "Response," p. 245.

19. On the roles of the Democratic caucus and other party units in the 1980s, see Smith, "Decisionmaking in Congress," pp. 225–28, 232.

20. On the tensions between decentralized, collegial, and centralized forms of decisionmaking that developed in the House during the 1980s, see Smith, *Call to Order*.

21. On the undesirable effects of ad hoc policymaking on tax policy, see Rudder, "Tax Policy" and "Fiscal Responsibility."

Bibliography

Government Documents

Administration of Ronald Reagan. "Tax Reform: Address to the Nation." *Weekly Compilation of Presidential Documents* 21 (June 3, 1985): 703–7.

Office of Management and Budget. *Budget of the United States Government, Fiscal Year 1976, Special Analyses*. Washington: Government Printing Office, 1975.

_____. *Budget of the United States Government, Fiscal Year 1987, Special Analyses*. Washington: Government Printing Office, 1986.

_____. *Budget of the United States Government, Fiscal Year 1990*. Washington: Government Printing Office, 1989.

U.S. Congress. *Congressional Directory*. 86th–99th Congresses. Washington: Government Printing Office, 1959–86.

_____. *Congressional Record*. Washington: Government Printing Office, 1974–86.

U.S. Congress. House. Committee on Ways and Means. *The Committee on Ways and Means: A Bicentennial History, 1789–1989*. Washington: Government Printing Office, 1989.

_____. *Hearings on Tax Aspects of the President's Economic Program*. 97th Cong., 1st sess. Washington: Government Printing Office, February 24, 25, March 3–5, 1981.

_____. *Ninety-Second Congress Legislative Record of the Committee on Ways and Means*. 92d Cong., 2d sess. Washington: Government Printing Office, January 2, 1973.

_____. *Ninety-Third Congress Legislative Record of the Committee on Ways and Means*. 93d Cong., 2d sess. Washington: Government Printing Office, January 2, 1975.

_____. *Report on H.R. 4242, The Tax Incentive Act of 1981*. 97th Cong., 1st sess. Washington: Government Printing Office, July 24, 1981.

_____. *Report on the Tax Reform Act of 1983*. 98th Cong., 1st sess. Washington: Government Printing Office, October 21, 1983.

_____. *Report on the Tax Reform Act of 1984*. 98th Cong., 2d sess. Washington: Government Printing Office, March 5, 1984.

_____. "Speech of Rep. Dan Rostenkowski to Economic Club of New York." Press Release, February 25, 1985.

U.S. Congress. Joint Committee on Taxation. *Comparative Summary of H.R. 4242*. 97th Cong., 1st sess. Washington: Government Printing Office, July 27, 1981.

_____. *Estimated Revenue Effects of the President's Tax Reform Proposal*. 99th Cong., 1st sess. Washington: Government Printing Office, July 26, 1985.

————. *General Explanation of the Tax Reform Act of 1986.* 99th Cong., 2d sess. Washington: Government Printing Office, May 4, 1987.

————. *Summary of H.R. 3838, Tax Reform Act of 1985, as Reported by the Committee on Ways and Means on December 7, 1985.* 99th Cong., 1st sess. Washington: Government Printing Office, December 9, 1985.

————. *Summary of H.R. 3838, Tax Reform Act of 1986, as Reported by the Senate Committee on Finance.* 99th Cong., 2d sess. Washington: Government Printing Office, June 5, 1986.

U.S. Congress. Senate. Committee on the Budget. *The Congressional Budget Process: An Explanation.* 100th Cong., 2d sess. Washington: Government Printing Office, March 1988.

Newspapers and Periodicals

Congressional Quarterly Almanac, 1959–86
Congressional Quarterly Weekly Report
National Journal
New York Times
Wall Street Journal
Washington Post

Books, Articles, and Unpublished Papers

Aaron, Henry J. "The Impossible Dream Comes True: The New Tax Reform Act." *Brookings Review* (Winter 1987): 3–10.

Aaron, Henry J., and Harvey Galper. *Assessing Tax Reform.* Washington: Brookings Institution, 1985.

Alexander, De Alva S. *History and Procedure of the House of Representatives.* Boston: Houghton Mifflin, 1916.

Almond, Gabriel, and Sidney Verba. *The Civic Culture.* Princeton: Princeton University Press, 1963.

Arnold, R. Douglas. *Congress and the Bureaucracy.* New Haven: Yale University Press, 1979.

————. "The Local Roots of Domestic Policy." In *The New Congress,* edited by Thomas E. Mann and Norman J. Ornstein. Washington: American Enterprise Institute, 1981.

Asher, Herbert B. "Committees and the Norm of Specialization." *Annals of the American Academy of Political and Social Science* 411 (1974): 63–74.

Bach, Stanley, and Steven S. Smith. *Managing Uncertainty in the House of Representatives.* Washington: Brookings Institution, 1988.

Barone, Michael, and Grant Ujifusa. *The Almanac of American Politics,* 1986. Washington: National Journal, 1985.

Beer, Samuel H. "In Search of a New Public Philosophy." In *The New American Political System,* edited by Anthony King. Washington: American Enterprise Institute, 1978.

Bessette, Joseph M. "Deliberative Democracy: The Majority Principle in Republican Government." In *How Democratic is the Constitution?,* edited by Robert A.

Goldwin and William A. Schambra. Washington: American Enterprise Institute, 1980.

_____. "Is Congress a Deliberative Body?" In *The United States Congress: Proceedings of the Thomas P. O'Neill, Jr., Symposium on the U.S. Congress. January 30–31, 1981*, edited by Dennis Hale. Chestnut Hill, Mass.: Boston College, 1982.

Birnbaum, Jeffrey H., and Alan S. Murray. *Showdown at Gucci Gulch*. New York: Random House, 1987.

Bolling, Richard. *House Out of Order*. New York: Dutton, 1965.

_____. *Power in the House*. New York: Dutton, 1968.

Bowler, M. Kenneth. "Changing Politics of Federal Health Insurance Programs." *PS* 20 (1987): 202–11.

_____. "The New Committee on Ways and Means: Policy Implications of Recent Changes in the House Committee." Paper presented at the annual meeting of the American Political Science Association, 1976.

_____. "Preparing Members of Congress to Make Binary Decisions on Complex Policy Issues: The 1986 Tax Reform Bill." *Journal of Policy Analysis and Management* 8 (1989): 35–45.

Bowler, M. Kenneth, Robert T. Kudrle, Theodore R. Marmor, and Amy Bridges. "The Political Economy of National Health Insurance." *Journal of Health Politics, Policy and Law* 2 (1977): 100–133.

Brady, David W. *Congressional Voting in a Partisan Era*. Lawrence: University Press of Kansas, 1973.

Brown, George R. *The Leadership of Congress*. Indianapolis: Bobbs-Merrill, 1922.

Ceaser, James W. "Direct Participation in Politics." *Proceedings of the Academy of Political Science* 34 (1981): 121–37.

Clapp, Charles L. *The Congressman: His Work as He Sees It*. Washington: Brookings Institution, 1963.

Clausen, Aage. *How Congressmen Decide: A Policy Focus*. New York: St. Martin's Press, 1973.

Conable, Barber B., Jr. "Aspects of Legislative Persuasion: Congress." *National Tax Journal* 32 (1979): 307–11.

_____. *Congress and the Income Tax*. Norman: University of Oklahoma Press, 1989.

Conable, Barber B., Jr., and Joseph Pechman. "Tax Philosophy: An Interview with Barber Conable and Joseph Pechman." *Public Opinion* 8 (February/March 1985): 2–7.

Conlan, Timothy J., David R. Beam, and Margaret T. Wrightson. *Taxing Choices: The Politics of Tax Reform*. Washington: CQ Press, 1989.

Conlon, Richard P. "Response by Richard P. Conlon." In *The United States Congress: Proceedings of the Thomas P. O'Neill, Jr., Symposium on the U.S. Congress. January 30–31, 1981*, edited by Dennis Hale. Chestnut Hill, Mass.: Boston College, 1982.

Cooper, Joseph. "Congress in Organizational Perspective." In *Congress Reconsidered*, edited by Lawrence C. Dodd and Bruce I. Oppenheimer. New York: Praeger, 1977.

_____. "Organization and Innovation in the House of Representatives." In *The House at Work*, edited by Joseph Cooper and G. Calvin Mackenzie. Austin: University of Texas Press, 1981.

———. "Strengthening the Congress: An Organizational Analysis." *Harvard Journal on Legislation* 12 (1979): 307–67.

Cooper, Joseph, and David W. Brady. "Institutional Context and Leadership Style: The House from Cannon to Rayburn." *American Political Science Review* 75 (1981): 411–25.

———. "Toward a Diachronic Analysis of Congress." *American Political Science Review* 75 (1981): 988–1006.

Crook, Sara Brandes, and John R. Hibbing. "Congressional Reform and Party Discipline: The Effects of Changes in the Seniority System on Party Loyalty in the U.S. House of Representatives." *British Journal of Political Science* 15 (1985): 207–26.

Davidson, Roger H. "Breaking Up Those 'Cozy Triangles': An Impossible Dream?" In *Legislative Reform and Public Policy*, edited by Susan Welch and John G. Peters. New York: Praeger, 1977.

———. "Committees as Moving Targets." *Legislative Studies Quarterly* 11 (1986): 19–33.

———. "The New Centralization on Capitol Hill." *Review of Politics* 50 (1988): 345–64.

———. "Representation and Congressional Committees." *Annals of the American Academy of Political and Social Science* 411 (1974): 48–62.

———. "Two Avenues of Change: House and Senate Committee Reorganization." In *Congress Reconsidered*, 2d ed., edited by Lawrence C. Dodd and Bruce I. Oppenheimer. Washington: CQ Press, 1981.

Davidson, Roger H., and Walter J. Oleszek. "Adaptation and Consolidation: Structural Innovation in the U.S. House of Representatives." *Legislative Studies Quarterly* 1 (1976): 37–65.

———. *Congress Against Itself.* Bloomington: Indiana University Press, 1977.

———. *Congress and Its Members.* Washington: CQ Press, 1981.

Davidson, Roger, David M. Kovenock, and Michael K. O'Leary. *Congress in Crisis.* Belmont, Calif.: Wadsworth, 1966.

Davies, David G. *United States Taxes and Tax Policy.* Cambridge: Cambridge University Press, 1986.

Davis, Eric L. "Congressional Liaison: The People and the Institutions." In *Both Ends of the Avenue*, edited by Anthony King. Washington: American Enterprise Institute, 1983.

Derthick, Martha. *Policymaking for Social Security.* Washington: Brookings Institution, 1979.

Derthick, Martha, and Paul J. Quirk. *The Politics of Deregulation.* Washington: Brookings Institution, 1985.

Dodd, Lawrence C. "Woodrow Wilson's *Congressional Government* and the Modern Congress: The 'Universal Principle' of Change." *Congress and the Presidency* 14 (1987): 33–49.

Dodd, Lawrence C., and Bruce I. Oppenheimer. "The House in Transition: Change and Consolidation." In *Congress Reconsidered*, 2d ed., edited by Lawrence C. Dodd and Bruce I. Oppenheimer. Washington: CQ Press, 1981.

Drew, Elizabeth. *Politics and Money.* New York: Macmillan, 1983.

Edsall, Thomas Byrne. *The New Politics of Inequality.* New York: Norton, 1984.

Ellwood, John W. "Budget Reforms and Interchamber Relations." In *Congressional Budgeting*, edited by W. Thomas Wander, F. Ted Hebert, and Gary W. Copeland. Baltimore: Johns Hopkins University Press, 1984.

———. "The Great Exception: The Congressional Budget Process in an Age of Decentralization." In *Congress Reconsidered*, 3d ed., edited by Lawrence C. Dodd and Bruce I. Oppenheimer. Washington: CQ Press, 1985.

———. "The Politics of the Enactment and Implementation of Gramm-Rudman-Hollings: Why Congress Cannot Address the Deficit Dilemma." *Harvard Journal on Legislation* 25 (1988): 553–75.

Ellwood, John W., and James A. Thurber. "The Politics of the Congressional Budget Process Re-examined." In *Congress Reconsidered*, 2d ed., edited by Lawrence C. Dodd and Bruce I. Oppenheimer. Washington: CQ Press, 1981.

Eulau, Heinz, and Vera McCluggage. "Standing Committees in Legislatures: Three Decades of Research." *Legislative Studies Quarterly* 9 (1984): 195–270.

Fenno, Richard F., Jr. *Congressmen in Committees*. Boston: Little, Brown, 1973.

———. *Home Style*. Boston: Little, Brown, 1978.

———. "The Internal Distribution of Influence: The House." In *The Congress and America's Future*, edited by David B. Truman. Englewood Cliffs, N.J.: Prentice-Hall, 1965.

———. *The Power of the Purse*. Boston: Little, Brown, 1966.

Ferejohn, John A., and Morris P. Fiorina. "Purposive Models of Legislative Behavior." *American Economic Review* 65 (1975): 407–16.

Fiorina, Morris P. *Representatives, Roll Calls, and Constituencies*. Lexington, Mass.: Lexington Books, 1974.

Fleming, James S. "Re-establishing Leadership in the House of Representatives: The Case of Oscar W. Underwood." *Mid-America: An Historical Review* 54 (1972): 234–50.

Froman, Lewis A. "Organization Theory and the Explanation of Important Characteristics of Congress." *American Political Science Review* 62 (1968): 518–27.

Furlong, Patrick J. "The Origins of the House Committee on Ways and Means." *William and Mary Quarterly* 25 (1968): 587–604.

Galloway, George B. *History of the House of Representatives*. New York: Thomas Y. Crowell, 1961.

Gilligan, Thomas W., and Keith Kreibel. "Complex Rules and Congressional Outcomes: An Event Study of Energy Tax Legislation." *Journal of Politics* 50 (1988): 624–54.

Goodwin, George, Jr. *The Little Legislatures*. Amherst: University of Massachusetts Press, 1970.

Greenstein, Fred I. "Change and Continuity in the Modern Presidency." In *The New American Political System*, edited by Anthony King. Washington: American Enterprise Institute, 1978.

———. *Personality and Politics*. Chicago: Markham, 1969.

———. "Personality and Politics." In *Handbook of Political Science*, Vol. 2, edited by Fred I. Greenstein and Nelson W. Polsby. Reading, Mass.: Addison-Wesley, 1975.

Hall, Richard L. "Participation and Purpose in Committee Decision Making." *American Political Science Review* 81 (1987): 105–27.

Hamilton, Alexander, James Madison, and John Jay. *The Federalist*. Edited by Clinton Rossiter. New York: New American Library, 1961.

Hansen, Susan B. *The Politics of Taxation*. New York: Praeger, 1983.

Hasbrouck, Paul D. *Party Government in the House of Representatives*. New York: Macmillan, 1927.

Havemann, Joel. *Congress and the Budget*. Bloomington: Indiana University Press, 1978.

―――. "The Congressional Budget Process and Tax Legislation." In *The Congressional Budget Process After Five Years*, edited by Rudolph G. Penner. Washington: American Enterprise Institute, 1981.

Hess, Stephen. *Organizing the Presidency*. Washington: Brookings Institution, 1976.

Hinckley, Barbara. "Policy Content, Committee Membership, and Behavior." *American Journal of Political Science* 19 (1975): 543–57.

―――. *Stability and Change in Congress*. 4th ed. New York: Harper and Row, 1988.

Huitt, Ralph K. "Congressional Organization in the Field of Money and Credit." In *Fiscal and Debt Management Policies*. Englewood Cliffs, N.J.: Prentice-Hall, 1963.

Huitt, Ralph K., and Robert L. Peabody, eds. *Congress: Two Decades of Analysis*. New York: Harper and Row, 1969.

Huntington, Samuel P. *American Politics: The Promise of Disharmony*. Cambridge, Mass.: Belknap Press, 1981.

Ippolito, Dennis S. *Congressional Spending*. Ithaca: Cornell University Press, 1981.

Jacobson, Gary C. *The Politics of Congressional Elections*. Boston: Little, Brown, 1983.

Jewell, Malcolm E., and Chu Chi-Hung. "Membership Movement and Committee Attractiveness in the U.S. House of Representatives, 1963–1971." *American Journal of Political Science* 18 (1974): 433–41.

Jewell, Malcolm E., and Samuel C. Patterson. *The Legislative Process in the United States*. 3d ed. New York: Random House, 1977.

Jones, Charles O. *Clean Air: The Policies and Politics of Pollution Control*. Pittsburgh: University of Pittsburgh Press, 1975.

―――. "Congress and the Making of Energy Policy." In *New Dimensions to Energy Policy*, edited by Robert Lawrence. Lexington, Mass.: Lexington Books, 1979.

―――. "House Leadership in an Age of Reform." In *Understanding Congressional Leadership*, edited by Frank H. Mackaman. Washington: CQ Press, 1981.

―――. "How Reform Changes Congress." In *Legislative Reform and Public Policy*, edited by Susan Welch and John G. Peters. New York: Praeger, 1977.

―――. "Joseph G. Cannon and Howard W. Smith: An Essay on the Limits of Leadership in the House of Representatives." *Journal of Politics* 30 (1968): 617–46.

―――. *The Minority Party in Congress*. Boston: Little, Brown, 1970.

―――. "Representation in Congress: The Case of the House Agriculture Committee." *American Political Science Review* 55 (1961): 358–67.

―――. *The United States Congress: People, Place, and Policy*. Homewood, Ill.: Dorsey Press, 1982.

Kantowicz, Edward R. "The Limits of Incrementalism: Carter's Efforts at Tax

Reform." *Journal of Policy Analysis and Management* 4 (1985): 217–33.

King, Ronald F. "Tax Expenditures and Systematic Public Policy: An Essay on the Political Economy of the Federal Revenue Code." *Public Budgeting and Finance* (Spring 1984): 14–31.

Kofmehl, Kenneth. "The Institutionalization of a Voting Block." *Western Political Quarterly* 17 (1964): 256–72.

LeLoup, Lance T. *The Fiscal Congress*. Westport, Conn.: Greenwood Press, 1980.

Light, Paul. *Artful Work: The Politics of Social Security Reform*. New York: Random House, 1985.

Lipset, Seymour Martin, and William Schneider. *The Confidence Gap: Business, Labor and Government in the Public Mind*. New York: Free Press, 1983.

Loomis, Burdett A. "The 'Me Decade' and the Changing Context of House Leadership." In *Understanding House Leadership*, edited by Frank A. Mackaman. Washington: CQ Press, 1981.

Lowenberg, Gerhard. "The Role of Parliaments in Western Democracies." In *Modern Parliaments*, edited by Gerhard Lowenberg. Chicago: Aldine Atherton, 1971.

Lowi, Theodore J. "American Business, Public Policy, Case Studies and Political Theory." *World Politics* 16 (1964): 677–715.

———. "Representation and Decision." In *Legislative Politics U.S.A.*, edited by Theodore Lowi. Boston: Little, Brown, 1964.

Maass, Arthur. *Congress and the Common Good*. New York: Basic Books, 1983.

McCubbins, Matthew D., and Terry Sullivan, eds. *Congress: Structure and Policy*. Cambridge: Cambridge University Press, 1987.

MacFarland, Andrew S. *Common Cause*. Chatham, N.J.: Chatham House, 1984.

Malbin, Michael J. "Factions and Incentives in Congress." *The Public Interest* 86 (Winter 1987): 91–108.

———. *Unelected Representatives: Congressional Staff and the Future of Representative Government*. New York: Basic Books, 1980.

Manley, John F. *The Politics of Finance*. Boston: Little, Brown, 1970.

———. "Wilbur D. Mills: A Study in Congressional Influence." *American Political Science Review* 63 (1969): 442–64.

Mann, Thomas E., and Raymond E. Wolfinger. "Candidates and Parties in Congressional Elections." *American Political Science Review* 74 (1980): 617–32.

March, James G., and Johan P. Olsen. "The New Institutionalism: Organizational Factors in Political Life." *American Political Science Review* 78 (1984): 734–89.

———. "Popular Sovereignty and the Search for Appropriate Institutions." *Journal of Public Policy* 6 (1986): 342–70.

Martin, Cathie Jo. "Business Influence and State Power: The Case of U.S. Corporate Tax Policy." *Politics and Society* 17 (1989): 189–223.

Masters, Nicholas A. "Committee Assignments in the House of Representatives." *American Political Science Review* 55 (1961): 345–57.

Mayhew, David R. *Congress: The Electoral Connection*. New Haven: Yale University Press, 1974.

Mikva, Abner J., and Patti B. Saris. *The American Congress: The First Branch*. New York: Franklin Watts, 1974.

Morrison, Edward F. "Energy Tax Legislation: The Failure of the 93d Congress."

Harvard Journal on Legislation 12 (1975): 369–414.

Moynihan, Daniel Patrick. *The Politics of a Guaranteed Annual Income.* New York: Random House, 1973.

Nie, Norman H., Sidney Verba, and John R. Petrocik. *The Changing American Voter.* Cambridge: Harvard University Press, 1979.

Oppenheimer, Bruce I. "Policy Effects of U.S. House Reform: Decentralization and the Capacity to Resolve Energy Issues." *Legislative Studies Quarterly* 5 (1980): 5–30.

———. "Resolving the Oil Pricing Issue: A Key to National Energy Policy." In *American Politics and Public Policy*, edited by Allan P. Sindler. Washington: CQ Press, 1982.

Ornstein, Norman J. "Causes and Consequences of Congressional Change: Subcommittee Reforms in the House of Representatives, 1970–1973." In *Congress in Change*, edited by Norman J. Ornstein. New York: Praeger, 1975.

———. "The Open Congress Meets the President." In *Both Ends of the Avenue*, edited by Anthony King. Washington: American Enterprise Institute, 1983.

Ornstein, Norman J., and David W. Rohde. "Political Parties and Congressional Reform." In *Parties and Elections in an Anti-Party Age*, edited by Jeff Fishel. Bloomington: Indiana University Press, 1978.

Ornstein, Norman J., Thomas E. Mann, and Michael J. Malbin. *Vital Statistics on Congress, 1987–1988.* Washington: CQ Press, 1987.

Owens, John E. "Extreme Advocacy Leadership in the Pre-Reform House: Wright Patman and the House Banking and Currency Committee." *British Journal of Political Science* 15 (1985): 187–205.

Parker, Glenn R., and Suzanne L. Parker. *Factions in House Committees.* Knoxville: University of Tennessee Press, 1985.

Pastor, Robert A. *Congress and the Politics of U.S. Foreign Economic Policy, 1929–1976.* Berkeley: University of California Press, 1980.

———. "The Cry-and-Sigh Syndrome: Congress and Trade Policy." In *Making Economic Policy in Congress*, edited by Allen Schick. Washington: American Enterprise Institute, 1983.

Patterson, Samuel C. "On the Study of Legislative Reform." In *Legislative Reform and Public Policy*, edited by Susan Welch and John G. Peters. New York: Praeger, 1977.

———. "The Semi-Sovereign Congress." In *The New American Political System*, edited by Anthony King. Washington: American Enterprise Institute, 1978.

———. "Understanding Congress in the Long Run: A Comment on Joseph Cooper and David W. Brady, 'Toward a Diachronic Analysis of Congress.'" *American Political Science Review* 75 (1981): 1007–9.

Pechman, Joseph A. *Federal Tax Policy.* 5th ed. Washington: Brookings Institution, 1987.

Penner, Rudolph G., ed. *The Congressional Budget Process After Five Years.* Washington: American Enterprise Institute, 1981.

Penner, Rudolph G., and Alan J. Abramson. *Broken Purse Strings: Congressional Budgeting 1974 to 1988.* Washington: Urban Institute Press, 1988.

Peterson, Paul E. "The New Politics of Deficits." In *New Directions in American*

Politics, edited by John E. Chubb and Paul E. Peterson. Washington: Brookings Institution, 1985.

Polsby, Nelson W. "The Institutionalization of the U.S. House of Representatives." *American Political Science Review* 62 (1968): 144–68.

———. "Legislatures." In *The Handbook of Political Science*, Vol. 5, edited by Fred I. Greenstein and Nelson W. Polsby. Reading, Mass.: Addison-Wesley, 1975.

———. "Studying Congress Through Time: A Comment on Joseph Cooper and David W. Brady, 'Toward a Diachronic Analysis of Congress.'" *American Political Science Review* 75 (1981): 1010–12.

Price, David E. *Policymaking in Congressional Committees: The Impact of Environmental Factors*. Tucson: University of Arizona Press, 1979.

Ray, Bruce A. "Committee Attractiveness in the U.S. House, 1963–1981." *American Journal of Political Science* 26 (1982): 609–13.

Reese, Thomas J. *The Politics of Taxation*. Westport, Conn.: Quorum Books, 1980.

Reichley, A. James. *Conservatives in an Age of Change*. Washington: Brookings Institution, 1981.

Rice, Stuart A. *Quantitative Methods in Politics*. New York: Knopf, 1928.

Rieselbach, Leroy N. *Congressional Politics*. New York: McGraw Hill, 1973.

———. *Congressional Reform*. Washington: CQ Press, 1986.

Ripley, Randall B. *Majority Party Leadership in Congress*. Boston: Little, Brown, 1969.

———. *Party Leaders in the House of Representatives*. Washington: Brookings Institution, 1967.

Rohde, David W. "Committee Reform in the House of Representatives and the Subcommittee Bill of Rights." *Annals of the American Academy of Political and Social Science* 411 (1974): 39–47.

———. "Variations in Partisanship in the House of Representatives, 1953–1988: Southern Democrats, Realignment, and Agenda Change." Paper presented at the annual meeting of the American Political Science Association, Washington, D.C., 1988.

Rohde, David W., and Kenneth A. Shepsle. "Leaders and Followers in the House of Representatives: Reflections on Woodrow Wilson's *Congressional Government*." *Congress and the Presidency* 14 (1987): 111–33.

Rudder, Catherine E. "Committee Reform and the Revenue Process." In *Congress Reconsidered*, edited by Lawrence C. Dodd and Bruce I. Oppenheimer. New York: Praeger, 1977.

———. "Fiscal Responsibility and the Revenue Committees." In *Congress Reconsidered*, 3d ed., edited by Lawrence C. Dodd and Bruce I. Oppenheimer. Washington: CQ Press, 1985.

———. "The Policy Impact of Reform on the Committee on Ways and Means." In *Legislative Reform*, edited by Leroy N. Rieselbach. Lexington, Mass.: Lexington Books, 1978.

———. "Tax Policy: Structure and Choice." In *Making Economic Policy in Congress*, edited by Allen Schick. Washington: American Enterprise Institute, 1983.

Savage, James D. *Balanced Budgets and American Politics*. Ithaca: Cornell University Press, 1988.

Schick, Allen. *Congress and Money*. Washington: Urban Institute, 1980.

―――. "The Distributive Congress." In *Making Economic Policy in Congress*, edited by Allen Schick. Washington: American Enterprise Institute, 1983.

―――. *Reconciliation and the Congressional Budget Process*. Washington: American Enterprise Institute, 1981.

Schultze, Charles L., Edward R. Freid, Alice M. Rivlin, and Nancy H. Teeters. *Setting National Priorities: The 1973 Budget*. Washington: Brookings Institution, 1972.

Shelley, Mack, III. *The Permanent Majority: The Conservative Coalition in the United States Congress*. University: University of Alabama Press, 1983.

Sheppard, Burton D. *Rethinking Congressional Reform*. Cambridge, Mass.: Schenkman Books, 1985.

Shepsle, Kenneth A. *The Giant Jigsaw Puzzle: Democratic Committee Assignments in the Modern House*. Chicago: University of Chicago Press, 1978.

―――. "Prospects for Formal Models of Legislatures." *Legislative Studies Quarterly* 10 (1975): 5–19.

Sinclair, Barbara. "Agenda Control and Policy Success: Ronald Reagan and the 97th House." *Legislative Studies Quarterly* 10 (1985): 291–314.

―――. "Agenda, Policy, and Alignment Change From Coolidge to Reagan." In *Congress Reconsidered*, 3d ed., edited by Lawrence C. Dodd and Bruce I. Oppenheimer. Washington: CQ Press, 1985.

―――. *Congressional Realignment 1925–1978*. Austin: University of Texas Press, 1982.

―――. *Majority Leadership in the U.S. House*. Baltimore: Johns Hopkins University Press, 1983.

―――. "Purposive Behavior in the U.S. Congress: A Review Essay." *Legislative Studies Quarterly* 8 (1983): 117–31.

Smith, Hedrick. *The Power Game*. New York: Random House, 1988.

Smith, Steven S. "Budget Battles of 1981: The Role of the Majority Party Leadership." In *American Politics and Public Policy*, edited by Allan P. Sindler. Washington: CQ Press, 1982.

―――. *Call to Order*. Washington: Brookings Institution, 1989.

―――. "The Central Concepts in Fenno's Committee Studies." *Legislative Studies Quarterly* 11 (1986): 5–18.

―――. "New Patterns of Decisionmaking in Congress." In *The New Direction in American Politics*, edited by John E. Chubb and Paul E. Peterson. Washington: Brookings Institution, 1985.

―――. "O'Neill's Legacy for the House." *Brookings Review* (Winter 1987): 28–36.

Smith, Steven S., and Christopher J. Deering. *Committees in Congress*. Washington: CQ Press, 1984.

Smith, Steven S., and Bruce A. Ray. "The Impact of Congressional Reform: House Democratic Committee Assignments." *Congress and the Presidency* 10 (1983): 219–40.

Snowiss, Leo M. "Congressional Recruitment and Representation." *American Political Science Review* 60 (1966): 627–39.

Spohn, Richard, and Charles McCollum. *The Revenue Committees*. New York: Grossman Publishers, 1975.

Steinmo, Sven. "Political Institutions and Tax Policy in the United States, Sweden and Britain." *World Politics*, 41 (1989): 500–535.

Stevens, Arthur G., Arthur H. Miller, and Thomas E. Mann. "The Mobilization of Liberal Strength in the House, 1955–1970: The Democratic Study Group." *American Political Science Review* 68 (1974): 667–81.

Strahan, Randall. "Governing in the Post-Liberal Era: Gramm-Rudman-Hollings and the Politics of the Federal Deficit." *Harvard Journal on Legislation* 25 (1988): 593–609.

Sundquist, James L. *The Decline and Resurgence of Congress*. Washington: Brookings Institution, 1981.

_____. *Politics and Policy: The Eisenhower, Kennedy and Johnson Years*. Washington: Brookings Institution, 1968.

Surrey, Stanley S. "Our Troubled Tax Policy." *Tax Notes*, February 2, 1981, pp. 179–97.

_____. "Reflections on the Revenue Act of 1978 and Future Tax Policy." *Georgia Law Review* 13 (1979): 687–721.

_____. "A Tribute to Dr. Laurence N. Woodworth: Two Decades of Federal Tax History Viewed from This Perspective." *National Tax Journal* 32: 227–39.

Swenson, Peter. "The Influence of Recruitment on the Structure of Power in the U.S. House, 1870–1940." *Legislative Studies Quarterly* 7 (1982): 7–36.

Truman, David B. *The Congressional Party*. New York: John Wiley and Sons, 1959.

_____. *The Governmental Process*. New York: Knopf, 1951.

Turner, Julius, and Edward V. Schneier, Jr. *Party and Constituency: Pressures on Congress*. Rev. ed. Baltimore: Johns Hopkins University Press, 1970.

Unekis, Joseph K., and Leroy N. Rieselbach. *Congressional Committee Politics*. New York: Praeger, 1984.

Verdier, James M. "The President, Congress, and Tax Reform: Patterns Over Three Decades." *Annals of the American Academy of Political and Social Science* 499 (1988): 114–23.

_____. "The Tax Reform Act of 1986: Some Lessons About Policy Change." Paper presented at the annual meeting of the Association for Public Policy Analysis and Management, Austin, Texas, 1986.

Vogler, David J. *The Politics of Congress*. Boston: Allyn and Bacon, 1974.

Vogler, David J., and Sidney R. Waldman. *Congress and Democracy*. Washington: CQ Press, 1985.

Wahlke, John C., Heinz Eulau, William Buchanan, and LeRoy C. Ferguson. *The Legislative System*. New York: John Wiley and Sons, 1962.

Wander, W. Thomas. "Patterns of Change in the Congressional Budget Process, 1865–1974." *Congress and the Presidency* 9 (1982): 23–49.

Wander, W. Thomas, F. Ted Hebert, and Gary W. Copeland, eds. *Congressional Budgeting*. Baltimore: Johns Hopkins University Press, 1984.

Weaver, R. Kent. *Automatic Government: The Politics of Indexation*. Washington: Brookings Institution, 1988.

_____. "Controlling Entitlements." In *New Directions in American Politics*, edited by John E. Chubb and Paul E. Peterson. Washington: Brookings Institution, 1985.

West, Darrell M. *Congress and Economic Policymaking*. Pittsburgh: University of

Pittsburgh Press, 1987.

White, Joseph, and Aaron Wildavsky. *The Deficit and the Public Interest.* Berkeley: University of California Press, forthcoming.

Wildavsky, Aaron. *The Politics of the Budgetary Process.* Boston: Little, Brown, 1964.

———. *The New Politics of the Budgetary Process.* Glenview, Ill.: Scott, Foresman, 1988.

Witte, John F. *The Politics and Development of the Federal Income Tax.* Madison: University of Wisconsin Press, 1985.

Yager, Joseph A. "The Energy Battles of 1979." In *Energy Policy in Perspective*, edited by Craufurd D. Goodin. Washington: Brookings Institution, 1979.

Index

213